Merchant Saint

Other Books of Interest from St. Augustine's Press

Donald S. Prudlo, *Governing Perfection*

Bartholomew of the Martyrs, O.P., Donald S. Prudlo (translator), *Stimulus Pastorum: A Charge to Pastors*

Zbigniew Janowski, *Homo Americanus: The Rise of Totalitarian Democracy in America*

Leo Strauss, *Leo Strauss' Published but Uncollected English Writings*

Michael Davis, *Electras: Aeschylus, Sophocles, and Euripides*

D. Q. McInerny, *Being Philosophical*

Gabriel Marcel, *Toward Another Kingdom: Two Dramas of the Darker Years*

David Ramsay Steele, *Orwell Your Orwell: A Worldview on the Slab*

Gene Fendt, *Camus' Plague: Myth for Our World*

Roger Scruton, *The Politics of Culture and Other Essays*

Nalin Ranasinghe, *Shakespeare's Reformation: Christian Humanism and the Death of God*

Francisco Insa, *The Formation of Affectivity: A Christian Approach*

Daniel J. Mahoney, *Recovering Politics, Civilization, and the Soul: Essays on Pierre Manent and Roger Scruton*

Pierre Manent, *The Religion of Humanity: The Illusion of Our Times*

James M. Rhodes, *Knowledge, Sophistry, and Scientific Politics: Plato's Dialogues Theaetetus, Sophist, and Statesman*

Michael Franz (editor), *Eric Voegelin's Late Meditations and Essays: Critical Commentary Companions*

John von Heyking, *Comprehensive Judgment and Absolute Selflessness: Winston Churchill on Politics as Friendship*

Winston Churchill, *Savrola*

Winston Churchill, *The River War*

Winston Churchill, *My Early Life*

Merchant Saint
The Church, the Market, and the First Lay Canonization
Paul J. Voss and Donald S. Prudlo

St. Augustine's Press
South Bend, Indiana

Copyright © 2025 by Paul J. Voss and Donald S. Prudlo

All rights reserved. No part of this book may be reproduced, stored in a retrieval system, or transmitted, in any form or by any means, electronic, mechanical, photocopying, recording, or otherwise, without the prior permission of St. Augustine's Press.

Manufactured in the United States of America.

1 2 3 4 5 6   30 29 28 27 26 25

Library of Congress Control Number: 2024940219

Paperback ISBN: 978-1-58731-513-8
ebook ISBN: 978-1-58731-514-5

∞ The paper used in this publication meets the minimum requirements of the American National Standard for Information Sciences – Permanence of Paper for Printed Materials, ANSI Z39.48-1984.

St. Augustine's Press
www.staugustine.net

Table of Contents

Prologue vii
Acknowledgements xi
Abbreviations xii
Chapter 1: Treasure in Heaven 1
Chapter 2: Growing Pains 45
Chapter 3: A Good Man in the City 78
Sources for the Life of Omobono
   The Bull of Canonization — *Quia Pietas* 102
   Cum Orbita Solis 109
   Quoniam Historiae 124
   Labentibus Annis 135
Chapter 4: The Cult of Omobono and the Medieval Synthesis 145
Chapter 5: Merchants on Page and Stage:
   Literary Representations and the Creation of Stereotype 185
Chapter 6: The Purpose of Business and the Meaning of Work:
   An Economist Speaks 242
Conclusion 301
Index of Names and Terms 303
Index of Scripture 309

Prologue

"We have created new idols! The worship of the golden calf of old (cf. Ex 32:15–34) has found a new and heartless image in the cult of money and the dictatorship of an economy which is faceless and lacking any truly humane goal."[1] From the beginning of his pontificate, Pope Francis has denounced corruption and greed in no uncertain terms, often with a vehemence redolent of an Old Testament prophet. In his many off-the-cuff statements he has sometimes made his attacks so broad that it can seem that the whole of the capitalist system, along with freedom of trade and exchange and the life of business and entrepreneurship in general, has come under attack. Indeed it is not far off the mark to consider Francis as a type of Christian socialist, given his experiences with Argentinian Peronist statism and Liberation Theology.[2] While Francis eschews some of the heterodox implications of the latter movement, he has made his own its denunciations of Latin American capitalism, noted for its cronyism and corruption. Indeed Francis has moved far from the measured criticisms of liberal capitalism made by his predecessors. While certainly amplified by a media that works in out-of-context sound bites, still he has planted the seeds of confusion regarding the Church's perennial tradition regarding the Christian concepts of money, markets, and merchants.[3] While many tensions exist in that living tradition, we are

1   Address of Pope Francis to the new non-resident ambassadors to the Holy See: Kyrgyzstan, Antigua and Barbuda, Luxembourg, and Botswana, 16 May 2013.
2   Indeed his recent encyclical *Fratelli tutti* seems to confirm this observation.
3   For example, when Francis praised the vocation of the business person in his address to the US congress in 2015, few in the media took

convinced that it contains the tools necessary for the resolution of the troubled relation between the Church and commerce.

Francis undoubtedly draws from venerable wisdom that can be traced back to the prophet Amos in the Old Testament, denouncing those who live for this world only, who oppress the poor, and who deprive workers of their just wages. Such tropes are deeply embedded in the Western Christian consciousness, evident from the days of Christ Himself, through history all the way to Dickensian representations of heartless industrialists and vulture-like robber barons. Indeed such anti-market sentiments have continued well into the twentieth and twenty-first centuries, with examples ranging from Michael Douglas's slick worshipper of greed in *Wall Street*, to the "Occupy" movements and critics of income inequality. Most of these critics today still bear the mindset of various premodern economic models, ranging from Aristotle to seventeenth-century mercantilism, that declared wealth to be a zero-sum game. If someone got rich, that meant that someone else ipso facto became poor. The theoreticians of capitalism demonstrated the fallacy of such concepts, and established that wealth can be created by application of labor, efficiency, and ingenuity. Indeed, the astonishing creation of wealth since the twelfth century is empirically demonstrable.[4] Old attitudes die hard however. Of course—contrary to the partisans of laissez-faire capitalism—mere creation of wealth is not the only issue. First and foremost the Church is concerned with justice, and asks relevant questions about how this new wealth is used. In particular the Church is interested in how it can promote a civilization of human dignity and flourishing dedicated to Charity in its fullest sense of rightly-ordered loves.

The Church justly condemns and rails against the sins of

note. "Address of the Holy Father to the joint session of Congress," 24 Sep 2015.

4   For a short, popular account see "The Economic History of the Last 2000 Years: Part II," *The Atlantic*, 20 Jun 2012. http://www.theatlantic.com/business/archive/2012/06/the-economic-history-of-the-last-2000-years-part-ii/258762/.

avarice and selfishness. It has proven to be a tireless defender of the poor. Yet there is a deep and parallel tradition in the Christian Church that diminishes excessive charges leveled against the market economy. Christianity has ever been a religion of the happy medium. The Church holds together seeming paradoxes which, taken by themselves, become enervated heresies: faith *and* reason, Grace *and* freedom, One *and* Three, God *and* man. Christianity is a religion of both/and. From the beginning Christianity has refuted the twin errors of an excessive Platonic spiritualism on one hand and base materialism on the other. She knows that the proper ordering of the spiritual and the material are necessary for sanctification. In particular she has struggled against anti-material heresies. From Genesis to the present day, the Church has constantly meditated on the goodness of the material world, created by an all-good God. It is not food, drink, sex, or any other thing that is evil in itself. Rather they are the gifts of the good God. It is only in the perversion—in the sense of turning away—of our free wills that turn these goods into evils. The Church grappled against Docetism, Gnosticism, Catharism, and Puritanism, for anti-materialism has manifested itself in every age. These sought to fix the origin of the evil that we encounter in the material world itself. Christianity responded that not only was the world itself good, but that it had been recreated by the immanent participation of the transcendent God Himself in history, by the Incarnation in the womb of Mary. God Himself had taken on materiality, and had sanctified it by His presence. Indeed He willed that the ongoing sanctification of the human race take place by means of humble material elements: water, oil, bread, wine, human bodies. All religions are directed to primarily spiritual ends, but Christianity's great claim to distinctiveness is the value it places on the material world itself and how it orients such transient things towards eternity.

What this means is that the natural goods of this world, of any kind, are sanctifying if properly ordered in God. This includes the necessary social elements of human life itself, one aspect of which is the good of exchange. The fruits of such exchange are profit and wealth. From the beginning, as we shall demonstrate, Christian thinkers were able to make distinctions between unjust wealth and legitimate property and profit. While in their more hyperbolic moments they could rise to a pitch of anti-capital furor, their primary concern was the preservation of the human dignity and salvation of their subjects, be they rich or poor. The long meditation on wealth and justice throughout the Christian experience was crystallized in an astonishing way when in 1199 the merchant Omobono of Cremona became the first canonized lay saint.

This work will examine that Western Christian tradition from its earliest times to the present day, using St. Omobono as a touchstone for demonstrating that genius of Christianity at walking the middle line, without falling either into uncritical condemnation of money, markets, and wealth, or the excessive approbation of the rich and powerful at the expense of the poor. Chesterton understood this challenge better than many:

> This is the thrilling romance of Orthodoxy. People have fallen into a foolish habit of speaking of orthodoxy as something heavy, humdrum, and safe. There never was anything so perilous or so exciting as orthodoxy. . . . The Church in its early days went fierce and fast with any warhorse; yet it is utterly unhistoric to say that she merely went mad along one idea, like a vulgar fanaticism. She swerved to left and right, so exactly as to avoid enormous obstacles. . . . It is easy to be a madman: it is easy to be a heretic. It is always easy to let the age have its head; the difficult thing is to keep one's own. . . . To have fallen into any one of the fads from Gnosticism to Christian Science would indeed have been obvious and tame. But to have avoided them all has been one whirling adventure; and in my vision the heavenly chariot flies thundering through the ages, the dull heresies sprawling and prostrate, the wild truth reeling but erect.[5]

5   G. K. Chesterton, *Orthodoxy*, chapter 6.

Acknowledgements

I have received tremendous support while writing this book, but since I am abundantly blessed with deep, abiding friendships, these debts will likely be discharged as charity. I want to thank Randy Hain for his unflagging enthusiasm for the project. I'm grateful to John Riordan, Bill Harrell, and David McCollough for travel grants used for research in Cremona. Thanks also to Christopher Wells and Paul Beezley, both of whom endured long discussions about the first merchant saint. I am awed by the intelligence and productivity of my co-author; it was an honor to work with him. I benefitted from the extensive community of Catholic business professionals from Legatus, many of whom offered advice and encouragement. These business professionals carry the legacy of honesty, integrity, resilience, fidelity, and innovation exemplified by St. Omobono.

I dedicate this book to my family—my dear wife Mary, our children Joseph, Luke and his wife CarolAnne, Maria Rose, JohnPaul, Aquinas, and our adored grandson Norman Arthur.

Abbreviations

COS   *Cum orbita solis*, liturgical life of Omobono (ca. 1198)
LA   *Labentibus annis*, *vita* of Omobono (ca. 1230–1240)
PG   Patrologia Graeca
PL   Patrologia Latina
QH   *Quoniam historiae*, *vita* of Omobono (ca. 1270–1300)
QP   *Quia pietas*, Canonization Bull of Omobono of Cremona, Innocent III (1199)
ST   Thomas Aquinas, *Summa Theologiae*

Chapter 1
TREASURE IN HEAVEN

The relationship between Church and capital has not always been smooth. From the very beginning Christians have often been suspicious of the power of riches to corrupt, and only secondarily conscious of the potential for money to help. In the Old Testament, prophets thundered denunciations against the rich for the oppression of the poor and the weak. Even more explicit is the New Testament, with its cautions about the temptations involved in the accrual of wealth. Nor did Christianity evolve in a world that was primarily mercantile, for it was born among Jews who idealized the pastoral life and Romans who yearned for the farm. Through the Patristic era, the Fathers constantly refined the Church's attitude toward the rich and powerful, a group often—but not always—at odds with Christianity. The legalization of the Church brought new problems and tensions, as Christians moved into positions of power and dominance. The question of the proper use of wealth in a Christian society came to the fore.[1] However, nascent meditations in this direction were upstaged by the massive socio-economic upheaval of the barbarian migrations. During the early Middle Ages the complexity of the economy unraveled, the circulation of money decreased, and property came to be thought of primarily in terms of productive land. The status of the impetuous "rich young man" was shuffled to the back burner. It was only with the dawn of the commercial revolution that such questions again arose. How could a rich man be saved? Was not avarice a most deadly sin? Was there worth to be found in the merchant life? All of these problems came to a head during the central Middle Ages.

The Old Testament

The Old Testament provides ample evidence of a suspicion of wealth and power. Adam was to toil by the sweat of his brow in order to scratch a living from the earth (Gen 3:17–19). Though this was the root of the later Christian doctrine of the dignity of labor, that idea would take centuries to develop (only maturing in the social teaching of the Church following *Rerum novarum* in 1891). Nor did "tilling the land" provide an answer to the value of such seemingly "unproductive" work as that done by the merchant, clerical, or scholarly classes. Indeed the whole of the Pentateuch evinces a strong aversion for the settled urban life, a necessary precondition for the development of a solid mercantile culture. Cain the murderer was the first founder of a city (Gen 4:17) and later attempts at city building are met with divine disapproval, as in the case of Nimrod's Babel (Gen 11). The city was seen as the fount of evildoing and all forms of immorality, a common trope throughout the Judeo-Christian tradition, commencing with the destruction of the Pentapolis which included Sodom and Gomorrah (Gen 19). The predilection of the ancient Hebrews was instead oriented toward the pastoral life of the shepherd. The way of the shepherd not only kept one free from the defilement of the city, but it also insulated the Hebrews against the fantastical pagan fertility rites common to their agricultural neighbors such as the Phoenicians.[2] Throughout the Old Testament one of the preferred ways of speaking about God, the soul, and the spiritual life is the relation between shepherd and sheep. Deeply embedded in the Jewish consciousness, such a vision was bequeathed to the Christan world.

This preference was magnified by the lack of temporal power and outright persecution experienced by the people of Israel. Constantly menaced by rich, powerful neighbors, the Hebrews stubbornly maintained their religious identity in the midst of harassment by the polytheistic nations. Indeed it was only during the brief period of David's and Solomon's reigns that the Jews had any modest earthly power, along with its attendant and commensurate wealth. While Solomon did use that wealth to build the Temple of the Lord, it also corrupted him, turning him into an oriental potentate with numerous wives and concubines who imported their polytheistic deities along with them (1 Kg 11:4). The prosperity of the kingdom was eclipsed after Solomon's passing. The rest of Hebrew history was one of constant menace by neighbors and conquerors. In spite of that, the Jews found that a combination of worldly powerlessness added to their solid monotheistic identity came to be a bulwark against the loss of their nationhood. From this perspective one can begin to see how the Hebrew attitude toward wealth developed.

From the beginning the Torah recognizes the possible dangers of wealth and comfort. Deuteronomy explains: "When you eat and are satisfied, when you build fine houses and settle down, and when your herds and flocks grow large and your silver and gold increase and all you have is multiplied, then your heart will become proud and you will forget the Lord your God" (Dt 8:12–13). In a theme that will continue in the New Testament, wealth is seen as leading to the enervation of religious identity and toward an exaggerated self-reliance. It becomes even more dangerous when the pursuit of wealth leads to the further sin of jealousy, as in Psalm 73, where Asaph nearly loses faith when he considers the "prosperity of the wicked." The prophetic tradition in particular is devastating in its denunciations of the misuse of wealth. Amos—writing in the earliest of the prophetical books—rails continually against the depredations of the rich against the poor. "Woe to those who lie in beds of ivory, and stretch themselves on their couches . . . who sing idle songs to the sound of the harp" (Am 6:4–5). The use of wealth to oppress the weak is a constant motif of his forthright condemnations. Amos is decidedly caustic against those who would allude to their riches as evidence of divine favor, when in reality it was the unjustly oppressed poor who were righteous before God. The other prophets voice similar concerns about the debilitating effects of wealth on faith and hope. Later scriptural writings seemed to concur in these sentiments, down through even the Second Temple period. A specific passage which would prove troublesome later was "A merchant can hardly keep from wrongdoing, and a tradesman will not be declared innocent of sin" (Sir 26:29). Even the translations of the Old Testament provided fuel for the fire. The Greek Septuagint mistranslated a passage in Psalms as "Because I have known trading, I will enter into the powers of the Lord" (Ps 70[71]:15–16).[3] This mistranslation was later included in the *Vetus Itala* used by early Latin Fathers and thus entered into the breviaries and liturgical books of the Western world.

Further complicating the problem was the Old Testament attitude to the practice of usury, a teaching which would cast an astonishingly long shadow on the culture of the West. The Torah is crystal clear on the immorality of lending at interest to other Jews, a practice which would become decisive for the development of complex market economies (Lv 25:36–37; Dt 23:19–20). However, this did leave open the practice of lending at interest to someone outside of the Chosen People, a loophole which later generations of Jews would embrace, particularly in social situations where their economic opportunities were limited. One should note that this proscription of usury was not limited to Judaism; similar prohibitions can be found in most Western cultures, a stigma that continued well into modern times.[4]

In spite of this, one can also sense a counterpoint running in a minor key through the Old Testament: that of wealth justly gained and rightly used. Those who were wealthy and yet commended as righteous before God—including the Patriarchs, such as Abraham and Jacob—is one thing that is often noted, but rarely explored. Abraham is blessed by God, and this includes (but is certainly not limited to) wealth in an earthly sense. Indeed he is described as a rich man, but one whose wealth exists to provide a foundation for the generations to be born from him. Both David and Solomon are praised lavishly for using their extraordinary riches in the construction of the Lord's Temple at Jerusalem. The use of wealth for the subvention of divine worship will become a perennially recognized pious act for wealthy people in nearly every period of the history of the Jewish people, an approbation that would continue under Christianity. There was never a time in which such actions by those of means did not merit praise. The prescriptions of the Torah imply the existence and de facto tolerance of economic inequalities in the Hebrew community, by commanding the support of poor neighbors by their richer ones (Lv 25:35–38). While condemning usury, Deuteronomy enjoins Jews to lend to one another in dignity and in justice (Dt 26:10–13). The Psalms constantly praise the generosity of the righteous rich, as opposed to the wicked who are covetous and forgetful of God (particularly Psalm 37). Indeed Psalm 112 suggests that the generous rich are an allegory for God Himself in His free munificence (Ps 112:3–5). Reflecting the sober, material mentality of their Egyptian origins, the book of Proverbs too is a thesaurus for the rich who wish to live an upright life. Such themes recur repeatedly. What receives condemnation in the Old Testament is fraud and avarice, particularly of the type that results in the oppression of the poor. The rich are to support the worship of the Jewish community and are to use their wealth to display generosity. They are also not to become comfortable in the idea that their wealth comes from their own merits, but rather are counseled to receive it as a continual gift of God for the good of themselves and the community as a whole.

The Old Testament also lays down the common teaching of the just existence of private property. Besides the grant to have dominion over the earth and subdue it in Genesis, most of the Patriarchs are spoken of as retaining, using, and bequesting private property to their heirs. Indeed the Old Testament has special curses reserved for those who wrongfully move property markers (Dt 19:14, 27:17, Prv 22:28 and 23:10, and Job 24:2). Indeed it is in this context that we see the denunciations against the oppression of the poor. The poor are entitled their *just and equitable* wages, which presumes that the proprietor has the means to effect such payment. Private property is accepted as normative throughout the Old Testament, not least in the commandment that forbids stealing. Such a prohibition can only be understood in light of just and proper possession by people of their own goods. Note also that the Old Testament does not absolutize this as a right (indeed the modern language of "rights" is alien to the scriptures) but speaks of it as normative, a just allocation of the goods of the earth for the benefit of the community, which necessarily implies private ownership and just exchange. The chief question about wealth then is one of use and intention, rather than the goodness of the object itself.

The Classical Tradition

Such ambivalent attitudes toward wealth were not unusual in the ancient Western world. Indeed, before the rise of capitalism people lived within an economic system best described as a primitive type of premarket economy, which was governed by the patron-client system. In this model hospitality and generosity were the key virtues. Wealth was for display and for giving away, for attracting retainers and clients, which in turn made one a powerful patron before the community. Commercial activity was thus subordinate to socio-cultural needs. Greed was considered the worst type of bad form, utterly socially unacceptable. When one acquired wealth one's object should be to display it and then give it away, thus attracting renown as a liberal and great-souled (or *magnanimous*) man. This was to be distinguished from pure charity, for the clients were expected to be loyal to the patron and to render service when requested. In the ancient world there was never any sentiment that approached the Christian idea of free alms for the indigent (unless one counts the expedient distribution of bread to prevent revolution). On the contrary, the wealthy were to spend their money freely on the support of their city and country, funding the military and paying for buildings of general utility, which redounded to the glory of their peoples. Indeed this was the attitude of the ancient Roman aristocrats of the early Republic, who were expected to spend twenty or more years in unremunerated military and civic service to the city. They did this because the root concept of the premodern world was the priority of the community and the common good. It was only with the coming of modernity that the shift from family, tribe, and city to atomic individuals comes about, an idea which must be kept in mind as we trace critiques of wealth in the premodern world.

The Greek philosophers in particular rejected wealth, choosing instead to live a life seeking the perfection of the soul and the higher good of wisdom. Some, such as Diogenes the Cynic, were openly hostile to the conventional acquisition of riches. Socrates himself was perpetually poor, and Plato and Aristotle were little better off. Indeed both of these repeated the common condemnations of usury, with Plato calling it "vulgar" and Aristotle more specifically calling it "unnatural." Plato understood the necessity of the life of merchants in his *Republic* yet considered that all who practiced such activity necessarily became corrupted.[5] For him there was a hierarchy of necessary occupations, and traders were far from the top of the list. Aristotle was in agreement with the tenor of Plato's criticism. In his conception money was a dead thing; it could produce nothing of itself, and so making money off of money alone was intrinsically immoral. Famously, Aristotle was unimpressed with merchants as a whole, saying that the "life of money-making is a constrained kind of life" when compared to the life of seeking wisdom in contemplation.[6] This was because wisdom is an end in itself, whereas wealth is only a means to other ends. Merchants were distracted from the things that mattered most, though Aristotle's account of the virtues seems to imply that such a life of wisdom must have a modest amount of economic means available to it for its full flowering.

In spite of all of that, it was Aristotle who provided the classic defense of private property. He repudiates Plato's communism, elucidated in *The Republic*, as incommensurate with the diversity of human affairs and lauds the advantages of mutually beneficial transactions. Private property dovetails with human nature, it is traditional to all human societies, and it produces the basic foundations for the practice of virtue lived in a community.[7] By and large however, the philosophers of the ancient world counseled moderation. They praised care for the soul rather than the body and evinced a general scorn for the things of earth. Indeed, this was something which united philosophers across schools, for Peripatetics, Cynics, and Stoics could all agree that the material world was of less importance than the spiritual, the soul more dignified than the body, that fickle fortune which brought wealth or poverty was to be scorned, and that care for material wealth was at best undignified. It would be a position which would attract many in the young Christian movement.

THE NEW TESTAMENT

An heir to all these meditations, the New Testament seemingly comes out even more strongly against the accumulation of wealth than previous traditions.[8] In the Gospels we are introduced to God made man in the context of a poor, working-class family. Even before Christ's birth we hear Mary singing with the voice of a prophet of Old, "the poor He has filled with good things, the rich he has sent away empty" (Lk 1:53). Her husband Joseph is a carpenter, a productive laborer, who nonetheless is unable even to procure a place for his wife to bear their child. In accordance with the Mosaic law they make the offering for their first born at the Temple using the sacrifice of birds because of their lack of money (Lk 2:24). Christ then becomes incarnate into a world of poverty and labor, in the unremarkable village of Nazareth, in the marginal and impoverished region of Galilee. The Gospels will retain this preference for the poor, for the rural, and for the downtrodden. Christ will retain this poverty into His active life and preaching, for the "Son of Man has nowhere to lay His head" (Lk 9:58, Mt 8:20). His modest means are on full display at His crucifixion, as the soldiers cast lots for his few possessions, and as He gives his mother into the care of others, having been unable to leave anything to her Himself.

Yet it is the words of Christ which have echoed down the ages as regards wealth, money, and work. It would be otiose to list all the warnings, menaces, and condemnations of wealth in the Gospels, yet an attempt at an outline must be made. The Lucan version of the beatitudes continues the leitmotif begun in the Magnificat. "Woe to you rich, for you have your consolation" (Lk 6:24). Echoing Amos and Psalms, Luke brings forth the contention that the blessings of this life have been conferred on the rich for the small good that they have done.[9] This gospel is notable also for its references to the transitory nature of human wealth. "Sell what you have and give alms.... For where your treasure is, there will be your heart also" (Lk 12:33, 34). It is also the only gospel that has the famous parable of *Dives and Lazarus*, which for our present purposes, is worth quoting in full:

> There was a rich man, who was clothed in purple and fine linen and who feasted sumptuously every day. And at his gate lay a poor man named Lazarus, full of sores, who desired to be fed with what fell from the rich man's table; moreover the dogs came and licked his sores. The poor man died and was carried by the angels to Abraham's bosom. The rich man also died and was buried in hell, being in torment, he lifted up his eyes, and saw Abraham far off and Lazarus in his bosom. And he called out, "Father Abraham, have mercy upon me, and send Lazarus to dip the end of his finger in water and cool my tongue; for I am in anguish in this flame." But Abraham said, "Son, remember that you in your lifetime received your good things, and Lazarus in like manner evil things; but now he is comforted here, and you are in anguish. And besides all this, between us and you a great chasm has been fixed, in order that those who would pass from here to you may not be able, and none may cross from there to us." (Lk 16:19–26)

This parable became one of the most enduring images in the whole of the Western tradition. The rich man who died and was "buried in hell" became a key point for moralizing preachers in the Patristic period and into the Middle Ages. Indeed, in the final commendation of the Catholic Requiem Mass, the deceased was commended to be received by "Lazarus, who was once poor," that he might have eternal rest.[10] It became reproduced countless times in stained glass, in books of hours, and in paintings. Even Shakespeare's Falstaff makes reference to him, "but I think upon hell-fire and Dives that lived in purple; for there he is in his robes, burning, burning."[11] Suffused with these dire impressions, one can see the background against which the traditions of the West developed.

While Mark and Matthew are not as notable in their antipathy toward wealth, the general tenor of disapproval is still present. All three gospels record the parable of the Widow's Mite, which was of more value than the ostentatious offerings of the rich (Mk 12:41, Mk 12:41, Lk 21:1). In all three we find Christ's admonition to the Apostles to go out preaching, making no provision for the morrow, and not to travel with any money in their purses (Mt 10:9, Mk 6:8, Lk 9:3). Finally all three concur in the famous passage whose harshness has caused any number of attempts to explain it away through the Church's history. "Amen, I say to you, it will be hard for a rich man to enter the kingdom of heaven. Again I tell you, it is easier for a camel to go through the eye of a needle than for a rich man to enter the kingdom of God" (Mt 19:23–24, similar in Mk 10:24–27, and Lk 18:24–27). Even the disciples hearing this marveled, but Christ only comforted them thusly, "With men this is impossible, but with God all things are possible" (Mt 19:26). This is not a ringing endorsement of the accumulation of human wealth. Christ appears in every gospel purifying the Temple by force. While this episode is open to a variety of interpretations, the overall sentiment is clear. The worship of the Lord should be pure and undefiled by corruption of whatever form.

In terms of advice for living life, perhaps the most affecting story in the gospels is the tale of the rich young man, so eager and so committed. He asks the Master what he must do to obtain eternal life. Christ tells him to follow all the commandments. The man proudly proclaims that he has always observed them, and asked then what was still lacking in his search for perfection. Intrigued by the man, Christ went further: "If you would be perfect, go, sell what you possess and give to the poor, and you will have treasure in heaven; and come, follow me." Christ had given the recipe for Christian perfection, utter conformity to the will of God by the abandonment of earthly possessions and attachments. Yet, in one of the most melancholy passages in the Gospels, the rich young man turned and "went away sorrowful, for he had many possessions" (Mt 19:22). In this call to perfection Christ had laid out one of the most significant principles of Christian sanctity. Anyone may reach heaven by following the commandments outlined in revelation, however those who sought perfection—that is, perfect conformation to Christ the Head—must empty themselves like Him. Here is the classic distinction between commandments, which all must follow, and the counsels of evangelical perfection. Voluntary poverty then was to be a decisive element of a higher vocation, a more perfect way of life. But here was the key: riches, in themselves, were not bad. They were simply less perfect, for those possessing them still had a path to salvation and sanctity, just not one equal to the path of a person who had undertaken the counsels of perfection. It is notable that the Gospel of John, written around the year 100 AD, contains almost none of the above admonitions about poverty and wealth. It is not that Johannine Christianity disagreed with them in principle. It is simply that the Christians had progressed to a new point in Church history, being fully present in a gentile world, engaged in various occupations and businesses, and having more pressing issues to deal with, such as establishing the reality of the Incarnation against contemporary Christian heretics.

Yet in the Gospels—just as in the Old Testament—there is a quiet testimony to the "righteous wealthy." Christ in particular called some, like Matthew, who were from the more propertied and learned classes. He gathers around Him those who labor, including those who had been driven to work in ignominious and even sinful lines of business. He praises people like Zacchaeus, the chief tax-collector of Jericho. Unlike the "rich young man," Zacchaeus continued to pursue Christ, and he gave away half of his goods to the poor. This is notable. He did not give all his wealth and yet is still blessed by Christ, who said "today salvation has come to this house" (Lk 19:1–10). It is all the more notable that this passage appears only in Luke's gospel, thus making more complex the effort to understand that evangelist's message about material possessions. Immediately after this in Luke, Christ preached the parable of the Good Steward, who is entrusted with talents and turns a tidy profit for his Master, and is praised: "well done, good and faithful servant." However the man who buried his money is handed over to be killed (Lk 19:11–27, also Mt 25:14–30). While the meaning of this parable goes far beyond a simple narrative of monetary investment, one should note the context in which Christ chooses to tell the story. Other examples can be found. Christ does not disdain the houses of the rich, and opens His public ministry at a marriage banquet where there is much carousing, sanctifying both human celebration and the principal vocation of the lay life (Jn 3). Christ does not disdain to receive the timorous Nicodemus, the wealthy Pharisee (Jn 3). He is good friends with Lazarus, Mary, and Martha of Bethany, who have a house and give ample hospitality to Him and His Apostles. When the woman anoints Christ in Bethany with expensive oils, it is the traitor Judas who is scandalized, saying that such was an extravagance that should have been sold for the poor. Christ rebukes him, "For you always have the poor with you, but you will not always have me" (Mt 26:11). This is a very interesting passage which speaks of the providential ordering of economic life, of the permission to worship Christ with precious and expensive gifts, and gives a challenge to those who see only the earthly and material plight of the poor. Finally there is the rich man, Joseph of Arimathea, a secret follower of Christ. Without him the body of Christ would have remained unanointed by precious spices and would not have found a place of rest before the Resurrection. All of these considerations make it imperative to see that one is not dealing with a simplistic binary dichotomy between rich and poor; rather the truth is much more subtle, and would take centuries of reflection to unfold completely.

It is natural that the Book of Acts, authored by Luke, would continue the general negative themes surrounding wealth and money. The early Christian Church was poor and the small community lived in the expectation of an imminent return of Christ. For this reason they resided communally near the Temple in Jerusalem and when people joined the nascent movement they abandoned all their wealth at the feet of the Apostles so that the Church leaders could distribute it to those who needed charity the most. We see this in an arresting and shocking way in Acts 5 when a couple named Ananias and Sapphira hold back some of the money which they had committed to donate to the Church. Peter calls them out for their fraud, and they are struck dead instantly in a manner redolent of the wonders of the Old Testament. A commitment to serve God and promises made to the Church were serious business, something which Luke does not hesitate to reinforce with such a stunning story. Another negative episode takes place in chapter 8. Simon the Magician sees the wonders that Peter and John are working in the name of Christ, and desires to possess their power. He offers them money for the free gift of God and Peter curses his name because of it. "May your silver perish with you, because you thought you could obtain the gift of God with money!" (Act 8:20). The seriousness of this offense was such that it gave its name to the notorious crime of *simony* which is the attempt to buy, sell, or traffic in holy things, which are the gratuitous gifts of God. Luke once again reiterates his opinion that the Church and money do not mix felicitously.

Yet in spite of all the foregoing, there is no call in the Gospels or in Acts that private property ought to be abolished. While they continue with the Old Testament idea that everything is a gift from God (thus undercutting the Lockean idea that private property is inherently natural), they maintain prohibitions on stealing and praise those who use their means to subsidize the Church and the poor. Private property is to be maintained; it does not contradict the commandments, though some make a more perfect choice to leave such earthly goods for the sake of holiness. As in the Old Testament, the New underscores that the problem is not with wealth itself, it is rather in the manifold temptations to sin to which it can draw people.

While Paul does not deal with economic details at much length, some of the later epistles make the primitive Christian position very clear. And 1 Timothy is a famous example, which reiterates the prophetic warning about the danger of riches. With wealth comes temptation and a plethora of opportunities to engage in sins that are simply inaccessible to the poor. The letter then comes to the one of the most famous quotations about our subject in the whole tradition, "The love of money is the root of all evils" (1 Tm 6:10).[12] Yet 1 Timothy also gives hope for a new path, a holy way of being wealthy in the world. "Charge the rich of this world not to be high minded, nor to trust in the uncertainty of riches, but in the living God, who gives us abundantly all things to enjoy, to do good, to be rich in good works, to give easily, to communicate to others, to lay up in store for themselves a good foundation against the time to come, that they may lay hold on the true life" (1 Tm 6:17). That this passage follows hard upon the dark sentiments uttered against greed is significant. It is a plan for those who are in the world, who have chosen the less perfect way, to live well and to benefit the Church community with their generosity and largesse.

Not all the epistles are as balanced or sanguine about the possibilities of business. The letter of James is more direct; indeed one can call it a New Testament version of the prophet Amos. It is a rousing defense of the poor against the oppression of the rich. "Let the lowly brother boast in his exaltation, and the rich in his humiliation, because like the flower of the grass he will pass away. For the sun rises with its scorching heat and withers the grass; its flower falls, and its beauty perishes. So will the rich man fade away in the midst of his pursuits" (Jas 1:9–11). He rails against respect of persons based merely on external wealth, particularly in the Eucharistic celebration. The "poor in the world" are "rich in faith," and are oppressed by the lawsuits and blasphemies of the wealthy (Jas 2:5–6). Finally James works himself up to a frothy pitch of prophetic indignation: "Go now, ye rich men, weep and howl in your miseries, which shall come upon you. Your riches are corrupted and your garments are motheaten. Your gold and silver is cankered and the rust of them shall be for a testimony against you, and shall eat your flesh like fire. You have stored up to yourselves wrath against the last days" (Jas 5:1–3). The reason for this is that they have defrauded their laborers of their just wage, a sin that cries to heaven for vengeance. The book of Revelation speaks in a similar vein, but this time with Apocalyptic consequence at the forefront. "You say, I am rich, I have prospered, and I need nothing; not knowing that you are wretched, pitiable, poor, blind, and naked" (Rev 3:17). Riches will profit nothing on the last day, indeed they will deceive their possessors into a false sense of security. In a powerful image, and perhaps the one most directly related to the profession of merchant in the New Testament, the author of Revelation speaks of the Scarlet Whore of Babylon, by whom "the merchants of the earth have been made rich by the power of her delicacies" (Rev 18:3). Her fall is described in vivid, indeed overwhelming detail, in a passage remarkable for its attention to various practices of the mercantile class: "The merchants of these things, who were made rich, shall stand afar off from her, for fear of her torments, weeping and mourning. And saying: 'Alas! alas! that great city, which was clothed with fine linen, and purple, and scarlet, and was gilt with gold, and precious stones, and pearls. For in one hour are so great riches come to nought....' And they cast dust upon their heads, and cried, weeping and mourning, saying: 'Alas! alas! that great city, wherein all were made rich, that had ships at sea, by reason of her prices, for in one hour she is made desolate'" (Rev 18:15–19). The scriptures then offered quite an array of sentiments for the Christian Church to meditate upon in the coming centuries.

THE EARLY CHURCH

The Bible is the book of the Church, slowly put together over the course of centuries by a process of discernment, assessment, and selection. Of foremost importance in this process of "canonization" of the texts of scripture is that we must take note of the attitudes of the earliest followers of Christ, in particular the writings of those called the Fathers of the Church. Robert Wilken makes the prescient point, "any effort to mount an interpretation of the Bible that ignores its first readers is doomed to end up with a bouquet of fragments that are neither the book of the Church nor the imaginative wellspring of Western literature, art, and music."[13] Without an interpretive tradition drawn from those who actually received the oral preaching of the Apostles and assembled the canon, we degenerate into privately construed proof texts hurled back and forth. While the Old Testament had an interpretive tradition (later augmented by the Christians), the early Church *was* the interpretive nexus of the bible.[14] So then in interpreting the difficult and sometimes apparently contradictory ideas that have been noted above, we need to see what the first believers of the Christian tradition had to say about them.

One of the characteristics to note in the first century of the Church—apparent even in the pages of the New Testament—is the gradual move away from imminent eschatological expectation to a more permanent type of evangelical mission. Attendant upon this were the considerations of how a Christian was to live in a largely pagan world. These drove the first great development of Catholic theology and are apparent in the later texts of the New Testament, such as Ephesians, the letters to Timothy and Titus, and the Johannine literature. Already Christianity was penetrating into every corner of pagan society, all the while continuing a desultory struggle against Judaism and Judaizers, and at the same time attempting to meet heterodoxies within its own ranks. One of the earliest extra-biblical texts, earlier even than some books of the New Testament, was the highly respected First Letter of Clement to the Corinthians, dated between 90–95 AD.[15] It is an exceptionally early and precious witness to the development of the Christian tradition. Clement was the fourth bishop of Rome, having been ordained by St. Peter. It is a ringing call to fidelity, order, and charity in the Corinthian Church. He issues an appeal for humility and reciprocal service, which however does not entail the abolition of wealth, rank, or social status. "Let the strong not despise the weak, and let the weak show respect unto the strong. Let the rich man provide for the wants of the poor; and let the poor man bless God, because He has given him one by whom his need may be supplied."[16] Clement takes it as providential that, just as there are different gifts in the Church, so there are different socioeconomic states, and each is ordered toward the good of the other. One often discerns a struggle in Christian history between order and equality, indeed one can see Paul struggling with the concepts in his letters. Yet the Fathers, like Paul, realize that in fact it is one of the paradoxes of Christianity that both must be maintained for a just and holy society. The *Didache*, written at some point around the composition of 1 Clement, makes special note of avarice as a sin, and is insistent that the Church be free from greedy men and those who simoniacally charge for holy things, but does not castigate those who have money in any way.[17] Once again we see a balanced view that understands that the equality of Christians in their common nature and baptismal re-creation in Christ does not exclude genuine and useful distinctions in order.

Another early text is the *Shepherd of Hermas* which, though it has a complicated textual history, is the work of one person writing between 130–150, though some argue for an earlier date.[18] A first version was written during a time of persecution. By that time, many Christians had prospered in the Roman peace and had become quite comfortable in their wealth, yet when the persecutions came, it led them to apostatize. "These are they that have faith, but have also riches of this world. When tribulation comes, they deny their Lord by reason of their riches and their business affairs."[19] Here we see increasing anxiousness about the temptations which come with wealth. The author himself notes that he has lost much property by expropriation, and that this has brought him closer to God. Note however that these rich are considered to be in the Church during times of peace and are not charged with any sin. The pleasures and comforts of the world though, while legitimate and sometimes useful, can be an impediment to holiness. During a later redaction of *The Shepherd*, and after the storm of persecution had passed, the author became more measured in his comments about wealth. "Their riches have darkened and obscured them a little from the truth. When therefore the Lord perceived their mind, that they could favor the truth, and likewise remain good, He commanded their possessions to be cut off from them, yet not to be taken away altogether, so that they might be able to do some good with that which has been left to them."[20] He continues with this theme, which dovetails with that of the divine pruner who chastises those whom He loves for their own good. The riches are not to be removed completely. The solution for the author is for the rich to live in such a way as to spend their wealth on the Church and on the poor, living simply and piously so as to preclude the possibility of apostasy under the conditions of persecution.

The previous three documents were, for a long time and in many places, considered to be inspired Sacred Scripture, some of them well into the fourth and fifth centuries. As such they also provide a privileged window through which to examine the attitude of the Church toward wealth. Many writers on early Christianity tend to ignore these orthodox, yet extra-biblical texts which had the authority of scripture in many places. And yet the same scholars occasionally accord absurd importance to minor, unorthodox, gnostic texts which never had any substantive circulation, nor were ever received as scripture by the broad Church. Many of these were written by Gnostic heretics who were dualists: people who believed that a dark God had created the material world, so that everything involved in the tangible cosmos was essentially evil. Of course these "gospels" condemn earthly life, marriage, family, commerce, and human society. The Church struggled mightily against these anti-life messages, for She knew that the world was created by God Himself, who saw that it was good, and who created male and female in His own image and likeness. Further than that, the early Christian Church mightily defended the Incarnation of the Son of God, the signal doctrine which sets Christianity apart from every other religion on earth. Not only was the world good, but it was also sanctified by the presence of the transcendent God at a certain place and time, in a discrete human body. Nature had been re-created, as it were. Now the humble things of the material world were channels of divine supernatural grace: water, wine, bread, oil, human sexuality. Christ came to sanctify every area of human and bodily life, which included the life of the family and the labor of the worker. It was this the heretics denied, and every anti-human and anti-life ideology from that day to the present has borne a whiff of this Gnostic dualism.

The second century as a whole was a healthy time for the Church, as it was for the empire in general. Subject to general toleration by the polytheistic Romans, there were only sporadic and local outbreaks of persecution. Christians took advantage of the Roman Peace to evangelize and grow in numbers, while attending to the same professions that they had practiced before their conversion. Christian soldiers remained soldiers, Christian married couples remained married, and Christian laborers and merchants continued to pursue their various trades. One of the most prolific and interesting Fathers of the Church was a writer named Clement of Alexandria (ca. 150–ca. 215).[21] Like his contemporary St. Justin Martyr, he had continued in earnest the importation of the genius of Greek philosophy in defense of the Christian faith. He was the instructor of Origen (184–253), the first systematic theologian in the Church's history. Like Origen, his work is daring and thoughtful, a stirring testimony to the power of reason harnessed to the Christian faith. Clement is the first Christian to pose an extended answer to the problem of wealth in his work *Quis Dives Salvetur?* (Who is the the rich man that shall be saved?) Clement is a model of moderation, like all of the Church Fathers. Paradoxes like rich and poor must be balanced in order to arrive at the whole truth. Indeed Christianity is full of these: God and Man, Three and One, Faith and Reason, Freedom and Grace. To emphasize one over the other is to turn a partial truth into a whole heresy. Therefore Clement takes the Aristotelian doctrine of the mean and applies it to the Christian moral life. For instance, drunkenness is a vice, but so also is abstemiousness. Drink should be taken in moderation in accord with its end or purpose: with friends, for conviviality, nourishment, and medicine. Here lies virtue: the fulfillment of our natures as rational animals. So also does he treat wealth. Wealth sought for its own sake is a perversion of its proper end. Greed is a vice, along with its opposite prodigality, or needless, heedless wastefulness. Liberality is the virtue proper to those who possess money, which involves a rational balance between giving and acquiring.[22]

To this classical vision Clement adds his Alexandrian Christianity, which emphasizes a spiritualizing or allegorical reading of the scriptures. We have been so used to searching the bible for its literal meanings in the contemporary world, we neglect the very real and often deeper levels of significance contained in the text and discerned particularly among the Fathers of the Church. These allegorical readings helped them to identify Christ in the pages of the Old Testament. In Clement's Platonic philosophical world, the spiritual meaning of the text was all important. When analyzing Christ's words to the rich young man, he alludes that it would essentially be social and religious suicide to take them as a literal commandment to all. "How could one give food to the hungry, and drink to the thirsty, clothe the naked, and shelter the houseless, for not doing which He threatens with fire and the outer darkness, if each man first divested himself of all these things?. . . Riches, then, which benefit also our neighbours, are not to be thrown away. For they are possessions, inasmuch as they are possessed, and goods, inasmuch as they are useful and provided by God for the use of men."[23] For him, Christ's words had a spiritual meaning of detachment from the things of this world, and a focus on the higher, spiritual goods. One is to employ one's riches toward the common good, for the poor and in works of mercy, without thereby destroying one's own patrimony. It is the attitude of the soul which is important; riches are a means and not an end, a teaching both in accord with Plato and with the Scriptures.[24] Many in later history, and even today, would cry out that Clement's exegesis robs Christ's words of their radical immediacy. There is some truth to that. It is Christ however who made the distinction between salvation and perfection in the story of the rich young man. Clement, like the other Ante-Nicene Fathers, knew that there was a call to the abandonment of earthly goods in favor of a closer conformation to Christ, but that was a counsel of perfection, not a commandment of salvation. Clement, in making the distinction, was perhaps not thinking in these terms, since the theology of the counsels of perfection had not yet been made plain in the monastic movement, but what he did was establish the ability for Christians of all social classes, including the rich, to "live soberly, piously, and justly in this world" (Tit 2:12).

Later Church thinkers showed more ambivalence when compared to Clement's extraordinarily positive vision of the uses of earthly wealth. Tertullian (ca. 155–ca. 240), a brilliant African writer—the first to work extensively in Latin—is balanced in his view of the role of Christians in the world. However, later in his life he fell into the heresy of Montanism, which was in essence a puritanically fundamentalist view of Christianity. In his heretical period one finds strong condemnations of those who lived in the world, who pursued the military life, who were wealthy or merchants, or even those who married. "Is trading fit for the service of God?" Tertullian asked. "Certainly, if greed is eliminated, which is the cause of gain. But if gain is eliminated, there is no longer the need of trading."[25] Those who engaged in such actions (or who indeed had any relation to the world at all and who did not hold themselves aloof) were surely damned. The Church unreservedly condemned Montanism as a heresy and, in spite of his brilliance, accorded Tertullian neither the title of saint nor that of Church Father. His later views were too extreme, and condemned the greatest part of humanity to the flames. St. Cyprian of Carthage (ca. 200–258), another representative of the radical Christianity of North Africa, has similar sentiments, but in the end hews to orthodoxy. Like the author of *Hermas* he is concerned that the weight of wealth becomes a burden during persecution, leading some to apostatize for fear of losing it. Such as these "think of themselves as owners, rather, it is they rather who are owned: enslaved as they are to their own property, they are not the masters of money but its slaves."[26] Yet it was the attachment to wealth that caused the fall, and not the wealth itself, a trap into which Cyprian never falls. His anger in *De Lapsis* is with apostates who demonstrated many reasons for abandoning the Church, in addition to wealth. So in a real sense he stands apart from the bitter denunciations of Tertullian, while never forgetting to remind the rich of the burden that holds them bound. The remedy, for Cyprian, is alms given to the Christian poor, through the instrumentality of the bishop, expiating the sins of the wealthy, and creating solidarity in the Christian community.[27]

In spite of criticisms like this, the world of Ante-Nicene Christianity was far from condemning wealth, nor did it seek to abolish private property in anticipation of a sort of Christian communism. Indeed the Ante-Nicene Church is surprisingly positive toward the possibilities of wealth, and the means necessary to acquire it. Wealth was a necessary part of divine providence, meant to engender salvation for its bearers, and it was succor for the poor. It could be retained in service to the community as a whole. There was then no "Constantinian fall" as detractors of the Church would have it; indeed it would be the Post-Nicene period which would develop critiques of wealth which would sound strange to the sub-Apostolic Fathers.

The Golden Age of the Church Fathers

In 313 the emperors Constantine and Licinius met and enacted the Edict of Milan. It legalized Christianity after nearly 250 years under the Neronian decree which proposed the death penalty for followers of Christ (though it was only enforced sporadically). This new edict granted general toleration to the Church, and it restored possessions which had been expropriated by the state in the previous 70 years. That last part is important. It is clear that the Churches of the Mediterranean had possessions, sometimes of significant size and worth, before the dawn of the Great Persecutions in 250 AD.[28] Property was not alien to Christianity. When Pope St. Sixtus II was killed in 258, and his deacon

Lawrence ordered to hand over the wealth of the Church, he showed the Romans the widows, orphans, sick, and poor who were supported by the property holdings and alms of the Church of Rome. The Church had and kept property for the very reasons adduced by Clement of Alexandria: for the protection of the poor and weak, and so that it could enact the works of mercy called for by Christ. Indeed one can and must say that the Church and wealth coexisted much more easily before the legalization than after. In addition to the privileges above, Constantine granted large amounts of money to build new churches, and donated much land in Rome to the Church, notably the Lateran Basilica, which became the "First Church" of Christendom and the cathedral of the papacy. Further, Constantine built massive edifices over the tombs of the apostles Peter and Paul, and left the Church in peace and much wealthier. In fact the Christian bishops were busy appropriating the old Roman civic devotion of the pagan wealthy. It was now to be directed to Christian endowments, both in terms of Church building and in charitable organizations for the poor. Christianity was migrating to a new form of civic pride, one which was focused on the City of God (though which did not thereby exclude a devotion to one's own home or territory).[29]

There was undoubtedly a downside to Christianity's stunning victory against pagan Rome. When Christianity was legalized in 313, finally becoming the official state religion in 380, it no longer required heroic witness to become and remain a Christian. From 64–313 AD Christianity was technically punishable by death. There were local and sporadic—but very bitter—outbreaks of persecution in the second century. The period between the Decian persecutions of 250 and the final climax of the Diocletian persecutions of 313 were general and led to the death of thousands of martyrs. These men and women were drawn from all ages and all conditions of society, and many who were wealthy and of noble blood suffered and died alongside slaves for their commitment to Christ. To be a Christian in this age was heroic, and could often lead to torture and death. Now, as Tertullian said, the "blood of the martyrs is the seed of the Church." For every martyr that was killed, dozens of people converted to the faith, moved by their example and wanting to unite themselves to a faith which inspired such courage. In the end the persecutions backfired on the Romans, leading to the victory of the cross.

Almost overnight, the victory of Constantine changed everything. Now the persecutions had ended, and the emperor and his family had become Christian. Now, not only was it safe to acknowledge one's Christianity publicly, it also became socially advantageous. One can imagine that the quality of those professing the Christian faith dropped significantly over the course of the fourth century. And yet for all that, Christians were still dedicated to the search for perfection. There was no greater perfection or witness than the conformity to Christ in martyrdom. "Greater love has no man than this, that a man lay down his life for his friends. You are my friends if you do what I command you" (Jn 15:13–14). Now that the ages of persecution had passed (at least temporarily), how was one then to "Be perfect, as your heavenly Father is perfect"? (Mt 5:48). Many had begun asking themselves this question, including a "rich young man" named Anthony.

Anthony (251–356) was a wealthy youth from Egypt, descendant of an ancient Christian family of landowners (once again showing the place of wealthy Christians in the Ante-Nicene period). One day as a young man Anthony heard the biblical pericope, "If you would be perfect, go, sell what you possess and give to the poor, and you will have treasure in heaven; and come, follow me" (Mt 19:21). Yet this rich young man answered differently than that one in the gospel. Anthony divided his landholdings, reserved a portion of wealth for his sister, and gave the proceeds to the poor. He then retired to the desert as one of the first hermits, seeking the life of perfection by abandoning anything which might distract him from God, whether it be self-will, family, or money. In doing this he pioneered the practices of monasticism, which would later be augmented by men like Pachomius, Basil, and Benedict into the common life of poverty, chastity, and obedience.

This monastic revolution rocked the Church, as men and women by the thousands abandoned settled life and sought a path of greater perfection. Yet this movement was no gnostic dualism, no rejection of the material world as evil. Once again the distinction must be borne in mind. The Church never condemned marriage; indeed, Christ had come to sanctify it and raise it to the dignity of the sacrament. Yet Christianity also pointed to a better way: the virginity of Christ and Paul's calls to chastity (1 Cor 7:9). So it is not that the married state was evil. No, indeed marriage was good, but virginity was *better* for it was a more perfect way— a *via perfectior*—to union with God. It was similar to self-will. Rightly directed free will was a good, for it was the very freedom with which the creator endowed us as part of being created in the image and likeness of God. However, obedience and abandonment of self will was a *better* way. To apprentice oneself to a spiritual master, and to be directed in the ways of God, was a surer and safer path to holiness. Finally, as we have seen, there was no condemnation of wealth as such, merely cautions about the temptations and sins that it could occasion. Therefore there was a better and more perfect way, that of voluntary poverty. By detachment and divesting, one removed the potential obstacles in one's path toward union with God. So this development must not be seen in terms of binary dichotomies, but rather in the light of a distinction between *good* and *better*. In their eagerness to promote this evangelical ideal, however, very often some of the Church Fathers, particularly those who became monastics themselves, could sometimes tend toward hyperbole in their description of the common life of holiness, and they gave birth to a literary form called *contemptus mundi*, or the contempt of earthly things, singing the praises of the cloister, often to the detriment of those who lived the quotidian Christian life outside of its walls.

The Church of the fourth and fifth centuries was drawn strongly by this monastic ideal but, as always, remained balanced in its public presentation of the faith.[30] This did not, however, prevent them from castigating the rich and the powerful, for with the toleration of Christianity came new opportunities for political and military authority. While Christianity's newfound social acceptance gained it converts, not all of these were as concerned as Anthony with living the life of religious perfection. During these centuries Christian attitudes toward wealth and the market became quite fixed for nearly a millennium, and would form the basis for considerations of money well into the Middle Ages. In particular there was a growing awareness of the commonality of the world's goods: that all material wealth was a gift from God, held in common in necessities, but appropriated privately by just convention. This became particularly pointed in the discussion over provisions for the poor. The idea that there were common goods that included the necessities of human life came to the forefront here and would become the universal teaching of the Church. For example, St. Basil of Caesarea (329/330–379) speaks to the rich, "The bread which you hold back belongs to the hungry; the coat, which you guard in your locked storage-chests, belongs to the naked; the footwear mouldering in your closet belongs to those without shoes. The silver that you keep hidden in a safe place belongs to the one in need."[31] Basil's target here is avarice, that deadly sin of the premodern world, for it denies that all things are gifts from God and uproots human solidarity. It is a ringing call to almsgiving, the duty of those with wealth, "What keeps you from giving now?... The hungry are dying before your face. The naked are stiff with cold. The men in debt are held by the throat. And you, you put off your alms, till another day?"[32] The duty, indeed the salvation of the rich is the succoring of the poor, for the rich are the stewards of wealth so that through it they might become the ministers of God. Indeed, Basil's language is strong; it seems that the superfluous wealth of the rich is the *right* of the poor, and many other Fathers would agree. Ambrose (340–397) has this to say in his consideration of riches: "You are not making a gift of your possession to the poor person. You are handing over to him what is his."[33] Ambrose was eager, as were other bishops, to encourage solidarity with the poor by blurring artificial, socially inherited categories of "otherness" so as to incorporate the poor as brothers and members of the Christian community.[34] Gregory of Nyssa (ca. 335–ca. 395), adducing the universal Fatherhood of God and the universal brotherhood of man, excoriates the rich for hoarding the inheritance of one's own family members. Use for him is permitted, but not abuse.[35] John Chrysostom (ca. 349–407) speaks similarly of the wealthy. Nothing in this world is truly our own, but we have been given superintendence over some things for our own good and the good of all. In terms of wealth, "if you enjoy it alone, you too have lost it: for you will not reap its reward. But if you possess it jointly with the rest, then will it be more your own, and then you will reap the benefit of it."[36] John uses the image of the body. We are all one body, each with separate offices and functions, but which must use those functions in order to be of service to all. Sometimes he speaks even more strongly, "the rich are in possession of the goods of the poor, even if they have acquired them honestly or inherited them legally."[37] Jerome (ca. 347–420) is the most direct, as was his wont. Disgusted with the machinations of ecclesiastical politics in Rome, he retired to a cave in Bethlehem in order to undertake his monumental translation of the Bible. Wanting no part in the newly realized political and economic power of the Church, he encapsulated a latent fear in post-Constantinian Christianity. The Church, he claimed, "has grown great in power and riches and has shrunk in spiritual energy."[38] He, perhaps more than any other Father, contributed to the domination of the monastic mentality in the mind of the West. To the widow Hedibia, he wrote "All riches come from iniquity, and unless one were to lose, another could not gain. Hence the common adage seems to be very true, 'The rich man is unjust or the heir of an unjust one.'"[39] Jerome seems to intimate the absolute impossibility of a rich man's being saved at all here, and so the only possibility for the rich man is complete abandoning of wealth. Of course those familiar with Jerome understand his habitual exaggeration, for it runs like a current through all his work.

It seems that quite a shift had taken place, indeed an inversion of the usual story of Constantinian corruption. Whereas the early Church was favorable to wealth and private property, we see the fourth-century Fathers seeming to overthrow that understanding in favor of a more literalistic type of abandonment of earthly riches. The story is not so simple however. The Church after 313 was encountering and responding to a new situation. There had always been wealthy Christians in the past, but the greatest threat then, as seen from *Hermas* and Cyprian, was that the weight of their riches would make them more likely to apostatize. Now that the danger of persecution was past, Christians had entered into positions of social and political power, thus multiplying the temptations and opportunities to sin. This had led to increasing concern about the position of the wealthy in a Christianized society. Added to that was the new impetus toward voluntary poverty in monasticism. The monks had a privileged place from which to attack wealth and its potential depredations, for they themselves had foregone their money for a more perfect life. Yet an astonishing and unexpected thing happened; society itself came to be drawn toward the monks. As much as Anthony sought to leave public life, so much more did Christians trail out into the desert after him to seek his prayers and advice. A spiritual division of labor was being constructed which would endure well into the Middle Ages. The laity supported the monasteries in their material needs, while the spiritual specialists aided the laity by their prayers and advice. A symbiosis was then created that gave the monks a leadership position in society, one with unquestioned moral authority. In order to prick the conscience of a fallen world, the monks often bit the hand that fed them.

Indeed the Church continued to demonstrate that it was not contrary to riches in themselves. A new heretical movement appeared in the 300s called the Eustathians, probably after Bishop Eustathius of Sebaste. Like Tertullian, he had hardened into a puritanical position regarding the Christian life. Indeed, in many periods of Church history puritanical movements have arisen, which had the common trait of confusing the evangelical counsels of poverty, chastity, and obedience for commandments. Probably disgusted by the stream of converts for less than religious reasons, Eustathius decided to take action himself. Trained in a monastic environment he attempted to mold a new Christianity by making the world into one large cloister. He condemned marriage, the eating of meat, and the management of temporal goods by worldly bishops. He encouraged women to abandon their husbands and for parents to have no care for the material needs of their children. He encouraged his followers to fast always, including on days of mandatory feasting, such as Easter and on Sundays. Most of all, however, he condemned material wealth. The Council of Gangra met at some point during the third quarter of the 300s and condemned all these as errors in no uncertain terms. Of particular interest is the Synodical epilogue, which reinforces the distinction between counsels and commands.

> We do, assuredly, admire virginity accompanied by humility; and we have regard for continence, accompanied by godliness and gravity; and we praise the leaving of worldly occupations, [when it is made] with lowliness of mind; [but at the same time] we honour the holy companionship of marriage, and *we do not condemn wealth enjoyed with uprightness and beneficence*; . . . and we approve of gathering together in the Church itself for the common profit; and *we bless the exceeding charities done by the brethren to the poor, according to the traditions of the Church*; and, to sum up in a word, we wish that all things which have been delivered by the Holy Scriptures and the Apostolical traditions, may be observed in the Church.[40]

The normal, everyday occupations of Christians are guaranteed here. Marriage, family, business, and wealth are all affirmed, with the proper distinction between "good" and "better" maintained. Eustathius' too-vigorous defense of a monastic lifestyle as necessary for salvation was absolutely condemned, even though it would continue to appear in various guises through the centuries.

In spite of their occasional hyperbole, the Post-Nicene Fathers too were nuanced in their assessments of wealth and business.

John Chrysostom, who was unstinting in his speaking of truth to power, even pauses to reflect sometimes on his harsh language. "I am often reproached for continually attacking the rich. Yes, because the rich are continually attacking the poor. But those I attack are not the rich as such, only those who misuse their wealth. I point out constantly that those I accuse are not the rich but the rapacious. Wealth is one thing, covetousness another. Learn to distinguish."[41] Learn to distinguish indeed! For this is the cardinal rule in the Church's mission; any overemphasis of one truth to the detriment of another leads to the deformation of the whole and the formation of heresies. This has its roots in the Incarnational reality defended by the Church as Her central doctrine. The world is good, the things of this world are good, the wealth accrued by a legitimate use of the world which has been vouchsafed to us is good. It is the perversion of the free human will which introduces disorder into nature. It is not the sexual act that is bad, but our perversion of it from its proper ends. It is not the wine that is evil, but our bad wills which turn to sin. Nor is wealth in itself sinful, but rather its misuse, particularly to oppress the poor. This is what those Christian fundamentalists of every age miss, be they sexual puritans, pacifists, or advocates of poverty for its own sake. Chesterton put it best when he described the paradoxical nature of Christianity, where straying too far to one side or the other was to leave orthodoxy behind. Even the crotchety St. Jerome is forced to remark that, "A wise man with wealth has a greater reputation than one merely wise."[42] He goes on, "wealth is not an obstacle to the rich man who uses it well. . . . The example of Abraham, as well as daily instances about us, is a proof of this; the one was a friend of God in the midst of great riches."[43] It should be remembered that these Fathers were living the last age of the Roman empire in the West. The socio-economic classes had hardened considerably, and the wealthy were concentrating their riches, aggressively collecting debts, and using their leverage to persecute the poor. In such a situation it is understandable that Church thinkers would react strongly, yet always return to the golden mean: that it was use and not nature that made riches evil.

The turn of the fifth century saw massive conversions to Christianity, notably among the old Roman families and new men recently risen. They continued to enjoy their wealth as Christians, while accommodating themselves to the new modes of thought about riches being developed at the time. Peter Brown draws our attention to Paulinus of Nola (ca. 354–431), a rich Christian who had abandoned his ancestral lands to move to southern Italy and patronize the shrine of St. Felix. In a certain sense he became the fellow citizen of Felix, and spent his not inconsiderable wealth in constructing a cultic center for the saint. To Paulinus wealth was a balance that had to be transferred. It was symbolic of the transitory nature of earthly life. But still Paulinus was convinced that you *could* take it with you. This was accomplished by taking earthly riches and putting them to the service of God, the Church, and the saints. The massive expenditure he made at Nola were in a certain sense earnest money which would be returned thirtyfold in heavenly glory. He even called it "Spiritual commerce" or "Spiritual business"—*Commercium Spirituale*. Though it sounds a bit impious to modern Christian ears, Paulinus and those like him were convinced that they could purchase heaven, for in so doing God could work the impossible, and allow them to pass through the eye of a needle. Wealth spent for the Church and for the poor was never wasted, but returned with the greatest interest imaginable.[44]

Augustine (354–430), as in nearly all things, sees the farthest. His account of wealth is similar to many of the other Fathers and yet penetrates far more deeply. Like the older Fathers and even Jerome, he asserts the example of the patriarchs against those who would maintain a literalist reading of the evangelical counsels, in this case certain Pelagians. Apparently some of them claimed that, "If the rich remain in their riches, they shall not be able to enter into the kingdom of God." Augustine responds that Abraham, Isaac, and Jacob had copious riches, and yet entered into the heavenly kingdom. The reason that "Dives" did not enter into paradise was on account of the pride which he had in his riches and his dismissal of the needs of Lazarus. One will not be condemned for riches, he says, but only for impiety. He shall receive condemnation for unjust riches. But he who uses his riches well will receive even more from the Lord.[45] This is a recurring theme of Augustine. It is the use rather than the possession which can lead to sin and damnation. "I do not say, 'you are damned if you have wealth,' but 'you are damned if you presume on such things,' if on account of them you are prideful, if you see yourself as great because of them, if you ignore the poor because of them, if you forget the common human condition because you have so much more vanity. For then it is necessary that God pay you back on the last day, and who shall render these things to nothing in His city."[46]

In spite of his capacious mind and learning, it is unfortunate that Augustine was hampered by his limited linguistic abilities. He had to rely on the *Vetus Itala* version of the Greek Septuagint with its misapprehension of Psalms 70 (71):15–16, "Let them not know tradings." In his commentary on the Psalms, Augustine makes some ambivalent remarks on this passage, "Let traders hear and change their life; and if they have been such, be not such. . . . Let Christians amend themselves, let them not trade."[47] He betrays some uneasiness with this obvious meaning, though. He imagines a dialogue with a trader who has brought goods from a faraway place, asking him for his intrepidity and risk whether the "worker is worthy of his reward" (Lk 10:7). Here Augustine hews to the great tradition and to his own metaphysics of evil, for he recognizes that the fraud and deceit sometimes practiced in trading lies in the perverse will of the merchant and not in the nature of trade itself. Indeed it is not only merchants who commit fraud, it can be committed in any field. Augustine gives examples of seamstresses, cobblers, and farmers engaging in fraud, indicating its root in the human will and not in the life of a merchant by its very nature. In the end it is the merchant who admonishes Augustine, "Look then, O Bishop, how you understand the tradings which you have read in the Psalm lest perchance you do not understand, and yet forbid me trading. Admonish me then how I should live, if well, it shall be well with me. One thing however I know, that if I shall have been evil, it is not trading that makes me so, but my iniquity." Augustine allows himself to be chastened by his imaginary interlocutor, and transposes the presumed biblical imprecation against trading into an astonishingly positive statement about the value of the merchant life.

Augustine also analyzes the order of society when seen from the perspective of providence. He considers both the rich and the poor to be that way by the will of God Himself. He says:

> So when God made the poor—since he did not wish that they might have goods—when he makes the poor he tests the rich. For thus it is written, "The rich and poor have met one another" (Prv 22:2). Where do they meet each other? In this life. For this one is born, that one born, they find each other, they meet one another. And "The Lord is the maker of them both" (Prv 22:2). The rich man, that he might help the poor man, the poor that he might test the rich. And that everyone might give from his necessities, let them not do this, that he might suffer dire straits. This we do not say. Your surpluses are others' necessities. You heard it when it was read in the gospel, "And whosoever shall give to drink to one of these little ones a cup of cold water on account of me, he shall not lose his reward" (Mk 9:40). The kingdom of heaven is put up for sale, and He wishes its price to be one cup of cold water. But when it is the poor man who gives alms, then his alms ought to be one cup of cold water. He who has more, let him do more. That widow gave two minas (Mk 12:42). Zacchaeus gave half of his wealth, and in order to redress his fraud, reserved another portion. For those alms benefit those who change their way of life. For you give to the poor of Christ so that you might atone for your past sins. Yet if you gave like that so that you might be permitted to sin always with impunity, you do not feed Christ, but you attempt to bribe the judge.

> Therefore give alms so that your prayers might be heard, and God might speed you to life changed for the better. And you who change in this life, shall be changed for the better. And through alms and prayers many past sins will be blotted out, and future goods come to you forever.[48]

Riches and poverty are sent from God Himself, who is omnipotent and omniscient. They are there for testing. Nor is one to exhaust one's own wealth in supporting the poor, but rather to give from one's excess. In a certain sense the rich are to be a gift to the poor, to enable them to meet their lives' necessities, yet without putting trust in such riches. Earlier in the sermon he warns the rich not to trust in their wealth, nor to use it as a cause for pride. All that they have received is from God and will return thence. A commonly used phrase in Augustine for the poor is *laturarii*, or porters. The poor become not passive receptacles for Augustine, but work out their own salvation as spiritual merchants. They are the ones who are the agents of the rich in transferring their wealth to the Kingdom of God; they are the moneychangers, who turn the coin of the earth into the treasure of heaven.[49] This created a radically new calculus of almsgiving. No longer was magnanimity the province of the rich alone, but more humble possessors could lay up treasure in heaven proportional to their means. One need only recall the gesture of the Widow's Mite in the gospels. Brown calls this a "flattening" of the hierarchy of giving. It allowed average Christians to lay up treasure by their own modest gifts. For "every gift, however small, brought about nothing less than the joining of heaven and earth."[50] Augustine preaches powerfully using the language of the gospel regarding the necessity of laying up treasure in heaven, and cleverly weaves the concept in mercantile terms. The poor work out their salvation by receiving alms, the rich by giving it. There is no necessity for absolute abandonment of wealth, for such inequalities were within the very providence of God Himself.

Some have said that Augustine is remarkable in his appreciation for wealth and the merchant life. Perhaps he simply thought it through more. After all he came from a middle-class family of strivers and achieved the office of Bishop. During the fourth and fifth centuries the Bishops had to undertake substantial temporal duties, including managing the patrimony of the Church and acting as adjudicators in small claims cases.[51] His intimate familiarity with the Christian laity had insulated him from some of the more strident criticisms of wealth made by his monastic colleagues. His long struggle with the problem of evil had focused his attention away from evil having a positive existence in natures (the dualistic error of his youthful Manichaeanism) toward the fixing of evil as a disorder in limited, free wills. Sin could be found in any Christian vocation, and in spite of the special temptations brought by money, in no way was wealth intrinsically evil, any more than liquor, sex, or food were. Augustine could see the benefits of mercantile trade, even from a human perspective. He chooses not to cast society in terms of class warfare between rich and poor, but rather uses the old distinction between the "rich" and the "wise." The foolish rich sought only to acquire; Augustine and his friends sought the philosophical life of wisdom that used wealth with moderation.[52] He also recognized the necessity of the rich in supporting the Church and the poor, and indeed made a shift to recognizing that the vocation of the rich lay precisely in their wealth. The use they made of it would determine their eternal destination. Augustine's focus on the freedom of the individual will (all under the omnipotent providence of God) can be seen in his stunning *Confessions*. It was he who brought to the attention of the world the incarnational revolution of Christianity. Individuals, rich or poor, were no longer cogs in a machine, valuable only in the aggregate for the use of the powerful. No, rather the drama of salvation played out in the universe of each individual soul. Christianity had brought a revolution of individuality which would become a hallmark of the West, even though the Church always embedded the individual within the range of the reciprocal social relations of Church, city, and family. It will be Augustine's insight that will permit the innovation made possible in the scholastic thought of the central Middle Ages, though not before a long period where the monastic elements of the critique of wealth completely held the field.

Early Medieval Developments

The Fathers of the Church thus wove a complex tapestry regarding the West's appreciation and trepidation over money, trading, and wealth. Their meditations paralleled similar developments in Judaism. The Talmud relates that a rabbi was asked why God doesn't support the poor, if He loves them. The rabbi replied, "So that through them [by giving alms] we [the rich] may be saved from the punishment of Gehinnon."[53] Neither faith could have foreseen, however, the coming of a new religious force, whose ideas on such things would be both radically simple and quite opposed to the established Christian tradition. Muhammad was born into the trading city of Mecca, a member of the powerful Quraysh tribe who controlled the markets and trade routes of southern Arabia. He married a prosperous tradeswoman named Khadijah, and took active part in the trading life himself, even while he was receiving the revelations later written down in the *Quran*. From the very beginning of the religion trading and the merchant life were honored and praised, both in the *Quran* itself, and in the Hadith, or traditions, which grew up around its interpretation. Some ideas would be familiar to the Judeo-Christian tradition. For instance, Islam asserts the universal dominion over all things by God, while maintaining that humans enjoy a right to the use of property as the agents of Allah. As long as property is justly acquired, it may be enjoyed without sin.[54] Fraud and deceit are to be excluded from all commercial life. Indeed, Muhammad is reported as condemning avarice in strong terms, "the slave of the dinar is miserable."[55] Here is where the comparisons largely end. There is no call to asceticism or renunciation of property within the religion, other than the communally sanctioned fasts and alms. Mendicancy is seen as exceptionally dishonorable, and work is a requirement.[56] The religion explicitly permitted profit-seeking for its own sake. As long as the wealthy fulfill their religious duties, and do not try to avoid fighting by use of wealth, then they are permitted to own and enjoy their goods. Indeed, one of the primary reasons for the Islamic expansion was the legitimate enjoyment of spoils promised by the *Quran*.[57] The heaven of Allah is seen to be a material paradise, comparable to the blessings of earthly wealth. In the end, there is no counterbalancing tradition in Islam that is similar to the New Testament counsels of renunciation. Wealth and its use, omitting fraud and corruption, are affirmed. Indeed, in an early Hadith it is recorded, "From Abdullah Ibn 'Umar—may Allah be pleased with him—that Allah's messenger [Muhammad]—peace and prayer of Allah be upon him—said, 'The trustworthy, honest Muslim merchant will be with the Prophets, the honest men, and martyrs on the Day of Resurrection.'"[58] Islam quickly conquered an area from the Atlantic Ocean to India, and when the tide of conquest slowed, established a mercantile system and empire that was far advanced beyond its Christian counterpart, for there was no contrary intellectual or religious tradition to challenge it. No tension existed. Al-Ghazali puts it thus, "The truthful tradesman will resurrect on the Resurrection Day with the truthful and the martyrs."[59] While this certainly materially benefitted the Islamic world, the absence of the salutary tensions in the Christian tradition prevented the kind of serious and thoughtful development on the moral role of riches on society.

While Islam was rapidly expanding the West was contracting. Islam took over the majority of land in the eastern Byzantine empire, not to mention the Christian territories of north Africa and Spain. In the meantime barbarian groups had migrated into western Europe. Long familiar to the Romans, these peoples sought land and settlement rights in imperial territory. Gradually they took over the political remnants of Roman authority and created a network of successor states with new ruling elites.[60] It took the Church several hundred years of patient labor to bring these new peoples into the fold of orthodox Christianity. With the collapse of the old Empire the economic networks began to constrict. Old trading routes were extinguished, especially because of Islam, throwing people back upon their own local resources. The availability of exchangeable commodities decreased. There was no longer any Roman army or navy to protect travelling merchants, and the Muslims had sealed off trade to the east, making the long-distance trading of the Roman era but a distant memory. The Muslims would keep this near-monopoly on far eastern trade until the ages of exploration in the 1400s.

Several economic consequences followed from these events. First, as the trading economy of the late antique period waned, the concept of gift economy gained renewed traction.[61] This more primitive economic form had clear basis in human nature, and some resonance with the Christian tradition. It was an economy of largesse. Wealth existed to be displayed and given away in order to show one's liberality and magnanimity. Of all of these hospitality came to be seen as the cardinal virtue. In a very real sense, it was a hearkening back to pre-Christian economics described both in Greece and in the Old Testament. The new Germanic peoples constructed their social ties through complicated rituals of reciprocal gift exchange. As Peter Brown has outlined, the Christian concept of charity could be elided with these ideas of gift. The precise prices and values calculated within a complex market system are simply not there anymore (most prices were fixed locally and differed from town to town). Because of this, the culture was thereby insulated not only from the accumulation of wealth for its own sake, but also the from the attendant temptations and sins denounced by the Fathers. Indeed, the voices of the next half-millennium would be quite silent about the dangers of wealth to the Christian community, largely because these problems were essentially nonexistent.

This gift economy can be witnessed in any number of places, in Gregory of Tours (538–594), in *Beowulf*, and all the way through to the Nordic sagas. Great kings distributed their wealth liberally and lavishly to their clients, and characters who hoarded wealth were almost pitied rather than excoriated (i.e., the monster Grendel). Christianity did exert some influence however. Burial of wealth in treasure troves was forbidden, and the new Christians were encouraged to make the "heavenly transfer" described by Augustine and Paulinus of Nola. In the case of the early Middle Ages this involved the creation of monasteries and the endowment of the shrines of the saints. The introduction of this concentrated wealth began a slow circulation through the territories of western Europe, gradually increasing the amount of specie available for exchange. From the seventh century mercantile trade began to reawaken.[62] Indeed, the Carolingians had again begun to stabilize silver coinage to supplement the base metal money that had been enough for the previous several centuries. Unfortunately the Carolingian moment fizzled out, and Europe would have to wait generations for the promise of a commercial revolution to bear fruit. For indeed the majority of Europe had coalesced into quasi-independent local microstates, a peasantry surrounding primitive castles for protection. In spite of that trade slowly resumed, and towns arose which were not related to agricultural produce, but to the promotion of mercantile adventures.

Yet the pieces were moving. Minted coinage was expanding. The borders were becoming stabilized. Some cities in Italy had not ceased the practices of trade all through this period, in places like Genoa, Pisa, and Venice. Most of all though, Europe was on the edge of two of the most important transitions in the history of the world. By the year 1000 she was on the cusp of the second agricultural revolution, creating the means to produce a superabundance of food with much less labor, a development that would lead to the great commercial revolution and creation of the proto-capitalism whose effects continue to be felt to this day. Yet what of the response of the Church? Held in abeyance for nearly half-a-millenium, questions about greed, wealth, riches, and salvation would once again be aired, and the answers that were produced created a new path for the west.

Chapter 1 Endnotes

1. Two key works for understanding these developments are: Justo Gonzalez, *Faith and Wealth: A History of Early Christian Ideas on the Origin, Significance, and Use of Money* (New York: Harper and Row, 1990). This work is however tinged with more contemporary concerns about the place of the poor in current Christian theologies, but is useful for gathering relevant texts. Also, see Barry Gordon, *The Economic Problem in Biblical and Patristic Thought* (Leiden: Brill, 1989). For a very in-depth analysis with his usual perspicacity, see Peter Brown, *Through the Eye of a Needle: Wealth, the Fall of Rome, and the Making of Christianity in the West, 350–550 AD* (Princeton, NJ: Princeton University Press, 2012).
2. To give one example, see Dt 23:17.
3. The correct translation is "ὅτι οὐκ ἔγνων γραμματείας, εἰσελεύσομαι ἐν δυναστείᾳ κυρίου," "Quoniam non cognovi litteraturam, introibo in potentias Domini," "Since I did not know letters, I will enter into the powers of the Lord."
4. For a thorough examination see John Thomas Noonan, *The Scholastic Analysis of Usury* (Cambridge: Harvard University Press, 1957).
5. See Plato, *Laws*, 918.
6. Aristotle, *Nicomachean Ethics*, 1.v.8. 1096a.
7. Aristotle, *Politics*, book 2. For an analysis of the economic significance of his writings see, Scott Meikle, *Aristotle's Economic Thought* (Oxford: Clarendon Press, 1995).
8. See the analysis of Barry Gordon in *The Economic Problem in Biblical and Patristic Thought* (Leiden: Brill, 1989), esp. pp. 43–88.
9. A position discussed ably by Augustine, *City of God*, book XI, and in C. S. Lewis, *The Problem of Pain*.
10. *In Paradisum*, "Chorus angelorum te suscipiat, et cum Lazaro quondam paupere aeternam habeas requiem."
11. Shakespeare, *Henry IV, part I*, III.3, 33.
12. In reality such a sentiment was not original to 1 Timothy; centuries before Diogenes the Cynic had made the same claim, another instance of the dovetailing of Christian and Classical thought.
13. Robert Wilken, *The Spirit of Early Christianity* (New Haven, CT: Yale, 2003), xvii.
14. These considerations drove so much of the *ressourcement* and *Nouvelle Theologie* of the pre-conciliar period.
15. For an excellent introduction to these arguments see: J. A. McGuckin, "The Vine and the Elm Tree: The Patristic Interpretation

16 First Letter of Clement to the Corinthians, c. 38.
17 *Didache*, c. 3, 11, 15.
18 Johannes Quasten, *Patrology*. 4 vols. (Utrecht, 1972), I. 92–96.
19 *Shepherd of Hermas*, Vision 3.5.5.
20 Ibid., Parable 9.27.4.
21 For an introduction to Clement's economic thought, see Annewies van den Hoek, "Widening the Eye of the Needle: Wealth and Poverty in the Works of Clement of Alexandria," in *Wealth and Poverty in Early Church and Society*, ed. Susan R. Holman (Grand Rapids, MI: Baker Academic, 2008), 67–75.
22 Thomas sums up these virtues and vices exceptionally well in *Summa Theologiae*, II-II, q. 117–19.
23 *Quis Dives Salvetur*, c. 13–14.
24 McGuikin, 11, rightly notes the influence of the Stoic doctrine of "Right Use," that is, using thing for the end for which they were designed.
25 Tertullian, *On Idolatry*, c. 11.
26 St. Cyprian of Carthage, *De Lapsis*, 6:10–12.
27 Brown, *Through the Eye*, 43.
28 I profoundly disagree with contemporary historians who attempt to minimize the reality of early Christian persecution and the significance of the martyrs. E.g., Candida R. Moss, *The Myth of Persecution: How Early Christians Invented a Story of Martyrdom* (New York: Harper One, 2014). She ignores archaeology, art history, and near-contemporary historians in favor of an overemphasis on some unreliable hagiographical traditions. The book combines this approach with a modern political leitmotif that makes for bad history.
29 Brown, *Through the Eye*, 64.
30 Many of the later Patristic meditations on riches can be found edited and translated in: Walter Shewring, *Rich and Poor in Christian Tradition* (London: Burns, Oates & Washbourne, 1948).
31 St. Basil the Great, *Homily on the saying of the Gospel According to Luke, "I will pull down my barns and build bigger ones," and on Greed*, 7 (Patrologia Graeca 31, 277A), hereafter PG.
32 Ibid.
33 "Non de suo largiris pauperi, sed de suo reddis." St. Ambrose, *On Naboth* (Patrologia Latina 17, 747) hereafter PL, translated in Shewring, *Rich and Poor*, 69–82. Ambrose is perhaps the most direct theorist against natural private property among the Fathers. "Nature produced common rights, then, it is usurping greed that has

established private rights." Ambrose, *De Officiis*, 1.28.137. For this see the discussion in Brown, *Through the Eye*, 131–34. In a certain sense his radicalism is echoed centuries later in Rousseau's and communist theorists' considerations of private property.
34 Ibid., 129.
35 St. Gregory of Nyssa, *De Pauperibus Amandis* (PG 46:466), translated in Shewring, *Rich and Poor*, 63–68.
36 St. John Chrysostom, *Homily 10 on First Corinthians*, c. 7.
37 St. John Chrysostom, *Homily 11 on Lazarus*.
38 St. Jerome, *Vita Malchi*, (PL 23: 53C), cf. Brown, *Through the Eye*, xxv.
39 St. Jerome, *Letter to Hedibia*, Ep. 120.
40 Synod of Gangra, synodal epilogue. Italics mine.
41 St. John Chrysostom, *On the Fall of Eutropius*, 2.3.
42 St. Jerome, *Commentary on Ecclesiastes*, 7.12, trans. Richard J. Goodrich and David J. D. Miller (New York: The Newman Press, 2012), 85.
43 Cf. John A. Ryan, "The Church Fathers on Wealth and Ownership, Part III: St. Ambrose and St. Jerome," *The Common Cause*, Vol. 2, July–December 1912, 170.
44 Brown, *Through the Eye*, 235–36.
45 St. Augustine, Epistle 157.23 (PL 33, 686).
46 "Non dico: Damnamini, quia habetis; sed, damnamini, si de talibus praesumatis, si de talibus inflemini, si propter talia magni vobis videamini, si propter talia pauperes non agnoscatis, si generis humani conditionem communem propter excellentem vanitatem obliviscamini. Tunc enim Deus necesse est retribuat in novissima, et in civitate sua imaginem talium ad nihilum redigat." St. Augustine, *Ennarationes in Psalmos*, 72.26 (PL 36, 925–26).
47 *Ennarationes in Psalmos*, Psalm 70 (71): 15–17 (PL 36, 886). It is notable that Augustine does identify "letters" as being present in some codices, and provides an exegesis for that reading too. He freely admits that he does not know which one is the correct reading.
48 "Quando ergo Deus facit pauperes, quia ipse non vult ut, habeant, quando facit pauperes probat divites. Sic enim scriptum est: Pauper et dives occurrerunt sibi. Ubi sibi occurrerunt? In hac vita. Natus est ille, natus est et ille: invenerunt se, occurrerunt sibi. Et quis fecit illos? Dominus. Divitem, unde pauperem adiuvaret; pauperem, unde divitem probaret. Pro viribus suis quisque faciat. Non sic faciat, ut ipse patiatur angustias. Non hoc dicimus. Superflua tua necessaria sunt alii. Audistis modo, cum Evangelium legeretur: Quicumque dederit calicem aquae frigidae uni ex minimis meis

propter me, non perdet mercedem suam. Regnum caelorum venale proposuit, et pretium eius calicem aquae frigidae esse voluit. Sed quando pauper est qui facit elemosinas, tunc debet elemosina eius esse calix aquae frigidae. Qui plus habet, plus faciat. Vidua illa de duobus minutis fecit. Zacchaeus dimidium rerum suarum dedit, et ad reddendas fraudes suas, aliud dimidium reservavit. Elemosinae illis prosunt qui vitam mutaverint. Das enim Christo egenti ut peccata tua redimas praeterita. Nam si ideo das ut liceat tibi semper impune peccare, non Christum pascis, sed iudicem corrumpere conaris. Ergo ad hoc facite elemosinas ut vestrae orationes exaudiantur et adiuvet vos Deus ad vitam in melius commutandam. Et qui commutatis eamdem vitam in melius commutate. Et per elemosinas et orationes deleantur mala praeterita, et futura bona veniant sempiterna." Augustine, Sermon 39.4 (PL 38, 542).

49 The image is used in Sermons 25, 53A, and 60. See the engaging discussion in P. Allen and E. Morgan, "Augustine on Poverty," in *Preaching Poverty in Late Antiquity: Perceptions and Realities* (Leipzig: Evangelische Verlaganstalt, 2009): 119–70.
50 Brown, *Through the Eye*, 86.
51 See the exhaustive biography of Augustine in Peter Brown, *Augustine of Hippo: A Biography* (Berkeley, CA: University of California Press, 1967, 2013).
52 Brown, *Through the Eye*, 169.
53 Cf. Brown, *Through the Eye*, 236.
54 Some argue that this extends even to those outside the Islamic religion, see Surah 3:75.
55 Hadith quoted in Al-Ghazali, *The Niche of Lights*, trans. David Buchanan (Provo, UT: BYU Press, 1998), 46.
56 Al-Ghazali, *Iḥyā' 'ulūm al-dīn*, trans. Fazl-ul-Karim, 3.1.
57 Surah 48:20.
58 From Hadith collections: Ibn Maja (no. 2139), al Hakim (no. 2142), and ad Daruquthni (no. 17).
59 Al-Ghazali, *Iḥyā' 'ulūm al-dīn*, trans. Fazl-ul-Karim, 3.1.
60 For this process, see especially Patrick Geary, *The Myth of Nations: The Medieval Origins of Europe* (Princeton, N.J.: Princeton University Press, 2003).
61 While the monetary and trading economies did not wholly cease, the gift economy was a real phenomenon, encouraged by new Christian conceptions of Charity. See Lester Little's "From Gift Economy to Profit Economy," in *Religious Poverty and the Profit Economy in Medieval Europe* (Ithaca, NY: Cornell University Press, 1994), and

the writings of Arnoud-Jan A. Bijsterveld, especially his: *Do Ut Des: Gift Giving, Memoria, and Conflict Management in the Medieval Low Countries* (Hilversum: Verloren, 2007).

62 For this especially see Michael McCormick, *Origins of the European Economy: Communications and Commerce A.D. 300–900* (Cambridge: Cambridge University Press, 2001), 784–85.

Chapter 2
GROWING PAINS

Charlemagne's long reign (768–814) was a high point of the early Middle Ages. He brought security to the frontiers (including conquests that brought in significant revenue), good governance to his kingdom, and a nascent renaissance that paved the way for the establishment of the schools of medieval Europe. For economic markets to develop and mature all three of these elements were necessary: stability, justice, and learning. Though gold coinage had gradually fallen out of use by the end of the Merovingian age, the Carolingians were able to stabilize the value of the silver *denier*.[1] It was an indicator of the revival of trade and business that slowly revivified throughout the period.[2] Yet Charlemagne's great achievement did not long outlive him. Soon after his death new enemies began to appear on the horizon. The Vikings, emboldened by the death of the powerful warrior, began their devastating raids from the north, pouring down the river courses of continental Europe. In the east a new barbarian force had arisen: the Magyars (or Hungarians). To the south the Muslims, after a century of infighting, had coalesced once again, and began to raid in earnest along the Christian Mediterranean coast, even sacking the city of Rome itself in 846. Nor did the internal situation of the empire help. Charlemagne's son, Louis the Pious, engaged in a bitter and protracted civil war against his own sons, one that saw Europe permanently divided in 843 in the treaty of Verdun. The Church was little better off; after the rule of Nicholas I called the "Great" (858–867), there was to be no strong pope for nearly 200 years, with the papacy falling into terrible moral turpitude in the tenth century. Even the monasteries, which had preserved learning and the search for religious perfection during the days of the political dissolution of Rome, were waning in their observances. The majority of them had become relaxed and sought no longer the perfection desired so strongly by their forefathers Anthony, Basil, and Benedict. In this situation commerce could only advance by fits and starts, though it seems clear that, from the seventh century, a steady if slow improvement in economic conditions was able to manifest itself.

Early Medieval Society

Europe at the time was essentially a society of landholding rooted in a variety of interpersonal relationships based on loyalty and service, with some mercantile activity on the margins of the North Sea and the Mediterranean.[3] Society was fundamentally agricultural, focused on a manor which was intended to have all of the requisite necessities for the life of a small village, organized around a system of rents or payments-in-kind.[4] In spite of that there is clearly evidence of trade, at least on the local level within the Carolingian heartlands. A system of serfdom developed in which an individual owed a certain amount of labor to his local lord in exchange for protection, but was otherwise free to exercise his industry for the support of his family and to marry and associate within the village itself. In the ninth century, the imperial system broke down quickly and control reverted to these local units of government. Because of the level of political violence little external travel was necessary or possible. Some exceptions existed. In the first place the international Church was still there and—though it needed reform—it provided a unifying force for society along with the necessity of travelling on ecclesiastical business. It also supplied the one outlet for upward mobility in a socially stratified age, though within the clergy wealthy families dominated monasteries and bishoprics. Further, there was always the possibility of pilgrimage which could be undertaken by anyone in a society, either to local shrines or—as time went on—to the more distant and famous shrines of

Compostela, Rome, or even Jerusalem.[5] Pilgrimage kept the roads of early medieval Europe open and was one of key paths to sanctity open to the lay faithful. Another aspect that caused medievals to venture beyond their villages was church law. Canon law prohibited marriage within the fourth degree of consanguinity, but in the early Middle Ages this was often increased to seven (until restored to four by Lateran IV in 1215).[6] This included marriage with up to a sixth cousin. While customs varied from place to place, if one was going to keep Church law it was going to be imperative to travel outside of the village. While often ignored in practice, this would have the effect of encouraging exogamy and travel. Beside the peasantry though, the nobility continued to travel to assemblies, to war, and in practicing roving lordship over multiple territories. Outside of these cases however, the conditions for the creation of open markets in the early Middle Ages was quite limited.

All of this began to change, at first at a glacial pace, then like a torrent. In 909 two Benedictine monks named Odo and Adhegrin did the unthinkable. They abandoned their monasteries. One of the vows that every Western monk took was one of stability, or of permanent, lifetime affiliation with one monastery. Yet these monks were no renegades. The monastery they had left was relaxed and corrupt, with no intention of living the life of perfection or following the Benedictine charism. So they abandoned it and traveled to a remote valley in central Burgundy. There they founded the mighty monastery of Cluny and called to themselves all monks who wanted truly to live their calling. Other reform attempts had been tried, with limited local success, but none had the long-term influence of Cluny. They allied with the papacy, which granted them the privilege of exemption from unworthy bishops, thus allowing their ministry to develop unhindered. Within a hundred years the corrupt monasteries were depopulated, either being closed or put under the authority of Cluny, and were completely reformed. These became an engine for European progress into the next centuries. The search for perfection, it seems, was far from dead.

Civil society was beginning to stabilize itself as well. After a hundred years of depredations by the Viking raiders, Christendom realized that the best way to neutralize the northern threat was to co-opt them into European society by ensuring that they converted to Christianity. Through many twists and turns, through force of arms, cultural pressure, and missions the Viking world was gradually incorporated into the Church so that—by the early 1000s—the Vikings had been established as an integral part of Christendom. Their raids were over and the north was secure. A similar thing gradually happened in the east as Byzantine missionaries from the south and German missionaries from the west converged into the Slavic lands. One by one the tribes of eastern Europe became Christianized: Bohemia, Poland, Bulgaria, Hungary, and even Russia entered into the fold of the Church, thereby checking menace from the eastern paganism. In Spain the tiny Christian kingdom had not only survived but had begun to push back against Islamic occupation, continuing its 700-year-long *Reconquista* to take back the country Spain from the Muslims. Governments too were beginning to stabilize. Otto I became Holy Roman Emperor in 962, providing the first strong imperial leadership in central Europe since Charlemagne. Hugh Capet, though ruling just a small area around Paris, established a dynasty in 987 that would rule for over 800 years. England ended over two centuries of struggles between Angles, Saxons, and Danes with the Norman invasion of 1066. The pieces were falling into place.

One of the primary reasons for this stabilization was climatological. Beginning in the seventh century, Europe entered into the Medieval Warm Period. The bitter winters of the post-Roman age came to an end, and incessant rains began to fade away. The temperatures increased while the climate dried out. During this period, for instance, England was able to grow grape vines and produce its own wine. Greenland may indeed have been greener when the Viking navigators first arrived and when they landed in Labrador, they called it the "land of the grapevines." Conditions were ripe for an increase in agricultural production, even without the innovations in farming technology which came out of this period. Land in the Mediterranean region around Italy and Spain was soft and easy to plow. Ever since the ancient world it had been enough simply to turn the soil over lightly and to plant crops that achieved a reasonable yield. The tools used were called "scratch plows" from which we get our expression to "scratch the surface."[7] In the north however the soil was wet and heavy. It was extremely rich in nutrients, if only it could be accessed. As Europe dried out these became easier to plow but, coupled with advances in surface mining that allowed more iron to be produced, the medievals made one of the most significant breakthroughs in history: the heavy, wheeled plow. These iron-hardened plowshares could bite deeply into the soil, churning up nutrients which in turn created an increase in crop yields. Of further importance was a change in draft animals. In early medieval Europe the ox was the prime choice for plowing. While strong, they were slow and nearly impossible to turn, leading to extremely long strips of cultivated land. A horse, while a bit weaker, was of much greater utility. It was easy to manage, trainable, and had a multitude of other uses outside of plowing (for example it was rare to see a person riding an ox to market). The problem was the harness. Oxen were so strong that the harness could be placed around their necks. To do this to a horse would be to choke it. The invention of the soft harness changed everything. Now the soft collar could be placed against the breastplate of the horse, enabling it to pull with its whole weight and yet leave its neck free for movement and without restricting its breathing. It is estimated that these innovations allowed the horse to do 50% more work than an ox, even though it was less muscular.

Another innovation was the concept of crop rotation which involved the use of two, and then three, different divisions of a field. One part of the field was left fallow, which allowed it to be used for pasture, and to allow the nutrients to recharge. The introduction of legumes also allowed the soil to regenerate even while producing a crop. All of these produced such an astonishing surplus that it has been called the Second Agricultural Revolution, with effects that paralleled the achievements of the first during the neolithic period, which had allowed the first stable settlements in human history.

Revolutions Agricultural and Commercial

This surplus meant many changes for European society. In the first place, coupled with political security and rapidly stabilizing frontiers, people felt secure enough to begin to have more children. There is a close correlation between stability and family size in the premodern world and Europeans began to have large numbers of children. As an anecdotal example of this, Catherine of Siena (1347–1380) was the 23rd child of Giacomo di Benincasa and his wife Lapa, just before the Black Death put an end to European population growth. In any case the period between 900–1300 was the longest sustained period of growth of any culture in human history up to that point—a baby boom that lasted not 20 years, but 400. England, which had a population of 1.1 million in the Domesday book of 1086, had risen to 3.7 million by 1346. Increased food and a more varied diet helped to promote elevated life expectancy, though the rate of infant mortality was still exceptionally high. The increase of agricultural efficiency meant not only more food, but less labor needed to produce it. This created a surplus of residents in rural territories who were not necessary for agricultural work. These began to migrate to the cities around the year 1000, creating an urbanization at levels never seen before.

The generation of increasingly large agricultural surpluses led to questions about how to deal with them. Coupled with the innovations in farm machinery, significant achievements were made in gearing that allowed the production of flour and facilitated the brewing of beer. In both of these forms wheat and other cereal products had a much longer shelf life. They could be stored against times of want. The improved weather of the Medieval Warm Period meant that periods of plenty were far more common. Gradually, once the needs of the village had been satisfied, people began to look further afield in their efforts to profitably be rid of their excess surplus. Eventually regional markets developed in centralized locations along rivers and the remains of the road system. These provided temporary places to trade and barter, increasing the possibility for exchange and profit. These also necessitated the expansion of useable money, which was easily exchangeable and transportable. Farmers could sell their surplus regionally. They earned not only enough to support their families, but began to generate surplus income, which opened the way to the purchase of luxuries, at least for the upper classes. Such was what economists call a "virtuous circle" where rising surpluses and profits create heightened demand and allow increased specialization of labor, which in turn leads to technological and economic innovation, thus increasing the efficiency of production, resulting in increased wealth for the whole of the community. As the specialization of labor increased, and as farming efficiency lowered the need for agricultural workers, these temporary markets and fairs became progressively permanent, until they established themselves as towns. Older cities which had suffered during the middle ages, now found new life as they emerged as the economic nexuses of a burgeoning society, taking in the excess population from the countryside, and creating entirely new urban landscapes.

Trade began to increase dramatically and was centered around two primary axes, the city-states of north-central Italy and the coastal towns of Flanders. What we see developing is labor paid in wages, increasing profits, and the pooling of capital. This was the necessary groundwork for the achievement of the Commercial Revolution which established the precursors of modern capitalism and made possible the development of economic tools which would propel Europe later into the Industrial Revolution.[8] Between these areas vast commercial networks were spawned, connected by a rapidly improving road system and coastal sea lanes. The already existing cities in the Islamic world proved ready markets for increased European production. Many European towns banded together to create robust commercial leagues, bringing in astonishing wealth and attracting a population wholly dedicated to trade or industry. The presence of such numbers of people, the greatest concentrations since late Roman times, demanded the mobilization of the local economy for security, order, raw materials, and a regular supply of food. A stable system of exchanges was quickly regularized between city and country, and between the sources of raw materials and the commercial centers.

In order to manage this trade, innovations were needed. No longer could a merchant be expected to travel all over Europe with chests full of money, thus being subjected to robbers and highwaymen. Besides the slow increase of precious specie, first silver, and—in the thirteenth century—gold, enterprising individuals began to set up shop in the same markets where the merchants traded. There they specialized in exchanging and weighing money from different nations. More importantly, one could deposit sums of money with them and receive a letter of credit in return. This letter of credit could be exchanged wherever the bank had an affiliate stall in any of the markets of Europe. This freed the merchant from the burden of carrying his money with him, and increased the security he felt in making journeys and transactions. The concentration of wealth in these institutions enabled investment on a scale never before seen. Whereas a merchant might not have enough capital to undertake a potentially profitable journey, the banking houses did. Using their pooled capital, they bankrolled tremendous enterprises with the hopes of profit, thus propelling the expansion of trade and exchange far beyond what was possible even for the wealthiest merchant.[9] Other astute medieval entrepreneurs noted one of the reasons that merchants, a notoriously cautious band, were nervous about undertaking profitable but dangerous journeys. There was a real possibility a ship sent to Egypt for grain might never come back. These entrepreneurs stationed themselves at the port of Venice and began to take records. They noticed that 97 of 100 ships made it back to Venice. They devised a system whereby a merchant would pay 5% of the whole profit of a journey to these insurers. If the ship was lost, the insurance company paid out 100% of the cost, thus insulating the merchant from risk. If it returned, the merchant pocketed 95% of the profit, and the insurance company 5%, more than enough to account for the 3% of ships who were lost. This distribution of risk in the invention of insurance was critical to the spread of commercial wealth and the expansion of trade. Coupled with a decrease in risk came the creation of a whole new type of business, the insurance industry—without which a functioning complex market could not exist. Another innovation of this period was the joint-stock company (in the Middle Ages called *commenda*), which served to disperse risk while increasing the ability to bring wealth to bear on large-scale projects. What one merchant could never do on his own, 100 investors certainly could, with each being entitled to a share of the profits. Other breakthroughs had to do with such workaday issues as recordkeeping. How was one to keep track of a trading empire which ranged over thousands of miles? The medievals pioneered double-entry bookkeeping to ensure the veracity of trading records, a simple invention yet of incalculable significance in the success of the European protocapitalist project. The basis of our modern economic system was established in its entirety in the central Middle Ages. 500 years before Adam Smith laid down the principles of capitalist theory in *Wealth of Nations*, the practices that made it possible were pioneered, creating a rising cycle of prosperity that had made possible our modern industrial and technological age. While it was not capitalism *per se*, since it was not liberated from the social, cultural, and religious claims of the medieval world, it was precisely those claims which humanized it, and prevented many of the issues that later arose from the liberal capitalism of the nineteenth century.[10]

THE RISE OF THE CITIES

Yet with this revolution came unintended and unexpected consequences. A whole new socio-economic stratum had been created, never before seen in the history of any human culture. These independent townsmen stood outside the social preconceptions of their age. For instance, Alfred the Great (King of England, r. 886–899) had described the existence of three distinct orders.[11] The first estate was the clergy, or those who had received tonsure and exercised spiritual authority in Christendom. These were not only the great bishops of the Church, but also the thousands of monks who exercised proprietorship over much of the lands of Europe. These were known as "those who pray" for they had the responsibility of supporting the nobles and peasants by their spiritual exercises. Whether bishop or monk, though, the source of their wealth was the vast rural estates that sustained their offices. The second order was the aristocrats, who were known as "those who make war." They handled the civil government of society and were responsible for the protection of the Church and the peasantry. Fundamentally their power was also drawn from their rural estates. The final order was "those who work" or the peasants of the early medieval period. These were the serfs, tied to the nobility by bonds of loyalty and a desire for security. It was they who assured that provision was made for both the Church and the nobility, in exchange for protection, both material and spiritual. The people of the burgeoning towns of medieval Europe belonged to none of these classes. They were not aristocrats; indeed the early history of the communes shows how they displaced both the civil aristocracy and those bishops who were too closely aligned with that class. Yet neither were they peasants. They did not farm and bore no feudal allegiance to any rural lord. The legal principle (developed in the twelfth century) that a serf became free if he remained away from his village for a year and a day, gave rise to the German expression "Stadtluft macht frei" or "City air makes one free." These people were artisans, professional workers, skilled laborers, or employees in the blossoming industries of medieval Flanders and Italy. They were a new thing, a novel class. Slowly, almost imperceptibly, over the course of the 1100s, they undertook the civil management of their towns, coopting older episcopal-aristocratic regimes, and by mid-century, replacing them with models of broad civic participation.[12] They were independent of the old feudal life. Such a novel condition permitted Italy to form the first pure democracies since the time of the ancient Greeks. These were the "Burghers" of medieval Europe; they were the first middle class in all of history, that unique caste of entrepreneurial, creative, driven, and innovative individuals that are the health of modern economies, and without which a market system cannot thrive. For the first time in history a class of "white-collar" workers had been generated, who made their careers by moving money, keeping records, and by wielding words. They were notaries, scholars, merchants, bureaucrats, and bankers. They ushered in a new age of literacy and provided the raw material for the onset of a knowledge-based economy.

This was markedly different from what had come before. The specialties which these people employed had formerly been the province of an elite few. Now they multiplied and spread throughout Europe. Problems arose from this novelty. These professionals seemed not to produce anything of material use. Records, books, documents, contracts and the like seemed the simple manipulation of words for the achievement of profit. They were not like the solid farmers, carpenters, and millers of early medieval Europe. They were not established to fight, like the noble class. Nor were they clerics, who had engaged in those bureaucratic occupations in a manner subordinate to their spiritual end. They were difficult to place in the social order. Echoing the ancient criticisms of usury, this new middle class seemed unnaturally to make money from thin air. Their traffic in words and documents was a challenge to traditional preconceptions about the proper ordering of society and the economy. A host of new questions began to present themselves to the rapidly advancing civilization of medieval Europe, questions which touched on the moral fiber of Christian society itself. Money was "concentrated, mobile wealth."[13] It created the potential for the depersonalization of economic exchange. For example, now a knight could convert his feudal military duty from personal service in the lord's army to a cash payment, which in turn would allow the lord to employ mercenaries. The personal bond of loyalty is broken, becoming a common transaction rather than an interpersonal relation.[14] When one buys from a retailer, he or she has entered into an impersonal contract, rather than the former exchange of personal services. In this situation, one can begin to treat people as means rather than as ends in themselves. This has been a perennial concern of Christian social teaching up to the present day and must constantly be kept in mind as we analyze the approach of Christian intellectuals to this problem. The Church asks how technology, industry, capitalism, socialism, et al. affect *persons*. If there is a tendency to depersonalization, then human dignity can be compromised and so some practices can rightly come under the just censure of the Church.

There were further problems though. The rapid rise of cities brought whole new opportunities for vice which were utterly unavailable to the rural populations of early medieval Europe and disinterred the old Judeo-Christian suspicion against settled urban life. The first issue was the rise of temporary professions, such as those of students and prostitutes (often in a symbiotic relationship). Further, the immigrants to the cities all brought with them the perennial problems of cosmopolitanism. While they had access to culture and resources far beyond those available to their rural cousins, there was widespread alienation. Rapid urbanization could bring with it a cultural rootlessness, where people were sundered from the immemorial bonds of family, kinship, friends, customs, and their local churches. In this situation a universal Church could provide a stabilizing element that could eventually galvanize an urban population, given the right conditions. Another issue was that not all who came to the cities were able to find gainful employment. There was a precipitous rise in the numbers of the urban poor, appearing in concentrations greater than had been seen for nearly a millennium. This concentrated and visible poverty created new forms of religious life and charity, but not before generating a continent-wide crisis of conscience. Additionally these new forms of urban life and the necessity for the mobilization of capital brought back another venerable issue: that of usury. Bolstered by condemnations of the practice drawn from biblical revelation, the classical philosophers, and the

Fathers, the Church had little difficulty in proscribing the practice for Christians. To these thinkers, lending at interest attacked the idea of a society rooted in charity, with a commonality of goods for the sake of the Kingdom. But the Church held no such authority over the small Jewish communities of medieval Europe. Free from such restrictions, the Jews became some of the most well-known lenders and bankers in the Middle Ages. The friction, however, that can arise between lenders and borrowers was multiplied by the religious gulf between them, and Jewish success often led to many unfortunate episodes of anger and violence. As time went on and economic thought developed, Jews were driven from the more lucrative enterprises which became the domain of the great German and Italian banking houses. The Church would have to confront all of these issues, but in nearly every case, the traditional answers to these new questions were unsuitable, and developments had to occur.

It was the assumption of an older generation of scholarship that the Christian attitude to this development was unreservedly negative. "The attitude of the Church. . . toward commerce [was] not merely passive but actively hostile."[15] These were the words of the eminent social historian Henri Pirenne in the first half of the twentieth century. Pirenne developed a thesis on the progress of medieval economy that, while not without its detractors, has proven enduring.[16] He suggested that the sundering of the Mediterranean trade by the success of the Islamic invasions threw Europe back on its own resources, driving it to self-sufficiency and to innovation in politics and in the legal order. In spite of the correction of Pirenne by many scholars as regards the self-sufficiency of manors or the closing of seaborne trade by Islam, his initial apprehension of the attitude of the Church seemed right, on the surface at least. The Church had an immediate reason to be suspicious of the new monetary economy. In the atmosphere of increased wealth, people sought to turn their money into power, and they began to effect the corruption of the Church by the purchase of ecclesiastical offices. This practice of simony had arisen during the chaotic years after the collapse of the Carolingian Renaissance. It reached its heyday during the papal nadir of the tenth century. Within the context of the gift economy it had come to seem natural that a family would make an oblation to a monastery for the entrance of one of their children, or an ordinand make a gift to his ordaining bishop. As the monetary economy began to take off, however, its critics began to see such things through the lens of impersonal exchange. The "donation" of money in exchange for any sacred thing (ordination in particular) came to be seen as a damnable error, paralleling the grave sin of Simon the Magician in the book of Acts.

The Church Confronts Rising Prosperity

When the papacy began to regain traction in the mid-eleventh century, its reformers targeted simony in particular as a chief sin, and identified it as a violation of the gratuitousness of God's gifts, as a corrupting influence in the Church, and as evincing the sinful spill-over from the world of money-making. A perceptible shift occurred at the time. For nearly a millennium pride had been identified as the chief capital sin, because of its intellectual nature. In their eagerness to reform the Church though, thinkers began to advance the idea that avarice was the chief moral transgression. In particular St. Peter Damian (ca. 1007–1072/1073)—the tip of the spear of the Gregorian Reform—made avarice and the fight against simony the centerpiece of his campaign to reform the Church from top to bottom.[17] Peter was a purist, "First of all, get rid of money, for Christ and money do not go well together in the same place."[18] Of course to understand this one must realize how relentlessly corrupt much of the Church was in his time, from the perspective of the reformers. Peter Damian served in the office of a medieval prophet, perhaps using hyperbole, but for the end of addressing a massive rot in the Church that went to the papacy itself. While Peter Damian was certainly a standard bearer for the Gregorian reform, the main impetus came from the reformed monasteries of Cluny. Much like the monastic revolution of the fourth and fifth centuries, these monk-reformers had a picture of a Church that was framed by the image of the cloister. For them purification meant liberation from the tyranny of money, through the destruction of simony and the elimination of clerical concubinage. In so doing the Church would embrace once again chastity and voluntary poverty and so would attain perfection illustrated by the model of the monastery.

The Gregorian reform, beginning with Pope St. Leo IX (r. 1049–1054) and running through to the conclusion of the Investiture controversy in the 1120s, was an astonishing success. Simony was rooted out, clerical celibacy was reinforced, and the papacy was well and thoroughly purified. This new monastic vision of Christian and ecclesiastical perfection however did tend to leave many people behind. Besides the innumerable secular clergy and canons who had not taken monastic vows, there was also the laity who because of their state in life were incapable of following the evangelical counsels. This divide was exacerbated by the increasing wealth of the urban middle class, who were major supporters of the purification of the Church. For example the lay people of Milan had expelled their entire corrupt clergy in the 1070s. After the purification though, what was the status of the urban laity vis-a-vis holiness and salvation? In some ways the Gregorian Reform was a victim of its own success. It installed an enduring model of holiness that would last well into the twentieth century, but one that tended to leave out many of its most ardent supporters, the newly wealthy and educated laity. These began to look for new paths to holiness, for they were excluded from the vision of the Gregorian reformers themselves. It would take later generations and earnest efforts successfully to reintegrate them.

The period of the Gregorian reformers was also the age of the rediscovery of systematic law, both Civil and Canon. Gratian, the father of Canon Law, was very traditional in his choice of authoritative sources for his compilation, *The Harmony of Discordant Canons* (ca. 1140, it became the normative law text for the Catholic Church until 1917).[19] Gratian was not so much interested in innovation, as in streamlining and harmonizing the

Church's disparate, thousand-year-old traditions of jurisprudence. To that end he cited significant sources from the past, and established them as normative for years to come. One of the most famous of these is the assertion about the possibilities of holiness available to the merchant class. Gratian seemed to have no interest in following the complex tradition that we have traced thus far. Rather he cites a proof text from St. Leo the Great (in reality drawn from a spurious commentary attributed to Chrysostom) that became a commonplace in the Middle Ages and the inspiration for many a sermon excoriating the life of the market, "A merchant is rarely or never able to please God."[20] Yet the snippet of a quote from Leo misses the first part of the author's sentiment, that it is the *type* of exchange that either excuses or convicts, because there is either honesty or disgraceful activity in trade. Therefore even this document does not wholly condemn trade. Unfortunately it was only the end of the response that made it into the canonical collections. It was repeated constantly in sermons, works of spirituality, and even in theological tracts, being included even in the primary theological textbook of Peter Lombard.

At the very beginning of his definitive compilation of canon law Gratian underscored the traditional conception of the natural commonality of property in his very first distinction.[21] When discussing the different types of law he asserts that there are certain natural laws that are common to all. Under this rubric he includes the commonality of property and the common possession of all things.[22] This primitive communism was a position of most of the Church Fathers, as we have seen. The Ordinary Gloss (the standard commentary on canon law in the Middle Ages) explains that this can either mean that no one owns anything absolutely, by virtue of Divine law or decree, or that necessities must be shared in times of want.[23] Similar sentiments are scattered through the compilation. Citing Ambrose in *De Officiis*, he includes a canon that the hungry must be fed, and if one does not do it, one murders them.[24] Gratian also employs a spurious letter of St. Clement of Rome, which attempts to assert that the origin of wickedness was the division of the goods of the earth into "mine" and "yours."²⁵ Gratian relied on the tradition that he received in building his compilation. His authorities, and the later stature of his collection, would provide a formidable challenge for those theologians who worked slowly to develop economic doctrine, but at the same time his assembling of these difficult texts brought the matter to the forefront of discussion and paved the way for further resolution.

Other works significantly played upon these traditional themes. There were satires about the corruption wrought by money in the highest offices in Christendom. Two famous examples set the tone for much of the central Middle Ages. One was the *Translation of the Relics of Albinus and Rufinus*.²⁶ In this case the martyred saints are allegories for white (Albinus) and red (Rufinus) corresponding to silver and gold. At each stage of the proposal of these saints to the Curia in Rome, money had to change hands in order for the process to advance. The meaning of the work was clear. Money flowed like blood through the highest offices of the Church and corrupted them significantly. Another work that railed against the vice of greed was the Gospel *according to the Mark of Silver*, which was included in the *Carmina Burana*.

> And it came to pass that a certain poor cleric came to the Curia of the Lord Pope and cried out, saying, "Do you, at least, have mercy on me, you doorkeepers of the Pope, for the hand of poverty has touched me. I am indeed needy and poor. Therefore, I beg you to come to my aid." But they, hearing him, were exceedingly angry, and they said, "Friend, you and your poverty can go to hell. Get behind me, Satan, because you do not savor of money. Amen, amen, I say to you, you shall not enter into the joy of your lord [the Pope] until you pay your last coin."²⁷

Medieval moralists were no less harsh on the vice of avarice. Alain of Lille (ca. 1128–1202/1203), one of the most prominent scholastics of the twelfth-century renaissance, spoke of the transposition of the imperial acclamations "Christus Vincit, Christus Regnat, Christus Imperat" ("Christ conquers, Christ reigns, Christ commands"). In his day Alain said that the refrain had been changed to "Nummus vincit, nummus mundum regit, nummus imperat universis." "Cash conquers, cash rules the world, cash commands all things."[28] Indeed Alain had coined a new term for avarice, "nummulatria," or the "worship of money." Yet while Alain castigates the sin of avarice and takes great pains to discuss its deleterious effect, he says at the end "this discourse is not to disparage riches or the rich but rather seeks to sink its teeth into vice. I do not condemn property, riches, or the practices of the rich, provided that the mind, with reason as mistress, is in command."[29]

One is confronted with a massive disjunction that was opening during this period. On one hand, meditations on the use, value, and morality of the market system and the lives of merchants—a tradition silent for nearly a half a millennium—were being reconsidered. Such a reexamination had the misfortune of being brought up in the context of a wholesale purification of Church structures, in the context of a monastic-inspired movement. Just as Jerome and the Fathers of the fourth and fifth centuries were influenced by the monastic call to perfection via the road of individual poverty, so did such poverty become the model for the regeneration of the Church in the eleventh. However, it came at an inopportune time for European business, for during the same period the economic explosion was reaching its zenith. Wealth was being created more quickly and distributed more widely than ever before. Of course this would have occasioned the Church's consideration in any case, but at this time it was seen through the lenses of the Gregorian reform, which sought an utter purification from such sullying influences of the world, the flesh, and the devil.

It is fair to say that these teachings had a wide audience, and were taken seriously by the members of the new urban classes. Premodern Europe was an essentially Christian society, and while there were exceptions, the clergy tended to share the views of the Christian population. Theirs was no active social control exercised on a mindless multitude, rather their views reflected the views of society as a whole. The new urban middle classes and merchant aristocracy were quite happy to be profitable; they were comfortable, and they were able to provide for their families and cities. Yet something was profoundly troubling. Like their predecessors in the Christian tradition they too shared the traditional suspicion of money. They were aware of the temptations that it could lead to and the sins that now became possible because of it. They knew and shared the traditional attitude toward greed, and they retained the most humane aspects of the gift economy, now made more efficient by the rise of money. The urban elite had heard all of the Old Testament imprecations against deceit and defrauding laborers of their earned wages. With certainty they were familiar with the New Testament stories of wealth and riches. They saw them regularly depicted in paintings and sculptures in their places of worship, indeed many of the urban elite had been the very patrons who commissioned such representations from the tradition. Further, in a world rapidly becoming literate, they had the opportunity to read and ponder the very passages that made the images so powerful. In addition they heard the message of the Church proclaimed from the pulpits. While there was a disjunction, there was no dissonance. There was no dissent from the new urban laity, clamoring for a "change in doctrine" that would be friendlier toward the wealthy. Rather the wealthy and well-off collaborated in the anxiety about their newfound economic success. Remember it had been these new urban dwellers who had allied with the reform movements in Christianity that made the Gregorian Reform successful and led to a purified Christianity throughout much of Christendom. These people took Christianity seriously, and were "working out their salvation in fear and trembling" (Php 2:21). Camels and needles were ever before their mind's eyes. It was no simple story of condemnation and resistance, but of gradual growth of serious Christian meditation on the place of money and power in society that took place over hundreds of years and laid the groundwork for our own modern economy, developed in tandem with the Christian intellectual tradition.

Responses to Wealth

The urban laity had been involved in these reform activities from the beginning. Freedom from the necessity of subsistence farming brought them leisure, and urban concentration prompted an exchange of ideas that would have been impossible in the settled, agricultural settings of early medieval Europe. Combined together these led to urgent meditations on the correct observance of the Christian life, adapted to such novel conditions. Foremost on their minds was guilt about material wealth. When this was added to the rising tone of Church denunciations and the increasing visibility of the urban poor, such guilt could seem overwhelming. Foremost in the minds of medieval people was exactly the question of the Rich Young Man, "What must I do to inherit eternal life?" That the answer to that question in the gospel was so involved with the issue of the evangelical counsel of voluntary poverty was not missed by medieval Christians. How could one secure salvation while at the same time prospering materially in one's society? This pressing issue, involving questions of justice and salvation, generated a wide variety of responses.

In particular there were movements that drew on traditional answers to the problem. Two of these were found in the establishments of the Camaldolese and Carthusian religious orders. The Camaldolese were founded by St. Romuald (ca. 951–ca. 1027). Born to an aristocratic family, he had witnessed his father kill a relative in a duel about a piece of property. Being affected to his core by this event he sought the religious life, eventually moving from a Cluniac type of monasticism, to one of the most rigorous lives of religion possible, that of the hermit.[30] That his pivotal conversion experience was motivated by the lengths that men would go to defend private property was not missed by his contemporaries. The Carthusians were founded by St. Bruno (ca. 1030–

1101), who had been a wealthy scion of the urban nobility of Cologne. He found great success in the Church, being a master of theology, and eventually achieved the wealthy position of chancellor of the diocese of Reims. He participated earnestly in the Church reforms then being undertaken, but was brought to a spiritual crisis by his appointment as an Archbishop in Italy. With several companions he renounced all of his titles and withdrew to the mountains where he lived out the rest of his life in silence and penance, founding one of the strictest orders in the Catholic Church.[31] While both of these men were extraordinary, and indeed are saints, their heroism demonstrates the feelings of anxiety coursing through medieval Europe. While very few could follow their example, both Romuald and Bruno are key for understanding the mindset of those who found themselves in positions of power, and achieved an acute awareness of the precariousness of their spiritual conditions.

Romuald and Bruno had provided traditional answers within the context of a revered tradition. "Flee the world" in order to seek the cloister; it was a heavenly waiting room, a place of safety amidst the vicissitudes of the present age. By disengaging from the normal concourse of human life one preserved oneself free of the stain of sin, or even its possibility. That is not to say that the monastic life was easy—for the narrow path is difficult—but it was a surer way of higher perfection. Yet not all could abandon the city. The vast majority of Christians "married and were given in marriage." The bulk of the clergy were not hermits or even monks, they were the secular priests who served alongside the laity in the villages of medieval Europe. A way of ministering to this vast multitude would have to be found.

One of the key devotional ideals which appeared in the twelfth century was the "Imitation of the Apostles." Newly literate people, or simply those who meditated on the life of Christ and the Apostles, came to the conclusion that in order truly to follow Christ then one must live a life that approximated that of the Apostles.[32] In order to do this these would-be apostles had to determine just what type of life the original followers of Christ had led. What was clear about the Apostles was that, unlike the propertied and cloistered monastic orders which had dominated Christendom for nearly a millennium, the Apostles were wandering, untethered evangelists. They went from town to town proclaiming the good news of Christ. They also did this in poverty, disdaining the things of this world in an effort to empty themselves in the search for perfection. The life of the Apostles then had been that of poor, itinerant preachers of the Gospel. In order truly to imitate them and to pursue the perfection that Christ demanded of His followers, they could not wall themselves up in a monastery, taking a vow of permanent, lifelong stability. They had to be freed to wander the byways of Europe and beyond, living like the Apostles of old. Men such as this began to appear in increasing numbers throughout the 1100s. The twin focuses of this movement were poverty and preaching.[33] This was a breakthrough among the spiritual movements of the Catholic Church. Unmoored from the requirements of the cloister, these men were free to roam about at will. Their poverty and charismatic preaching style won them devotees, particularly in the growing cities of Europe. They developed cult-like followings, and whole towns would be depopulated as they poured out into the countryside to hear these charismatic missionaries. During this period the sermon became the "mass media" of the age—all of our contemporary methods of communication rolled into one.[34] Preaching could go on for hours, or sometimes over the course of days, with biblical stories and moral parables interspersed with news of the wider world.

Yet there was a flipside to this popularity. People identified in these itinerants a spiritual quality that was occasionally absent from the leaders of the Church, both episcopal and monastic. They practiced fearful austerities, had no personal property, reveled in the practice of poverty and, unlike monastics, did this in a dramatically public way. Such practices accorded them a type of moral authority, including an authority to preach, which was outside the normal course of Church law and ecclesiastical supervision. Men like Robert of Arbrissel (ca. 1045–1116) and Bernard of Tiron (1046–1117), though generally orthodox, began to attract the ire of the rich and powerful whom they sometimes denounced. During many periods of history the institutional Church sought to establish boundaries and clear lines of authority over these more prophetic and charismatic members; indeed, such efforts can be clearly discerned in the later letters of Paul and in the subapostolic Fathers. Even though these early preachers neither denounced the Church directly nor contradicted doctrine, still their moral authority was such that it was seen as threatening to many in power. Many of them operated in a hazy area of Church governance and were usually kept at arm's length by Church officials, while at the same time they were enthusiastically supported by the laity. It was ironic then that these preachers who were inspired by the success of the Gregorian Reform would generate such misgivings among Church leaders. The purification of the Church had released forces which, once unleashed, proved difficult to control.

That there was legitimate value to this movement is demonstrated by the efforts of the Church, over the course of a century, to streamline it and legitimize it within the structures of Christianity. One notable early example was that of St. Norbert (ca. 1080–1134).[35] Norbert, like Bernard and Robert, began as the son of a respected aristocratic family. He obtained position and revenues and eventually became a rich court chaplain to the emperor. After a near-death experience with a lightning strike he radically transformed his life and embraced extreme asceticism. Norbert was attracted by the life of the wandering preachers but, unlike many of them, sought and obtained papal permission for his itinerancy. He was impressed with the revitalization of the monastic orders by the Cistercians but, attracted by the new spirituality of the times, he sought a novel form of religious life that would combine the best aspects of the monks with the urban life of the new cities that was so familiar to him. He founded the Praemonstratensian canons, a society of active priests who would go out and preach and minister and then would then return to his cloister for spiritual refreshment and communal life. Norbert's solution was a sort of halfway house between the rural monasticism of the older orders and the flexible apostolate of the wandering preachers. He was later appointed Archbishop of Magdeburg for his efforts. Norbert represents the first of the efforts to create and maintain the new spirituality in line with the ecclesial needs demanded by the age.

POVERTY, PREACHING, AND HERESY

Yet not all who embraced the apostolic way of life were as concerned with the necessity of hewing to the instructions of the institutional Church. Men like Robert of Arbrissel had already come under suspicion. This novel manner of life generated questions on both sides of the issue. On the Church's part, it did not seem that these preachers fit within the established hierarchy of Christianity that had been stabilized for over a millennium. Neither did they behave like well-anchored monks, whose way of life was recognized as the apex of all paths to Christian holiness. Indeed, when one looked at the broad tradition, they did not fit in at all. In the very beginning of the *Regula* of St. Benedict, the normative rule for all Western monastics, the founder warned about monks called "gyrovagues" and "sabarites," who lived by their own counsel, out of the supervision of an abbot or spiritual master and, even worse, "spend their whole lives tramping from province to province," forsaking the rock of stability.[36] Benedict reserves his harshest condemnation for these wandering preachers. But one could go far earlier than Benedict's denunciations, all the way to the scriptures themselves. Paul repeatedly warned about those who would come preaching a "different gospel," or who would seduce the weak by their charismatic ways (e.g., 2 Tm 3: 1–8). It seemed to the members of the hierarchy that all of these warnings were coming to pass. The new preachers were dangerous and had either to be streamlined within some existing system or else hounded out of existence. From the perspective of the preachers of poverty, theirs was a claim to a higher calling. They asserted that they were living the actual life of the Apostles, while the "successors of the Apostles"—the bishops—lived in luxury and power. Their poverty and asceticism countered the laxity of the secular clergy and, unlike the monks, was lived openly in the towns of Europe. They began to refine critiques of the wealth of the Church and of the power achieved by ecclesiastics. While these were a staple of moralists throughout history, there was a fine line between critiquing the officeholder and denouncing the office itself. There were many bad bishops, but when one began to claim that the office of bishop itself was bad, then one had then crossed a line. Given the enthusiasm with which the new preachers gave their orations, coupled with a general lack of theological education, the path was open for forays into heterodoxy.

The interaction between poverty, purity, and heresy was a strong one. It gained purchase during the course of the 1100s. The guilt surrounding medieval questions about wealth, coupled with the reform impulse in Christianity, put a target squarely on the back of the institutional Church that had held property since well before the time of Constantine. Of course the wealth of the Church was largely for the subvention of the poor, the indigent, and the sick. It also provided the support for the spiritual works of mercy, such as perpetual prayers for the dead in purgatory (for a medieval Christian just as critical as the corporal works of mercy, if not more so). Only a portion was used for the personal wealth of churchmen, and indeed much of that flowed from their secular entanglements as royal officials and aristocrats. That wealth, however, was public. The Christian people had shown no compunction in showering their riches upon the Church when they saw it put to use in the feeding of the poor and for the creation of cathedrals and saints' shrines, yet when it served to undergird the worldly wealth of officeholders, it began to rankle. This was especially true as they heard repeated denunciations of the depredations of the merchant class and their small possibilities of salvation.

This tension asserted itself repeatedly. In the first half of the 1100s a man named Arnold of Brescia (ca. 1090–1155) came forward with absolutist ideals of Apostolic poverty, tied to radical egalitarianism. He formally espoused the heresy of Donatism, which stated that unworthy priests were incapable of performing the sacraments. Augustine had defeated Donatism in the 400s, asserting that it was Christ who performed the sacraments through the priest, even if he be unworthy or sinful. In so doing he saved the conception of the visible Church. In the atmosphere of the Gregorian reform though, the specter of Donatism haunted even orthodox efforts. Arnold merely brought it out into the open. The Gregorians had been happy to coopt urban discontent in the overthrow of simoniacal clerics in Milan in the 1070s, but by the twelfth century such positions had become dangerous. Taken too far they began to descend into heresy.

Other movements attempted to harness the connection between poverty and purity. The most arresting instance was the Cathars, an antimaterialist, dualist group. These took the critique of wealth to its ultimate limit. Not only was wealth evil, so was *all* of the material world. In their case a critique of Church excesses led them to a denial of the very fundamentals of human society, including a rejection of money, of the eating of flesh meat, and even the practices surrounding marriage and sexuality. Their movement was one of the most anti-life expressions in the whole history of Christianity. Yet much of their critique was merely taking their connection of poverty and purity to its logical conclusion. The world itself was evil, and in order to achieve salvation we must be at length freed from bodily life. This led to a rising cycle of denial regarding the goods of human society, and eventually culminated in their exceptionally esoteric ideology. But such heterodoxy was not normal; at no point did the number of Cathars in Europe ever exceed 1% of the population. It was a bridge too far for the common sense of the average medieval person to admit that the very things that made life good and a blessing from God, could be themselves evil. Indeed most puritanical movements have ended in this manner, by narrowing the "just" to the very few and by denying the genuine human goods of this world. This was true from Tertullian's Montanists, to the Cathars, to the Jansenists, to the perfectionist communities of America in the nineteenth century. They have ended up essentially denying the very thing which made Christianity unique: the doctrine of the goodness of creation exalted by the reality of the Incarnation.

Others attempted to preserve the practice and value of voluntary poverty, while at the same time attempting to stay within the boundaries of Church orthodoxy. They were not always successful. One of the most significant lay practices of the 1100s was the living of the "penitential life." By affiliating themselves to a monastery, one abandoned the possibility of family and wealth in order to atone for sins. These penitents, later *conversi* or *lay brothers*, remained laymen. Some began to affiliate together, and began to go under the name of the *Humiliati*.[37] Others were different in that they did not always abandon family life, but chose to go about in simple attire, to perform charity, and to preach the Catholic faith. This was yet another attempt by the laity to seek out a path of perfection within the world, but it yet still bore resemblance to the monastic practices of the cloister. The local churches, and eventually even the pope, were content to let them incorporate and to do charitable activities, but they were expressly forbidden to preach. This was because they lacked a theological education, and the experience of the previous century had shown the ease with which an uneducated preacher could fall into heresy. Many of them, because of their manner of life, and feeling spiritually neglected by the low quality of parish clergy around them, could not refrain from preaching, and so fell under the sentence of excommunication. They were, however, eventually reconciled and began to form a type of "third order" which would prove to be an enduring category of lay piety into the present day.

Perhaps the most salient example of this struggle for a spiritual home for the new middle class was the story of Waldo of Lyons (ca. 1140–ca. 1205). Waldo was a successful merchant in the burgeoning city of Lyons, in south central France, a key trading center between the Mediterranean world and the north. Waldo had been growing anxious about his wealth, particularly in light of a new saint's life that had become astonishingly popular at the time: the story of St. Alexis. This hagiographical romance, much embellished over the centuries, is of a rich young man of the fourth century who flees the possibility of wealth and marriage to live as a beggar in Edessa. Later, much changed, he returned to Rome and lived as an unrecognized mendicant under the stairs of his own family's house. Recognized only after his death, he became venerated as a saint. That this story became popular in the twelfth century tells us much about the social anxieties of the time; successful urban people were worried. Being serious Christians, they longed for salvation and for holiness, but how could they square the circle? Alexis provided one—albeit radical—answer.[38]

Troubled in mind, Waldo asked for priests to make some translations of the gospels into the vernacular. He meditated on these, being fired by the idea of Christian perfection. He asked a priest one day what was the best and surest path to salvation. He was answered with Matthew 19:21, the same passage that runs through so much of this history. "If you would be perfect, go. Sell all you have and give it to the poor, and you will have treasure in heaven." In 1176 he abandoned his wealth. This enraged his wife, who took the matter to the bishop. Deciding in her favor, Waldo was forced to leave much of his wealth to her, but after that she has happy enough to see the back of him. They agreed on a mutual separation and Waldo became a wandering beggar and preacher. He began to attract a following, and his disciples were known for their penitential preaching, calling people to repent of their sins. This was traditional enough, and the Church was willing to tolerate it. Yet many of his followers were uneducated, and particularly suffered from their odd readings of the vernacular scriptures. They began to venture involuntarily into doctrinal error. Waldo made an attempt to regularize his position, and travelled with his followers to the Third Lateran Council in 1179. There he appealed to the pope and the council to approve his movement. When they arrived they were interrogated by the sarcastic curialist Walter Map, who instead of approaching them with charity, made their examination a showplace for his own learning and rhetoric. Map made them a laughingstock, demonstrating their theological ignorance. They were forbidden to preach. It was then that Waldo made his definitive break, considering that preaching was a command of God, and that one was to obey God rather than men. He founded the Waldensian movement which, while not as doctrinally esoteric as the Cathars, nonetheless made the leap from a critique of Church wealth to a critique of the Church itself.[39]

The tragedy of Waldo is that he appeared much like the later figure of Francis of Assisi, and their stories are quite similar. Had the Church been more sensitive to the situation it would perhaps not be impossible to think of a "St. Waldo of Lyons." In any case Pope Innocent III (r. 1198–1216) recognized the short-sightedness of the approach of the Church during the Third Lateran Council. He would not make the same mistake when presented with the possibility of reconciling some of Waldo's followers or especially when presented by the new programs of men like Francis and Dominic. Yet even Waldo's answer was not a panacea for the place of the new middle class in the Church. Most of the answers of the 1100s had resulted in either 1) the abandonment of wealth and the incorporation into quasi-monasticism, 2) the renunciation of wealth for a life of wandering penitence and preaching, or 3) outright heresy. Was there no place for the merchant where he was? Could perhaps holiness be found in the life of the family, the life of the city, or even the life of business? In order to see we need to look at an axial figure in the history of holiness in the Catholic Church, to a contemporary of Waldo himself, the merchant Omobono of Cremona.

CHAPTER 2 ENDNOTES

1. Adriaan Verhulst, *The Carolingian Economy* (Cambridge: Cambridge University Press, 2002), 117.
2. For the Carolingian economy, see ibid. Also Michael McCormick, *Origins of the European Economy: Communications and Commerce, A.D. 300–900* (Cambridge: Cambridge University Press, 2010).
3. While this is usually called "feudalism," that is a 17th-century neologism. The reality is much more complex. See, Susan Reynolds, *Fiefs and Vassals: The Medieval Evidence Reinterpreted* (Oxford: Oxford

University Press, 1994); and, Elizabeth A. R. Brown, "The Tyranny of a Construct: Feudalism and Historians of Medieval Europe," *The American Historical Review*, 79.4 (Oct 1974), 1063–88.

4   For the wide variety of the forms of "manor" see, Verhulst, 43–45.

5   Diana Webb, *Pilgrims and Pilgrimage in the West* (New York: St. Martin's Press, 2001); and, Jonathan Sumption, *The Age of Pilgrimage: The Medieval Journey to God* (Mahwah, NJ: Hidden Spring, 2003).

6   See James Brundage, *Law, Sex, and Christian Society in Medieval Europe* (Chicago: University of Chicago Press, 1987).

7   For an overview of these technologies see: Susan Bolich, *The History of Farming Machinery* (Oxford: Oxford University Press, 2005).

8   Analyzed by Martha C. Howell, *Commerce Before Capitalism in Europe, 1300–1600* (Cambridge: Cambridge University Press, 2010). See also the foundational work by Robert S. Lopez, *The Commercial Revolution of the Middle Ages* (Englewood Cliffs, NJ: Prentice Hall, 1971).

9   Lopez says, "Unstinting credit was the great lubricant of the Commercial Revolution," ibid., 72.

10 Martha Howell describes formal capitalism as a "self-equilibrating, self-regulating, hegemonic market economy *out from the constraints of larger society.*" (italics mine) Howell, *Commerce Before Capitalism*, 10.

11 The concept of the three orders were drawn largely from the thought of the English king, Alfred the Great. For a thorough examination see Georges Duby, *The Three Orders: Feudal Society Imagined* (Chicago: University of Chicago Press, 1980).

12 For this process see: Chris Wickham, *Sleepwalking into a New World: The Emergence of Italian City Communes in the Twelfth Century* (Princeton, NJ: Princeton University Press, 2015).

13 Lester K. Little, *Religious Poverty and the Profit Economy in Medieval Europe* (Ithaca, NY: Cornell University Press, 1978), 33.

14 Howell and others stress the continuing importance of personal trust, public reputation, and kinship in the central Middle Ages; such personalizing features of the markets begin to break up slowly after 1300. Howell, *Commerce Before Capitalism*, 28.

15 Henri Pirenne, *Economic and Social History of Medieval Europe* (New York: Harcourt, Brace and Company, 1937), 48–49. Pirenne's influence on the development of the medieval economy is immense, and his theses have been significant in pushing the field forward, even as scholars abandon his positions. See his *Medieval Cities: Their Origins and the Revival of Trade* (Garden City, NY: Doubleday, 1927; 1956).

16 Pirenne still is a touchstone for debates in the field; see the breakdown of medieval economic history provided in Verhulst, 1–8. See

criticisms in *La fortune historiographique des thèses d'Henri Pirenne*. eds. G. Despy and A. Verhulst (Brussels: ABB, 1986), and *The Pirenne Thesis: Analysis, Criticism, and Revision*, ed. Alfred F. Havighurst (Boston: Heath, 1958).

17 For this see: William D. McCready, *Odiosa Sanctitas: St Peter Damian, Simony, and Reform* (Toronto: Pontifical Institute of Mediaeval Studies, 2011). For the place of Avarice in medieval thought see Jacques Le Goff, *La bourse et la vie: économie et religion au Moyen Age* (Paris: Hachette, 1997), and Albert O. Hirschman, Amartya Sen, and Jeremy Adelman, *The Passions and the Interests: Political Arguments for Capitalism Before Its Triumph* (Princeton, N.J.: Princeton University Press, 1977; 2013).

18 Peter Damian, Epistle iii.2, PL 144: 289. Cfr. Little, *Religious Poverty*, 36.

19 Gratian, *Decretum Magistri Gratiani*. 2nd ed. E. Friedberg. Corpus Iuris Canonici, Vol. 1 (Leipzig: Tauschnitz, 1879). First twenty canons edited and translated in: *Gratian: The Treatise on Laws with the Ordinary Gloss*, eds. James Gordley and Augustine Thompson (Washington, DC: Catholic Univ. of America Press, 1993). See also, Anders Winroth, *The Making of Gratian's Decretum* (Cambridge: Cambridge University Press, 2000).

20 "Mercator vix aut numquam potest Deo placere." *Decretum*, 1. D. 88, c.22. This statement was found in most canonical compilations previous to Gratian as well, but acquired normative status with his edition. It may be a paraphrase from an epistle by St. Leo the Great to the Archbishop of Narbonne, "quia difficile est inter ementis vendentisque commercium non intervenire peccatum." *Sacrorum Conciliorum Nova Amplissima Collectio*, ed. J. D. Mansi (Florence, 1761), 6.404. In fact the quotation is from the *Opus Imperfectum in Matthaeum*, erroneously attributed to St. John Chrysostom in the Middle Ages. In reality it is an Arian text, but the attribution to Chrysostom made it a significant theological locus of authority in the medieval period. PG 56: 839. The spurious passage goes on to say: "Therefore no Christian ought to be a merchant, and if he becomes one, he is to be cast out of the Church." That Gratian did not include the rest of the text is interesting, but it is difficult to make an argument from absence.

21 One needs to note that the medievals, lacking the type of textual and critical analysis that would find its origin in the Renaissance, relied on a number of spurious texts and biblical readings. They adduced these as authorities. This should not diminish their logical or theological achievements though. The medievals understood that

the argument from authority was the weakest of all arguments, which is why they sought to harmonize variant readings, and to offer substantive, rational arguments for their positions. Far from relying on authority, they used these as springboards to audacious and deeply reasoned insights into theology, philosophy, and law.

22 Gratian, *Decretum*, D. 1. C. 7.
23 Gratian, *Treatise on Laws*, eds. Gordley and Thompson, 6.
24 "Pasce fame morientem. Quisquis enim pascendo hominem servare poteris, si non paveris, occidisti." Gratian, *Decretum*, D. 86, c. 21.
25 "Sed per iniquitatem alius hoc dixit esse suum, et alius istud et sic inter mortales facta est divisio." Gratian, *Decretum*, P. II, Causa 12, c. 2.
26 *Tractatus Garsiae, or The Translation of the Relics of SS. Gold and Silver*, ed. Rodney M. Thomson (Leiden: E. J. Brill, 1973).
27 *Carmina Burana: Text und Übersetzung*, ed. Benedikt Konrad Vollmann (Deutscher Klassiker Verlag, Frankfurt am Main 1987), c. 44.
28 Alain of Lille, *Liber de Planctu Naturae*, PL 210.464. translated in, *Alain of Lille: The Plaint of Nature*, trans. James J. Sheridan, Medieval Sources in Translation 26 (Toronto: PIMS, 1980) 177.
29 Ibid., 184.
30 The life of St. Romuald was written by none other than St. Peter Damian, the spokesman of Gregorian purification. Id., *Vita beati Romualdi*, Fonti per la storia d'Italia pubblicate dall'Istituto storico italiano per il Medio Evo, 94 (Rome, 1957).
31 For Bruno and Romuald see: David Knowles, *Christian Monasticism* (New York: McGraw-Hill, 1968); and, C. H. Lawrence, *Medieval Monasticism: Forms of Religious Life in Western Europe in the Middle Ages* (London: Longman, 1984). The central Carthusian monastery of the Grand Chartreuse was made famous in the evocative film *Die grosse Stille* ("the Great Silence") by Philip Gröning in 2005.
32 The idea of an "Imitation of Christ" would not be developed until the *Devotio Moderna* of the 15th century, and would have seemed faintly blasphemous to medievals, suggesting that one could imitate He who was God Himself. It was safer to imitate His first followers.
33 Grado Merlo has coined the term "Pauperistic-Evangelical" to describe their commonalities, see, id., *Tensioni religiose agli inizi del Duecento: il primo francescanesimo in rapporto a tradizioni eremitico-penitenziali, esperienze pauperistico-evangeliche, gruppi ereticali e instituzioni ecclesiastiche* (Torre Pellice, 1984).
34 For this see: *Preacher, Sermon, and Audience in the Middle Ages*, ed. Carolyn Muessig (Leiden: Brill, 2002).

35 For Norbert see: John Capgrave and Cyril Lawrence Smetana, *The Life of St. Norbert* (Toronto: Pontifical Institute of Mediaeval Studies, 1977).
36 Benedict, *Regula*, c.1.
37 For this group see: Frances Andrews, *The Early Humiliati* (Cambridge: Cambridge University Press, 1999).
38 For the arrival and popularity of St. Alexis's cult in the medieval West see, Little, *Religious Poverty*, 40; A. Gieysztor, "Pauper sum et peregrinus: la légende de saint Alexis en Occident. Un idéal de pauvreté," in *Études sur l'histoire de la pauvreté*, ed. M. Mollat (Paris, 1974), 125–39.
39 For Waldensianism as a movement, see Grado Merlo, *Valdesi e valdismi medievali; itinerari e proposte di ricerca* (Turin: Claudiana, 1984); and, Gabriel Audisio, *The Waldensian Dissent: Persecution and Survival, c. 1170–c. 1570* (Cambridge: Cambridge University Press, 1999); and, Euan Cameron, *Waldenses: Rejections of Holy Church in Medieval Europe* (Oxford: Blackwell Publishers, 2000).

Chapter 3
A GOOD MAN IN THE CITY

Shakespeare's *Romeo and Juliet* begins unexpectedly for a tragic romance. In the piazzas of Verona two rival gangs hurl insults at one another and engage in desultory conflict, gradually rising to a pitch of violence that causes the death of many of the main characters of the play. The Bard had set his drama in the early years of the thirteenth century, dimly recalling historical events around the year 1215. What he had accurately depicted, however, was the astonishing amount of communal violence that plagued the cities of northern Italy during that period. The decline of German imperial power, as well as the corruption of the papacy in the tenth century, had forced the northern Italian towns to fall back on their own devices. Some became powerful maritime trading powers, essentially turning their backs on their own peninsula in search of treasure across the waters; these included cities like Genoa, Pisa, and Venice. However, the cities of Lombardy and Tuscany were different. Taking advantage of their strategic position located at the crossroads of the Mediterranean and near the north-south trade routes to Germany and France, they charted a new course. Freed of the interfering supervision of the imperial nobility and absent the rigid pattern of lord-vassal relations, they began to construct new visions of politics and civic life. Having never entirely lost the inheritance of the classical world, and more literate than the rest of Europe, the cities of the north began to engage in profitable trade, innovating the mechanisms of proto-capitalism as described in the previous chapters. The attendant prosperity began to attract people to the cities. These "new men" were neither nobles nor peasants. They made up a truly new thing in world history. Once again we see the bourgeoisie—the middle class—a group of entrepreneurs and adventurers, social climbers and merchant trailblazers. In them we see the first rise of the class so essential for the modern civilized world. Socially they were all roughly equal (though later disparities in wealth would lead to bifurcation between merchant princes and the working classes). Because of that they settled upon a form of government that had fallen into disuse for over a thousand years. They chose the path of communal democracy.[1] All citizens would be responsible for the care and upkeep of the city, and their business achievements would redound to the good of the whole of the *comune*, as the new political association was called. It was the purest form of political freedom that had existed since the city-states of ancient Greece. Of course, like their ancient forbears, these democracies did sometimes turn to vicious factionalism, as both Dante and Shakespeare made clear. It was to be a wholly new type of political life—tailored to new economic and social realities—and yet it was still shot through with deeply held Christian beliefs. The question was how both the institutional Church and ordinary Catholics would respond to the challenges posed by these novel conditions.

THE CITY

Developments in the city of Cremona are a study in miniature of movements that existed all over the northern part of the Italian peninsula.[2] Under the Carolingians, Cremona had been bound by a close relationship with the German empire. By the end of the eleventh century though it had grown independent, like many other Italian cities, driven both by economic necessity and the political neglect of the empire. It joined forces with the pro-papal party of Matilda of Tuscany to withstand German imperial pretensions—and to preserve communal freedom. Quickly there came to be bitter conflicts in the independent city, ones that mirrored developments in the other city-states. The population divided itself into a party that favored the German empire, called the "Ghibellines," and a party favoring the papacy, called the "Guelfs." Of course the politics was not that simple.[3] There were a host of local and regional political considerations that helped to determine allegiances. This dissension also did not imply an essentially religious split, for most of those on the Ghibelline side remained good Catholics. They simply preferred the political rule of the emperor to that of the popes. Cities could and did switch sides, and Cremona did so with some regularity. The political split in the city ran so deeply that the respective partisans came to congregate in wholly separate neighborhoods, with the pro-papal Guelfs in the "new" city, and the pro-empire Ghibellines in the "old" city. Yet both sides were politically opportunistic. When Frederick Barbarossa (1122–1190)—the strongest German emperor in centuries—descended from the Alps, Cremona immediately sided with him, taking the opportunity to acquire new territory from its neighbors in the process. The Cremonese assisted him in the destruction of Milan, the greatest city in Lombardy, in 1166. But the winds shifted and Cremona switched sides again, just in time to achieve victory with the Lombard league against Barbarossa at the Battle of Legnano in 1176, which had the ultimate effect of securing the independence of the Italian cities. Cremona's activities in this period appear to be remarkably self-serving, and the rapid switching of allegiances does not suggest the most stable of urban environments. Clearly there was much disorder in the city, so great indeed that it had effectively resolved itself into two distinct parts.

Yet the urban discord went deeper. The macropolitical conditions of the peninsula of Italy magnified internal civic disorder, ranging from the conflict between papacy and empire to the local rivalries with the towns that surrounded Cremona. Such an atmosphere of chaos served as a smokescreen for those who bore heterodox ideas, particularly those who professed Catharism, an anti-materialist dualism, and the radicalized Waldensians known in Italy as the "Poor of Lyons." The presence of both of these fed increasing discontent in the cities. This restlessness had several sources. There was the constant pressure of the Gregorian reform that demanded a purified clergy. To that was added increasing levels of education and demand for literacy that led to disdain for the lack of sophistication from the existing urban clergy. To top it off, wealth was flowing into the new cities, bringing with it unprecedented concentrations of money and influence. In the midst of an intensely Christian culture, this was a volatile situation. Guilt about material wealth ran deeply, fed by the many meditations and traditions noted in the previous chapters. Such a seething mass of ideas encouraged an unstable environment. From the Church's perspective, all of these developments were alarming. Scholastic thinkers asked themselves whether provision could be made in the Christian worldview for the bourgeois and new-money merchants. Would the new middle classes shift their worldviews toward these purveyors of new and heretical ideas? Could there be any way of usefully integrating these new religious realities into the fabric of existing Christianity?

The Bishop

Into this charged environment came Sicard of Cremona (1155–1215), one of the ablest bishops of the twelfth century.[4] He was Cremonese by birth, but proved such an exceptional student that he was sent to the University of Bologna for extensive studies, where he probably befriended Lothario dei Conti, the future Pope Innocent III (r. 1198–1216). He returned to Cremona in 1183 as a subdeacon, but his promise was so great that within two years he was raised to the episcopate, which he held in that city for the next thirty tumultuous years.[5] He wrote a famous *Mitrale* describing the liturgical life of medieval Italy, as well as writing both historical and canonical works. An extremely active bishop, he attempted to hold his fractious city together by focusing them on foreign enemies. He endeavored to be a builder of consensus by engaging in works of peacemaking, coordinating with the universal Church, and cultivating the religious life of his people. He worked his whole life in attempting to unify his restive community, a position made more difficult by his identification with the "old" city and the more ancient episcopal/noble nexus of power. He was one of those rare prelates who was able to unite the pastoral, the scholarly, and the political in a generally happy union.[6] It would be Sicard who was the motivating force behind the presentation of his fellow townsman, Omobono, for canonization by his friend Innocent III.

Our earliest knowledge of Omobono comes most likely from the work of Sicard himself. Three lives of Omobono exist from the hundred years after the saint's death.[7] The first one is entitled *Cum Orbita Solis* (*COS*). While it is anonymous, scholars are all but convinced that the work is the product of Sicard's pen.[8] It was clearly written before the saint's canonization, and probably corresponds to the modern *positio*, or the story of the saint written by present-day scholars for the Dicastery for the Causes of Saints. It was the document designed to present Omobono to the Curia, later polished to provide the material for his liturgy as celebrated in Cremona. The second life is *Quoniam Historiae* (*QH*), which was anonymously written probably between 1230 and 1240. This is a more earthy life, which begins to delve into the social and religious milieu of the city, beginning to distance itself from the more formal *COS*. Finally there is a later life entitled *Labentibus Annis* (*LA*) which was written at some point during the last third of the 1200s. This *vita* completed the move away from a formalizing, clericalizing presentation of Omobono, and situated him strongly in his lay-merchant milieu. All of these lives are translated in the upcoming section, and will be discussed and analyzed separately. In them we see a transition unfolding over the course of 100 years, mirroring the developments occurring in broader Christian society: the birth of the concept of "saintly merchant."[9]

THE SAINT

Before looking at the lives of Omobono, we must try to present an outline of his life along with its social, political, and religious contexts.[10] Fifty years after his death he was said to be of the Tucenghi family, though this is not found in the earliest records.[11]

Scholars have placed his birth around the year 1117, for *QH* says that at the time of his death in 1197 he was around 80 years of age, and that he had spent fifty years in his profession from the end of his adolescence, and another fifteen in a penitential retirement. He lived among the upwardly mobile in the "new" section of the city made up of the rising bourgeoisie, within the parish of Sant' Egidio (St. Giles—a popular medieval saint and one of the "Fourteen Holy Helpers"). Born of a mercantile household, the *vitae* declare that he began his career as a tailor but later became a merchant and businessman of some means (*QH* 11, *LA* 2). The earliest life implies that he could have risen to have substantial success and wealth, and might have even gone on extended trading voyages, for he was among the "concourse of those who travel the land and sea" (*COS* 1). It seems that he was the only son of a middle-aged couple, themselves of the rising merchant estate. He followed his father's trade and became known among businessmen for his uprightness (*LA* 3). He married on the advice of his family and had at least two sons, one of whom he named Monaco. As was common in premodern society, he lived under the rule of his father even after his marriage, and did not come into the possession of his family's goods until his father had died. With that, he became proprietor of the family business and inherited the townhouse, as well as a small vineyard outside of the city walls that he used for extra income. Even if he was a merchant of only modest success, he was solidly planted within the middle class of Cremona.

It was around the time of his inheritance that Omobono's life took an unexpected turn, and he experienced a religious conversion. He began to meditate on the transitory nature of earthly things, a common ordeal for Christians seeking perfection in every age of the Church. All of the scriptures, meditations, and interpretations spoken of in previous chapters crowded in upon him. The negative bias against the merchant life, the difficulty of salvation for the rich, and the dangers of luxury and greed began to occupy his thoughts. He began to question whether or not he would be saved. While he had always been virtuous and had followed the laws and fasts of the Church with precision, like all saints he sought a deeper life of holiness. Much like the rich young man, he had followed all the commandments since birth. But what of perfection? Could he truly abandon all for Christ when was bound to the world in so many different ways? He had responsibilities for his property, to his wife and sons, and toward his city. He refused to abandon these, and it was precisely in this refusal that one finds the revolution of Omobono. He attempted to continue to be a good citizen and a good family man, while at the same time aggressively pursuing the life of holiness. Omobono turned first toward the commonly accepted medieval pattern of sanctity. He would become a lay penitent. Barred from the life of greater perfection in poverty and virginity, he embraced that common—and indeed at that time, only—path to holiness while remaining in the world. In his commentary on the Penitential Psalms, Innocent III—the pope who would canonize Omobono—outlined the necessary formula for lay sanctification. The pope said that one must have sincere faith in the Church and in the Trinity, one needed to follow the commandments, and one must perform the corporal and spiritual works of mercy.[12] In other words, orthodoxy and piety were the twin requirements. The problem that confronted Omobono was that in the 1100s the only accepted way of undertaking this was an abandonment of family and wealth in order to embrace a quasi-consecrated path.

The life of a lay penitent was one of the most popular religious manifestations of the Middle Ages.[13] Called by either the name "converts" (*conversi*) or "penitents" (*penitenti*) they traced their origins to the call for purification in the Gregorian Reform. As the Church and clergy were being sanctified, so the laity also came to bear similar hopes for themselves. The chief means of living out the penitential life was in ascetic practices that dated back to the very foundations of Christianity. These lay penitents would commit to extraordinary fasts and heroic works of charity in their attempts to mimic the religious life as closely as was possible, given their lay status. While many undertook to copy monastic practices, it was difficult to live in the world and attempt to be a monk at the same time. It was easier for *conversi* who were unmarried to affiliate themselves to a monastery as a lay brother, whose responsibility was to attend to the physical needs of the convent, and to say a certain number of Paternosters and Aves per day. This had been the old Christian pattern for widows whose husbands had passed away. Married penitents might take vows of chastity, but the Church demanded that these be mutually agreed upon, for the spouses had sexual rights over each other. A similar problem existed with wealth. We have already seen that the dispersion of Peter Waldo's patrimony was vigorously disputed by his wife, who had her own rights to support and property. Sometimes married penitents had spouses who were not on quite the same spiritual page. Interestingly, it was people in these types of situations who drove the development of new forms of lay holiness. A wife's or husband's refusal to become penitents together with their spouses caused the one seeking perfection to develop creative paths to holiness. These were consonant with both the retention of wealth and the rendering of the marital debt. Because of it a wholly new type of Christian life was being formed.

While these penitents would later coalesce into communities and, in the distant future, into third orders, penitence in the 1100s was largely an individual choice that sometimes resulted in unique manifestations of piety. In spite of their pioneering individualism, local penitents needed to distinguish themselves from wandering heretics, and so made it a point to affiliate themselves with the Church in some way, whether it was through a bishop, a monastery, or one's local parish. Having received this approval, penitents may have been distinguished by their sober clothing (or sometimes a penitential habit) and by their increased asceticism, but they remained in the world. They were not monks and continued to live a life in the city, becoming a "leaven" in the world. They continued their worldly paths and careers. They lived with their families and in their homes. Here was the recipe for a new stream of spiritual life in the Church. It was one that was neither clerical nor monastic (though it bore the marks of both of these at times) and was fully engaged in the secular life of the city. It would be this path that Omobono would make his own, and in so doing became a standard bearer for a novel path of holiness in the Church.

That medievals were solicitous for their own salvation is amply demonstrated by the eagerness with which they took up the penitential life. Yet they did not always do it at one go. As mentioned above, previous commitments were primary concerns in a society bound together by oath, vow, and personal loyalty. People united by communal and family ties were not able to renounce the world as completely as some did in the early Church. The townsmen clearly recognized Omobono as a virtuous man from the time of his entry into business, but it seems that his religious sentiments began to accelerate when the weight of property and responsibility began to bear down upon him following the death of his father. Before that time he had far fewer encumbrances. Even though married, he still lived in obedience to paternal authority under a roof not yet his by inheritance. Once his father had died, though, the conditions of his life brought him face to face with the same uncertainties running through the whole of bourgeois culture in the Middle Ages. "I am well off and comfortable. How then can I be saved?" Before his formal conversion to the penitential life, it seems Omobono took a series of steps in that general direction. What the early *COS* presents as a nearly instantaneous renunciation of the mercantile life, seems to develop over the course of time in the later works. He apparently became absent-minded at his trade and began to spend more time frequenting the churches of his city. Most notably he acquired a reputation as a fount of charity to all of the urban destitute, becoming widely known as the "Father of the Poor." He began to act more and more like a pious penitent, in particular by increased devotion to prayer and fasting and by dutiful attendance at the canonical hours celebrated in his local church. He was also assiduous in going to confession, a key indicator of the orthodox penitential life. He set himself apart proudly from anti-materialist heretics by continuing to live with his wife and pointedly eating meat on some days of the week and on feast days (*QH* 2). He was principally known for his attendance at the night watch, a particularly penitential hour prayed in the very early morning, perhaps around 2:00 a.m. He sometimes had to rouse his own parish priest for the night liturgy, at other times he simply appeared in church, the doors having unlocked of their own volition for him. The celebration of Matins was certainly seen as something with special penitential weight; many saints, such as St. Clare of Assisi and St. Thomas Aquinas, were noted for their devotion to this hour.[14] Yet there is something further to be seen here. Matins was the easiest hour to attend for someone who had both business and family responsibilities, for all the shops were closed and one's family members fast abed. It was a way to act in a penitential manner with as little inconvenience to the social fabric as possible. It is worthy of note that when the bell sounded for the other canonical hours during the work day, Omobono did not hasten to church, but rather retired to his vineyard to pray in private. That was a place of work, but one which he turned into an oasis of prayer (*QH* 3). Indeed the vineyard even became a place of spiritual combat, where the devil tormented him in private, until an apparition of St. Michael came to deliver him from the attacks.

The reasons for this privacy begin to come into focus in the later life of Omobono. His family was not thrilled with his newfound piety. His wife in particular began to harangue him. She attacked his inattentiveness at work from a perspective that merchant Christians could understand. She accused him of imprudence, a vice which should be foreign to successful businessmen. The family began to take note of his penitential practices and started to demand recognition as those to whom the holy man owed the production of his hands.[15] Omobono perceived this and began to take smaller and smaller portions at dinner. Yet he always managed to secret his food away in order later to distribute it to the poor. He also became something of a pious thief. He would raid the larder and take food and wine—and sometimes money—in order to give it to the poor. He considered that his excess was the property of the poor in any case (a position well supported by scholastic economists and thinkers back to St. Ambrose). His family members, however, had other ideas. They began to put the produce under lock and key. Omobono located the key and liberated more of his own stores to feed the indigent. His family began to make excuses for him as well. When he would give his clothing to the poor, they would claim that he had been waylaid by thieves. Indeed it seems in order to avoid their carping Omobono began buy into the ruse himself. There was a delicate balance to be maintained between penitent and patron and, while difficult, Omobono managed to walk that fine line.

He was a quiet man who preferred to perform his penances in private, especially in light of the demands made by his family.[16] His fasting and the wearing of a barbed penitential belt called a *cilice* were things that he could do individually without taking sustenance from his kin or drawing attention to himself. In a homely detail, *QH* recorded that he wished so little harm to come to living things that he would cross the street in order to avoid disturbing a bird that had landed there (a real proto-Franciscan moment, that) (*QH* 9). He did not like to proclaim his holiness at all, yet everyone recognized it.[17] When neighbors asked him to preach about the spiritual life, he would merely quote them the Golden Rule. This refusal to preach also underscored Omobono's difference from the loquacious and wandering heretical preachers. The Bull of Canonization contains a very interesting phrase that suggests that Omobono was a mediator for peace in the troubled city, stating that he would even omit attendance at his beloved Divine Office if there was a matter than involved such mediation. Omobono remained active politically in the *comune*, as a messenger of peace. The poor also clustered about him, knowing that he was a reliable source of alms. His business provided the means whereby he could support his family and the indigent at the same time, both from the produce of his work and the labor in his vineyard. Omobono had hit upon the key to the merchant piety that developed later. He had to keep working in order to keep giving alms. Abandonment of wealth was of little use to the poor; it was a singular and public act that might be done out of pride. Humble work, though, produced the very material needed for a consistent supply of alms to the poor. Indeed it seems that he used all of the surplus of his small plot of land outside of the walls for the subvention of the poor. Yet his wife (who remains unnamed in all extant sources) would not leave him in peace; *LA* constantly refers to her abuse and insults. He grew weary of the harangues but always triumphed over her by "humility and patience." *QH* 10 provides the unaffected detail that he was often angry with his family, but immediately regretted it and wept bitter tears. One can sympathize with the feelings of a man whose interests were seriously diverging from those closest to him, suffering from their refusal to understand his process of conversion. During his life he was reported as performing miracles. On two occasions additional bread and wine appeared in the pantry after he had given some to the poor, thus sparing him his wife's vicious tongue-lashings. Yet in the end, even his wife had to acknowledge her husband's holiness. He was respected by all in the town, he had opposed the heretics, and had served as a good citizen and neighbor in the city. In fact he was in all respects a good husband and father, in spite of his penitential eccentricities. She found she had little to complain about; she and her sons were provided for. At the end of her life, she said to her son, "Remember, that you will see many crowds come to venerate your father and if they knew him like I knew him, they would have venerated him even when he was alive" (*QH* 13). All in all, it was a stunning testimony of devotion from the person who had known him best and—at times—treated him the worst.

His wife having died, and with grown sons, Omobono was freed to undertake the more classical version of the life of a lay penitent. Omobono had cultivated very good relations with his parish priest and confessor, Osberto. This clergyman later traveled to Rome with Bishop Sicard and was the key witness in the canonization enquiry. It seems that Omobono was at least informally affiliated with his parish church as a lay penitent. He attended all the canonical hours, and one wonders if this might be an indicator of his having a working knowledge of Latin. Besides being a merchant, it was normal for lay penitents merely to pray repetitive prayers, while leaving the complex Divine Office to the clergy, but it seems that Omobono was quite devoted to the Hours. He continued to be active in the city, for it does not appear that he divested his properties and indeed most probably passed them on to his sons. Property was neither a burden nor a temptation for Omobono, but rather a necessary possession in order to pursue his love for the corporal and spiritual works of mercy. He fed the poor from his own profits, and he guaranteed them a Christian burial at their deaths. His very property ensured the possibility of a continuation of alms. What his heirs might do after his death was their own business; all he could leave them was the means to continue his work and his own good example.

Omobono's death happened in a dramatically pious way. It was an example of his devotion, and one that was recorded and remembered in all of the hagiography about him. Omobono had come to church, as was his habit, for the celebration of the night-watch of Matins on the 13th of November 1197. It was the feast of Saint Brice of Tours (known in Italy as San Brizio, a popular saint at the time in northern Italy). He decided, as he often did, to remain in Church until the celebration of the morning Mass. He prayed kneeling in front of a cross in the Church. The priest, probably Osberto, began to celebrate mass. When the priest began to recite the Gloria, Omobono prostrated himself in a cruciform position. This is not terribly surprising in itself. Not only were there no rubrics for the laity in the premodern mass, Omobono's neighbors and clergy were used to his pious idiosyncrasies in the Church. However, when he did not stand up for the Gospel (which was a normative practice) people began to take note. They came over to him and found him dead, in the shape of a cross, on the floor of the church he had loved so much.

Cult and Canonization

Omobono's reputation for holiness had preceded him. A popular cult is a necessary first step for the recognition of a public saint in the Church. This was made evident by the plaint of the poor of Cremona, who considered that they had lost their greatest benefactor. A multitude came for the funeral rites. It was then that miracles began to multiply, for besides the evidence of public cult, there also has to be the divine sign of approval in the accomplishing of miraculous deeds.[18] Omobono's friends and clients had witnessed his holiness in life, and they now saw the divine sign of approval in his death. Miracles multiplied and his fame began to spread locally.

It had been traditional in Christianity, at least since the 300s, for the local bishop to take charge of the management of local cults. Sicard quickly moved in and became the *impresario* (to use Peter Brown's term) for Omobono's burgeoning cult. He probably coordinated with the priest Osberto, pastor of Sant' Egidio. In all probability notaries were sent to Omobono's tomb to make careful legal records and documentation of the events that transpired there. Omobono may have remained only a local, episcopally authorized saint were it not for an event that propelled Sicard to a position of prominence in Italy.[19] On 8 January 1198, only two months after the death of Omobono, Sicard's friend and fellow student Lothario Conti was elected Pope Innocent III at the vigorous young age of 37. Innocent was a far-sighted, brilliant, and active pope, who used his pontificate to strengthen the position of the Church and to enhance the prestige of his office.[20] He became perhaps the most powerful pope in history, and one of the most famous leaders of the Catholic Church, whose legislation continues to be in force for millions around the globe. Sicard lost no time in hastening to his friend's court. In Sicard, Innocent had a reliable bishop in northern Italy who could effectively aid his cause against the pretensions of the German emperors and the efforts of the heretics. Sicard assembled a coterie of lay and clerical advocates, among them the priest Osberto, to go to Rome to lay the case for their saint before the new pope. Osberto proved to be the star witness, corroborating all that he knew of Omobono's holiness as his confessor and spiritual director for over twenty years. It is also possible that Sicard brought a document (today called a *positio*), entitled *Acta et obitus beati Homoboni* [Acts and death of Blessed Omobono]. Though the document is now lost, it is possible that it formed the basis not only for *Cum orbita solis*, but the canonization Bull itself.[21] Innocent was impressed that the cause had been backed by the entire ecclesial community of Cremona, and decided the case favorably. He proceeded to canonize Omobono just over a year after the saint's death, on 12 January 1199.

Many questions arise regarding this astonishing canonization. Why was Sicard so insistent on presenting his case to Rome? In the first place there was opportunity. His friend had become pope, and Innocent was willing to support the designs of a bishop whose allegiance he needed, and whose friendship he valued. Yet Sicard could have simply retained Omobono as a local saint, the likes of which could be found throughout the Christian world throughout the Middle Ages. Papal canonization at this time was relatively novel. It only came into spirited development during the pontificate of Alexander III (1159–1181). Before that, papal elevation of saints had been done only sporadically. Alexander would mold canonization into a tool of the papacy to propose universal veneration. People began increasingly to turn to Rome for the recognition of their holy men and women. Yet canonization was no sure thing, and came to be a significant financial burden on those prosecuting the cases. During this period the old spontaneity of veneration was still a central part of the process. Innocent seems to have wasted little time in deciding upon Omobono as the first canonized saint of his reign.

Sicard may have had several motivations in proposing Omobono. The first and most crucial was that Sicard and his people in Cremona were convinced that their fellow townsman was a real and genuine saint. This must be stated at the outset, even while other motivations might have come into play. Further, Sicard used his friendship with Innocent to secure a signal and paramount gesture that brought prestige to him personally and also to his community. To have a papally canonized saint was not only to achieve recognition at the highest level, but it also opened the possibility that the shrine of Omobono would become a place of significant pilgrimage (such as that of Thomas Becket). Though things did not quite transpire in this way, the possibility was certainly there. Sicard was recognized as a close associate of the pope, a reflected charisma that aided him in his local struggles in the city and within his diocese. Yet the most likely conclusion is that Sicard's main focus was in employing the cult of Omobono as a tool to unify the fractious city, not to mention underscoring his own authority.[22] Omobono had been a neighbor and peacemaker in the community, and could serve as a focus of devotion after death. He could unify the "old" and the "new" towns in common communal faith and pride. Because it seems that Sicard had been drawn from the older aristocratic side of the city, such an elevation of a "new" man would improve his relationship with the growing bourgeoisie. Things had reached such a point in the city that the "new" city had effectively seceded in 1197, electing its own podestà (a sort of term-limited city manager).[23] While Sicard's plans did not result in an end of the factionalism, they did provide a common center of civic pride.[24] One must say, however, that the canonization of a saint by the Roman See was quite a big gun to bring to that fight. Sicard, a canny politician and a sensitive pastor, merely saw the opportunity and seized it.

The question then remains concerning Innocent III's motivations. It is strange that, for his first canonization, he should have selected a humble man from Cremona, relatively unknown even in neighboring towns. Further, it is astonishing that he should have chosen a man from the new merchant classes, who was married, had children, and lived a life that did not embody the wholesale renunciation of property. In the history of sainthood there had never been a man like Omobono. There were many married people, but they had either been martyred (a different case altogether) or had been royals. There had been men and women of the world, but they had abandoned family and property and undertook the religious life, the more perfect way to heaven. In terms of saintly lay confessors, there really were not any. Innocent must have known the revolution in the idea of sanctity that this could have caused, but his canonization bull remains relatively traditional in attempts to understand Omobono's holiness.[25] The document is no manifesto on the dignity of labor or of spiritual approbation of the merchant life. It is possible that he was working with a more traditional notion of papal canonization, which was the mere authorization of an existing local cult. But, in reality, Innocent had bigger fish to fry. With Omobono he began a large-scale reimagining of the concept of sainthood and of canonization itself. Indeed one could say that the theology of canonization, as it continues to be operative in the Church today, was a result of Innocent's reimagining of sainthood in this bull. While it did not directly relate to the lay or merchant life, it established a pattern that would ensure that holiness be recognized at every level of the Christian life. Indeed, it has been recently argued that the revolutionary doctrine contained in the canonization documents are directly traceable to Sicard of Cremona, in his *Cum orbita solis* life.[26]

In the canonization bull of Omobono, Innocent had two main points to make.[27] The first was clearly to articulate a theology of public holiness in the Church. As candidates were increasingly being proposed to the Holy See for recognition, canonists and theologians in the curia began to consider the practices surrounding the recognition of public sanctity. For the first millennium of Christianity recognition had been spontaneous and local, a public cult that was accompanied by miracles usually managed by the local bishop. There was a problem though. What if someone had feigned their holiness and deceived the local church? With the increasing professionalization of theology and law, and with the rise of spiritual direction and private confession, many in the clergy were intimating that they had the requisite expertise to recognize sanctity, and in particular to distinguish it from false claims. There was indeed a danger that hypocrites could counterfeit sanctity and deceive the laity into honoring them with a public cult. Innocent demanded in *Quia Pietas* (Omobono's canonization bull, hereafter *QP*) that the public recognition of sainthood could only be accorded based on a life of systematic virtue.

The pope insisted that a heroic degree of virtue be demonstrated, in accordance with a person's vocation. That this requirement first appears in Omobono's canonization was a clear recognition that holiness could be found anywhere, as long as the virtues were heroically practiced according to a given state in life. Only the Church is authorized to make that determination, a contention that would lead to the rise of intricate canonization processes which continue to the present day. But works alone, even if systematically virtuous, were not enough. "Two things are necessary for one who is publicly venerated as a saint in the Church Militant: virtuous morals, and the power of signs, this means works of piety in life and the sign of miracles after death."[28] Miracles also were to be subject to ecclesial investigation, for demons can sometimes work miracles.[29] But Innocent knew that truly virtuous men would be recognized by God with genuine wonders, for men who consort with the devil may produce signs, but could never exhibit holiness of life. Both are necessary, and both are subject to analysis and evaluation only by the Church (eventually in the thirteenth century, only by the papacy). Omobono's canonization was a watershed moment in the history of public sanctity in the Catholic Church. Innocent also established the future form of canonization bulls, following up his theology with a brief biography of Omobono and a short list of miracles performed by him, all attested to by oath-bound witnesses and assessed by the pontiff himself. One could say that Omobono's was the first modern canonization.

There was another motivation in Innocent's intentions, and which could be seen unfolding in his later saintly elevations. At the dawn of his papacy a pair of heresies confronted Innocent that, while not numerous in adherents, threatened the very core identity of medieval Christianity. These were the anti-materialist Cathars and the wandering poor devotees of Waldo of Lyons. In the past the Church had experienced little success against them, and their numbers were growing in Christian heartlands such as Provence, Lombardy, and Tuscany. While Waldensian beliefs challenged the authority of the Church, Cathar tenets undermined the very foundations of society, civil law, marriage, and the family. Innocent would dedicate a major part of his career to a multi-pronged and highly successful campaign against these heretics. While he is most famous for the calling of the Albigensian Crusade, in reality he had a multifaceted approach to the problem. He was instrumental in offering paths to reconciliation for several Waldensian groups, which in turn became bulwarks against the Cathars. Recognizing the errors the Church had made with Waldo, Innocent knew he had to have a cadre of holy men and women dedicated to matching and exceeding the heretics in the practices of asceticism and poverty, and he provided the initial push that would lead to the later foundations of the mendicant orders, one of the conspicuous successes of medieval Christianity. Innocent also knew how deeply saints and sainthood were woven into the fabric of Christianity. The Christian people were deeply devoted to their holy men and women, and as such, they formed a heavenly vanguard against the pretensions of heresy. Innocent decided to deploy this heavenly army as the tip of the spear against the heretics. Saints were obedient sons and daughters of the Church, and in heaven they never ceased in their intercessions for Christians. By extension this meant that their prayers constantly went up against whatever heresies the Church then confronted. Innocent used his canonizations, starting with Omobono of Cremona, to enlist the saints as elite fighters against the heretics. All of Omobono's hagiographical accounts give brief but pointed testimony that he had confronted heretics during his life, but Innocent developed it into a cardinal aspect of his whole career.

Indeed there must have been heretics in Cremona. *LA* begins with the declaration that the city was overrun by them. While this is an exaggeration, it firmly fixed Omobono in an environment not only seething with political tension but also religious heterodoxy. Cathars and Waldensians used the cover of war and conflict to penetrate into the cities, locations that offered them relative anonymity. The rising middle classes, clamoring for a more serious spiritual life, were drawn to these wandering preachers and scornful of the sometimes short-sighted attitudes of their own urban clergy. Heretics often mimicked the pious lives of Catholics, participating in civic and religious rituals. Omobono had never had any truck with them however. He was reported as being a "despiser" of heretics, and he repeatedly opposed them by signs, miracles, and words, so that they were converted (*LA* 10). Innocent knew how powerful saints were as a bastion against heresy, and he makes it clear in *QP*, "so that the perversity of the heretics might be confounded when, coming to the tombs of the Catholics, they might see miracles spring forth."[30] In particular the Cathars were those who hated the material body, which they considered to be a creation of Satan, who was himself a god. Satan had created the whole of the material world, and souls had been imprisoned in bodies as a penalty for a spiritual "original sin." They therefore hated anything that had to do with the body, sex, sacraments, or any of the materiality that Christianity was immersed in so deeply. In short they were Anti-Incarnational; one could not conceive a more opposite heresy to orthodox Christianity. Yet the saints, like Christ, had bodies. From the earliest days of Christianity their bodies were placed in revered tombs. Mass was said there, linking the victory of the martyrs to that of Christ. Shrines were raised and pilgrimages began in order to bring living bodies into the physical presence of the dead body of the friend of God, whose bones would with certainty be raised unto immortal glory on the last day. Saints (along with sacraments) were some of the most stubbornly material components of Christianity, and as such they formed a flashpoint of conflict with the heretics.[31] As Innocent said, the Church encouraged prayers and pilgrimages to the tomb of a saint because there one witnessed astonishing things: dead material bodies healing living material bodies. A saint's tomb was meant to be a permanent sermon in favor of the Incarnation and against anti-materialism. Omobono's was one of the first cults officially deployed in this manner.

While Innocent was maintaining these new axioms of papal policy in canonization, the Cremonese rallied around their new saint, and he became a civic patron. It has been proposed that his cult was the result of a temporary efflorescence of cultic devotion, since there were no records of later miracle collections made at his tomb.[32] This did not matter too much to the townsmen or the bishop. They had their saint. The bishop and the town translated the saint's relics from his parish Church of Sant' Egidio on 25 June 1202, and placed them in a location of honor in the cathedral of the city. Indeed the canonization and the translation show the skill of Bishop Sicard at shepherding and maintaining a cult, and focusing civic devotion on the mother Church of the city.[33] In removing Omobono from his local church in the "new" town, he made Omobono the possession of the whole city, a living testimony to the reconciliation that Sicard desired so strongly. We will trace the later development of his cult, but now it remains to study the original documents of his life, collected together here.

CHAPTER 3 ENDNOTES

1 Daniel Waley, *The Italian City-Republics* (New York, 1978), 25–32, 102–15. Standard for this period is Giovanni Tabacco, *The Struggle for Power in Medieval Italy: Structures of Political Rule*, Cambridge Medieval Textbooks, trans. Rosalind Brown Jensen (Cambridge, 1989), 182–320.
2 Carla Bertinelli, *Cremona, città imperiale: nell'VIII centenario della nascita di Federico II* (Linograf, 1999).
3 For an in-depth discussion of the problems identifying the factions see: Daniela Medici, Sergio Raveggi, Massimo Tarassi and Patrizia Parenti, *Ghibellini, guelfi e popolo grasso*, Biblioteca di storia 26 (Florence, 1978).
4 For Sicard see: Ercole Brocchieri, *Sicardo di Cremona e la sua opera letteraria* (Cremona: Athenaeum cremonense, 1958). Also, Daniele Piazzi, "I tempi del vescovo Sicardo," in *Sant' Omobono nel suo tempo* (Cremona, 1999), 77–90.
5 See, Angelo Silvestri, *Power, Politics and Episcopal Authority: The Bishops of Cremona and Lincoln in the Middle Ages (1066–1340)* (Newcastle upon Tyne: Cambridge Scholars Publishing, 2015).
6 André Vauchez, *Omobono di Cremona (+1197): laico e sant : profilo storico* (Cremona: Nuova editrice cremonese, 2001), 16.
7 For Cremonese hagiography, see: M. R. Cortesi, "Libri, memoria e cultura a Cremona (sec. IX–XIV), in *Storia di Cremona. Il Trecento*.

Chiesa e cultura (VIII–XIV secolo). Eds. G. Andenna and G. Chittolini (Cremona, 2007) : 206–11.
8   Ibid., 26.
9   References to the lives will follow the abbreviations of the titles, *COS, QH,* and *LA.* They may be consulted in the translations in this book.
10 For this three works are absolutely indispensable: Daniele Piazzi, *Omobono di Cremona: Biografie dal XIII al XVI secolo* (Cremona, 1991); André Vauchez, *Omobono di Cremona (+1197)*; and, id. *S. Homebon de Crémone: "Père des Pauvres" et patron des tailleurs.* With collaboration by U. Longo, L. Albiero, and V. Souche. Subsidia Hagiographica 96 (Brussels: 2018).
11 This may or may not be the case; it was common in the later Middle Ages for prominent families to claim kinship with saints, as for example the cases of St. Dominic and St. Peter Martyr. However his relation to a merchant family, rather than a noble one, makes the claim more likely in his case.
12 Vauchez, *Omobono*, 24.
13 The best discussion of these is in: Augustine Thompson, *Cities of God: The Religious Life of the Italian Communes, 1125–1325* (University Park, PA: Penn State Press, 2005), 69–102.
14 See my "The Living Rule: Monastic Exemplarity in Mendicant Hagiography," in *Shaping Stability: The Normation and Formation of Religious Life in the Middle Ages*, eds. Krijn Pansters and A. Plunkett-Latimer, Disciplina Monastica 11 (Turnhout: Brepols, 2016): 229–44.
15 Indeed this was an Augustinian position. Those most due the support of our necessarily limited resources are first of all our family, friends, and neighbors. See: John Mueller, *Redeeming Economics* (Wilmington, DE: ISI, 2010), 133–53.
16 Indeed this quest for privacy was something quite unique in medieval Italy, where life was so much lived in common.
17 This is part of the classical irony of sainthood: the more one hides it, the more it blazes forth. The first hermits who went out to the desert to be alone, soon found the whole town coming after them for prayers, for advice, and for support. Out of charity they received them.
18 For useful examinations see, Roberto Paciocco, "'Virtus morum' e 'virtus signorum': La teoria della santità nelle lettere di canonizzazione di Innocenzo III." *Nuova rivista storica* 70 (1986): 597–610; and id., *Canonizzazioni e culto dei santi nella "Christianitas" (1198–1302)*. Medioevo Francescano, Saggi 11. (Assisi: Edizioni Porziuncola, 2006).

19 It did not become normative to propose candidates for devotion to the papacy until this time, and a definitive reservation of canonization to the popes was not achieved until 1634. By Omobono's time it was normal simply for a local bishop to authorize public devotion. See my *Certain Sainthood: Canonization and the Origins of Papal Infallibility in the Medieval Church* (Ithaca, NY: Cornell, 2015).
20 For Innocent, see John C. Moore, *Pope Innocent III: To Root Up and To Plant* (South Bend, IN: Notre Dame Press, 2009).
21 André Vauchez, *S. Homebon de Crémone*, 12. He also proposes that this work may indeed be *COS*.
22 This is the opinion of Vauchez, ibid., 7.
23 For events in the city at the time see Vauchez, *Omobono di Cremona*, 18–19. Also, Piazzi, "I tempi di vescovo Sicardo," 77–90.
24 See François Menant, *La Chiesa di Cremona nel XII secolo*, in *Sant'Omobono nel suo tempo. Conversazioni storiche* (Cremona, 1999): 29–44.
25 Mary Harvey Doyno attempts to argue that Innocent's primary concern in this bull was to "domesticate" saintly lay charisma, and to deflect the possibility it might challenge the institutional Church. If this is so the effort was both precocious (in that Omobono was one of the early public lay holy figures) and so precipitous as to be shocking, since the canonization happened within a year of the young pope's election. In any case her new work on lay sanctity is useful and interesting in contextualizing contemporary lay holiness. Mary Harvey Doyno, *The Lay Saint: Charity and Charismatic Authority in Medieval Italy, 1150–1350* (Ithaca, NY: Cornell, 2019), esp. 34–46. She also clearly recognizes that Innocent desired to deploy Omobono against heretics and in favor of civil peace.
26 This is the opinion of André Vauchez, *S. Homebon de Crémone*, 11–15; discussed in more detail in his, "Innocent III, Sicard de Crémone et la canonisation de saint Homebon (†1197)" in *Innocenzo III. Urbs et orbis*. Atti del congresso internazionale Roma, 9–15 sett. 1998. Ed. A. Sommerlechner. Nuovi studi storici 55 (Rome: 2003): 435–55.
27 For a more extended discussion see my: *Certain Sainthood: Canonization and the Origins of Papal Infallibility in the Medieval Church* (Ithaca, NY: Cornell, 2015), 63–66.
28 "Duo tamen, virtus videlicet morum, et virtus signorum, opera scilicet pietatis in vita, et miraculorum signa post mortem, ut qui reputetur Sanctas in militanti Ecclesia requiruntur." Innocent III, "Quia pietas" [Canonization of Omobono of Cremona], January 12, 1199.
29 Indeed Vauchez has called *COS* "a veritable treatise on miracles" written with scholastic precision. Vauchez, *S. Homebon*, 14.

30 "Sanctus etiam ab hominibus habeatur, et in hoc praesertim haereticorum confundatur perversitas, cum ad catholicorum tumulos viderint prodigia pullulare."
31 I trace all this in my book: *Certain Sainthood*.
32 Vauchez, *Omobono di Cremona*, 73.
33 Ibid., 76.

SOURCES FOR THE LIFE OF OMOBONO

BULL OF CANONIZATION – QUIA PIETAS

Note: The footnotes in this section are meant to accompany the text, not in the manner of an academic apparatus, but after the style of a medieval "gloss," that is, a commentary on the text meant to aid the reader.

Innocent's Bull of canonization represents a significant step in the reservation of saintly recognition to the papacy. In it Innocent outlines not only the life and miracles of Omobono, but also sets forth a comprehensive theory of public holiness in the Church. Innocent also gives a snapshot of the process of canonization at the time. Bishop Sicard and members of the comune *of Cremona—both lay and clerical—had come to present their petition to the new pope. Sicard's star witness was Omobono's own parish priest, confessor, and spiritual director, a priest named Osberto. In a canonization there is no better witness to a candidate's holiness than someone who had known the saint intimately. It seems Osberto's testimony was the clincher for Innocent. Innocent canonized Omobono with full liturgical honors, and then sent the following bull to the Cremonese on 12 January 1199.*

Innocent Bishop, servant of the servants of God, to his most beloved children, the clergy and the people of Cremona, Salutations and the Apostolic Benediction.

1. Since devotion toward God gives life, both here and in the world to come, the just and merciful God often glorifies in this life, and crowns in the future one, those whom He has

predestined to life.¹ He also promised to them, through the prophets, "I will give you praise, honor, and glory in the sight of all peoples" (Zeph 3:20), and He has Himself promised, "The just shall shine like stars in the kingdom of their Father" (Mt 13:43). For the Lord is marvelous in Himself, wonderful in His saints, wonderful in all His works, and He shows forth His power to us, He kindles the fading flame of charity in many people by the signs of His miracles, taking into His glory those who competed well in this world (cf. 2 Tim 2:5). In honor of their memory He renews signs and miracles (Sir 36:6, Ps 67:36), so that those who are saints in His sight may be regarded as saints among men. And this is principally so that the perversity of the heretics might be confounded when, coming to the tombs of the Catholics, they might see miracles spring forth.[2]

2. Even though, according to the testimony of the Truth, only final perseverance is required for the sanctity of souls in the Church Triumphant, "because he who perseveres to the end, he will be saved" (Mt 10:22),[3] two things are necessary for one to be venerated as a saint in the Church Militant, namely a holy life and the power of miracles, that is to say works of piety in life and the sign of miracles after death—these are

---

1 The pope here comments on the glorification of the saints made manifest by the will of God. He will not permit that His holy ones lie in obscurity.

2 In this model, saints are glorified by God because of the following reasons: 1) they increase His own external glory; 2) they have merited it by their free cooperation with grace; 3) that men might marvel at the gifts of God; and 4)—first seen here in Innocent's thought—to confute heretics.

3 One may make a distinction here between Saints with a "capital S" and saints with a "lowercase S." All who die in a state of grace, and who have been purified of the penalties for their sins, go to heaven and are genuine saints. "Capital S" saints are those whom the Church permits the faithful to venerate publicly.

required.⁴ For it often happens that the angel of Satan transforms himself into an angel of light (2 Cor 11:4) and certain of these are able to do good works, "that they might be seen by men" (Mt 23:5), and some even perform miracles, though their manner of life is evil, as we read of the magicians of Pharaoh (Ex 7:11–22), and also regarding the Antichrist (Mt 24:24; Rev 13:11–18) who would also if he could lead the elect into error with his false wonders.⁵ For this reason neither works alone nor miracles suffice, but when one follows upon the other, this offers true proof of sanctity, and moves us to venerate them as saints whom the Lord has shown worthy of such devotion through miracles. These two things are fully present in the words of the evangelist where, speaking of the apostles, he says, "But they going forth preached everywhere, by cooperating with the Lord, and confirming the word with signs that followed" (Mk 16:20). Indeed when he says there "cooperating with the Lord" he shows that they themselves were working, and what follows "the signs that followed," makes plain that God shone through them in miracles.⁶ This is how the Lord also works today in His saints, and shows His power with manifest signs, healing the sicknesses of men in commemoration of the dead, and that those are happier who die in the Lord (Rev 14:13) than those who still live in the world.

3. Truly, our venerable brother Sicard, your bishop, came into our presence with many religious men and other distinguished persons of his diocese, and humbly related to us the details of

---

4   Here is laid out the classic formula for public sanctity: 1) Genuine holiness of life, and 2) Divine confirmation of this by miracles after death.
5   Hypocrites may mimic goodness, and evil men may perform wonders with the aid of the devil. This is why both virtue and miracles are necessary.
6   Innocent's sophisticated exegesis preserves both the sovereignty of God in the performance of the miracles, and the genuine human cooperation that the saints exercise by merit.

the works and the manner of death of the holy man Omobono in name and in truth,[7] and we sensed the sweetness of the narrative and the odor of his holy behavior, and in faith we have examined and proclaimed God in all his marvelous works. For "like a tree which is planted near the running waters, which shall bring forth its fruit in due season" (Ps 1:3)—just as the present witness of these same men, both in person and through the written testimony, have made plain to us[8]—this saintly man meditated on the Law of the Lord day and night (Ps 1:2), so as to serve Him in fear (Ps 2:11) and, as the prophet says, rising in the middle of the night to praise Him (Ps 118:62), was always present for Matins. He frequented the office of Mass and the other Canonical Hours with the highest devotion, and remained assiduous in prayer, so that he sometimes was continually at prayer, or arrived early for the celebration of the Canonical Hours, unless he was delayed in the pursuit of peace in the city, for which as a man of peace he was solicitous, or there was an opportunity for almsgiving to the poor or some other work of mercy.[9] He had the habit of often prostrating himself before the cross of the Lord, and whatever work he did—standing, sitting, or lying down—others always saw him moving his lips in prayer. Among other things, he performed his works of piety toward the poor whom he housed, cared for, and fed in his own home, and toward other

---

7   A play on words, in Italian and Latin his name means literally "Good Man."
8   Innocent underscores the absolute necessity in canonization for the reliable testimony of worthy witnesses.
9   This is significant for Omobono as a lay saint. There were some aspects of the active life which constrained him beyond the contemplative life of prayer (proper to religious). These included the demands of charity and neighborliness. Innocent may not actually intend it here, but he is describing the "mixed" life of action and contemplation as the basis for lay holiness. The pope implies that at some times the pressing needs of charity or peacemaking constrain the layman beyond even the immediate need for prayer.

needy people, to whom in life he did not fail in his duties and after whose deaths he used to guarantee the benefit of burial, something to which he dedicated himself with devotion.[10] He did not frequent the company of worldly men, among whom he was distinguished like a lily among thorns, and he was a bitter despiser of heretics who with their pernicious doctrine infected that region. So he completed the course of a holy life when he arose for the celebration of Matins on the feast of San Brizio;[11] at the beginning of Mass he prostrated himself before the cross of the Lord, in his accustomed manner[12] and, while they sang the Angelic Hymn,[13] he had a blessed death.

4. Since it would be lengthy to number one by one what kind and how many miracles followed, and how many came to receive the gifts of healing at his tomb, we think that it is appropriate to recount only one which might lead to the edification of the Catholic faith. For when a certain possessed woman was led to his tomb and, lest any fraud be concealed, she was first sprinkled with unblessed water (which aspersion she calmly permitted), she then rejected the holy water. Similarly in a clearer manner, without her knowledge, she was presented with an unconsecrated host and received it, but later she was terrified by a consecrated host and refused it, she was freed through the merits of this same saint.[14]

---

10   Innocent stresses the completion of both spiritual and corporal works of mercy.
11   13 November 1197. St. Brice of Tours (ca. 370 – 444 AD), disciple of Martin of Tours. He was a saint significantly more popular in the Middle Ages than today, particularly in northern Italy.
12   In the premodern Mass there were no specific rubrics for the laity, who often clustered about the altar or around the pewless Church while services were ongoing.
13   The *Gloria*.
14   Not only is the sanctity of Omobono confirmed here, but also the potency of the devil, who is able to recognize the power of the Church in Holy Water and in the Host. Secondarily it reinforces the power of the clergy, which makes water holy and confects the Eucharist.

5. So that the sanctity of his life may be made more plain and worthy of belief, as we have examined above, although all doubt seems to be removed by the procession of signs through divine approval, and so that the proof of the miracles might not be vitiated by any fraud or deceit, we considered that we ought to make diligent inquiry as to the truth of the matter.[15]

In fact, we see the judgment of God shown clearly with credibility, as was related by the same bishop, uttered without deceitful delusion or hypocrisy, and through the testimony under oath of our beloved son Osberto, priest of Sant' Egidio[16] in Cremona, which was strengthened by an oath taken under the bishop. On this testimony, under oath,[17] he who was his spiritual guide for twenty or more years and who heard his confession many times, declared that the things that were recorded above by the bishop and other witnesses regarding the conduct of that holy man were true. He also made us more certain regarding his obedience and fidelity to prayer, vigils and in the fruits of penance, which he had imposed on him, and even going beyond that.[18] Also regarding those things that had been placed before us regarding miracles, by the oaths of all the foregoing who had come for this purpose, we received a fuller trust, so that by the declaration of the bishop

---

15 This will come to the common teaching, that only the Holy See is competent to judge in cases regarding the holiness of men and women, and the veracity of their miracles. It will speed the process of reserving canonization to the Holy See.
16 Saint Giles (ca. 650 – ca. 710) a hermit, famous as one of the fourteen Holy Helpers in the Middle Ages.
17 Note that this is the third time oath-taking is mentioned. One should remember how serious taking oaths was in the premodern world. To take an oath was in a certain sense to hold one's own soul up to heaven and declare "may God damn me to hell forever if I do not utter the truth of this matter."
18 The saint must exhibit *heroic* virtue, that is, he must go beyond what is merely required of a Christian.

together with the sure words of the priest, under the virtue of obedience, that following such divine and human judgements we might proceed in greater security.[19]

6. Since then we seemed to agree on both the uprightness of his life and on the power of his signs, in favor of the petition, for which by the above bishop and the aforementioned others strongly implored, with the consent of our brethren, after full deliberation with the archbishops and bishops whom we had summoned for consultation,[20] trusting in Divine Mercy and in the merits of the same saint, we decreed that he be added to the catalogue of the saints,[21] commanding that the day of his burial be celebrated every year as a feast among you and the other faithful of Christ.[22] Therefore we ask and order you in the Lord, commanding by means of this Apostolic Letter that, venerating the memory of the same saint, just as has been said, with worthy solemnity, that you may be able to gain eternal joy through his merits.

Given at the Lateran, the day before the Ides of January (12 Jan 1199).

---

19 This whole section addresses the problem that would cause grave controversy in the thirteenth century. What if the pope was led astray by false witnesses in depositions for sainthood? This was best prevented by assessing the trustworthiness of deponents, seeking independent corroboration, and imposing fearful oaths.

20 This consultation is always mentioned in canonization bulls and continues to be manifested in the consistories for the canonization of saints. Canonization, though a papal act, still is done in a collegial manner.

21 Innocent invokes divine aid and declares the canonization with extreme authority. This formula would quickly become augmented into the standard form for the definition of dogma in the thirteenth century, "we declare, pronounce, and define."

22 Though this bull is directed at the Cremonese, we here see evidence that Innocent is commanding the whole Church, a trend which began with the canonizations of St. Thomas Becket and St. Bernard in the 1170s.

Sources for the Life of Omobono

CUM ORBITA SOLIS

Cum Orbita Solis[23] is probably the work of Sicard of Cremona, dating from around the year 1200. As such it is very early, with Omobono's life still clearly in memory. It is a "Liturgical Life," meaning that it contains meditations and readings for use in the diocese of Cremona for the Matins night prayers of the Divine Office. During the night office, there would be psalms, interspersed with these readings. That the office has nine readings means that it was the most solemn feast possible in the Cremonese calendar.

This life is highly traditional in its approach to sanctity. That is a result of both its author and its audience. Sicard of Cremona was a bishop of the older, established part of the city. He moved in exalted circles (particularly after the election of his friend Lothario de' Conti as Pope Innocent III). He was educated at the finest universities of the era and as such had imbibed the traditional appreciation of the life of holiness as inherited by the Fathers and scholastic authors. In addition, the office was primarily intended for worship in the Cathedral, by the canons. The canons formed a sort of aristocratic court around the person of the bishop, and they were responsible for the solemnization of divine liturgy at the mother Church. They also probably came from more exalted backgrounds.

Both Sicard and his canons viewed holiness through the lens of the religious life and that of the clergy. As can be sensed in the text, there is a discomfort with the idea of a "lay" saint, and even more so with a merchant saint. We will see that this vita nearly bends over backwards to present Omobono as

---

23 After I made these translations, I was made aware of an unpublished work by the late James Powell, and Edward Peters was kind enough to forward it to me. Especially useful were his translations of *Cum orbita solis* and *Quoniam Historiae*. While they did not substantially alter my translations, they were useful especially since Powell had transcribed them from manuscripts. I am indebted to the pioneering work of James Powell in beginning to bring these texts to light.

a man who utterly abandoned secular pursuits to live as close to an ideal religious life as was possible while remaining in the secular world. It uses traditional forms to attempt to fit what is certainly the square peg of Omobono into the round hole of traditional, vowed religious life.

It should also be remembered that the audience for this life was largely clerical, and a clerical elite at that. They understood Omobono through their own lens. That this life was performed publicly only once a year, and in the dead of night, limited its reception. However, we must not think that it had no effect. Many more of the laity than is commonly thought had a smattering of Latin, the universal language of Christian culture, life, and faith. There were also quite a few who made it to the Matins night-watch, as we saw with Omobono himself. The later lives, as we shall see, are in some part a reaction against the saint's presentation in this text. It must be read against its traditional background to see how different the later lives are, and how great a revolution in the understanding of the market and of holiness is transpiring.

The beginning of the life of the blessed, holy, and most devout Omobono.

First Reading

When the course of the sun had made its transit through the Zodiac ninety-seven times after the 1100th year since the rise of the true Sun [Christ],[24] in Italy, in the city of Cremona, there was a man worthy of veneration by the name of Omobono, a "good man" in truth and in justice. Therefore, rejoice and be glad, Cremona, you have united one of your fellow-citizens to the heavenly court and city, trained in your ranks for the good fight. You have given a son to the Spouse, and now Christ has made him a coheir in the Kingdom of the Father, and for you he is established as an intercessor before the Father forever.[25]

---

24 Sicard is strutting a bit here.
25 The life begins with an appeal to civic pride and the centrality of

Although that King (Mt 22:1–4), who prepared the nuptial feast for his Son with slaughtered fattened bulls, and has invited him to the repast, yet from the end of his youth he went forth to the business of the market, having surrendered to the concourse of those who travel the land and sea.[26] But he who set him apart from his mother's womb (Is 49:1; Gal 1:15), who calls into being that which is nothing, and prefers what is weak (Mt 24:41), snatching him from the grindstone,[27] he called him to the nuptial bed, from familiarity with the perverse and depraved practices of the market to the state of blessed contemplation.[28]

---

    local sanctity. Cremona is blessed because heaven and earth are joined, one of its citizens—indeed a neighbor—is now a citizen of the eternal kingdom, a special friend of God, and advocate for his people.

26 Notice the increasingly negative tone. He "surrendered" to the market. Vauchez also considers this to be possible evidence of a good amount of wealth, since it implies international travel.

27 Sicard is making an elegant allusion to Gregory the Great's interpretation of Mt 13:8 and Mk 4:8 (the parable of the sower). Gregory proposes that the holy laity will receive 30 measures for labor at the "grindstone." Pastors will receive 60 measures for their labor in the fields of the Lord, while contemplative monastics (those who retire to the marriage bed of singular devotion to God) will receive 100. Sicard implies Omobono is passing from the 30 to the 100. Cfr. Vauchez, *S. Homebon*, 69n175.

28 Here we see the classical themes in their fullness. There are two kinds of life, the life of action and the life of contemplation. Ever since the ancient Greeks the life of contemplation was considered superior, because in it people seek true wisdom and union with God, rather than advancing merely temporal concerns. This was classically typified by the gospel characters Mary and Martha. Martha busied herself preparing everything that was necessary to feed and house Christ—in itself a good work. She was irritated that her sister Mary, who by all rights should be helping, sat at Christ's feet and drank in His words. Instead of rebuking Mary, He praises her. "Mary has chosen the better part, and it shall not be taken from her" (Lk 10:42). In Christian theology, the life of contemplation and withdrawal from the world has always been the more perfect way.

Second Reading

Oh wondrous dispensation of the creator! God has consigned all to sin, so that He might have mercy on all (Rom 11:32; Gal 3:22). He allows that the hundred sheep wander far from the pasture and pottage (Lk 15:4–7) and so weakened by unhealthy food and wounded by piercing rocks so that, weary from such a bitter experience, and knowing that one is unable to do anything himself (Jn 15:5), and, returning to the pastor of the sheep and the doctor of souls (1 Pet 2:25) borne upon mercy and truth, giving glory not to himself, but to the name of the Most High (Ps 118:67). For, casting out the darkness and being made fit for the gift of light, and after the bitterness of vices, he thus relishes with more spirit the sweetness of the virtues.

O great consolation for sinners! Do not fear, you who trade in money or are occupied in whatsoever kind of servile work.[29] Do not despair then yourself, who are mired in the wallow or are in deep mud, remember that sometimes the adulterer and the murderer[30] prophesy in soliloquy. Remember also that a tax collector became the disciple of the Lord (Mt 9:9). Pay attention that the Most High, through his mercy alone, drew blessed Omobono to Himself, so that where sin has abounded, grace may have superabounded (Rm 5:20), since it is difficult for one who practices business to divest himself of religious indifference.[31]

Third Reading

Then when Saint Omobono put off the old man and put on the new (Eph 4:22–4), he abandoned the business of the world and became a merchant for the kingdom of heaven (Mt 13:44–45). For some steal the kingdom of heaven cunningly (Mt 11:12), still

---

29 Sicard here makes what he probably considers to be a marvelous condescension. Even traders and handcrafters can be saved!
30 Allusion to King David.
31 An echo of the commonplace, that makes its way even into Canon Law, "A merchant is able to please God only with difficulty." *Decretum* Pars 1, D. 88, c. 11.

others, who are invited, enter it promptly, and others, without wanting, are driven by force.[32]

For the hemorrhaging woman stole it, when by her faith touching the back of the hem of the Lord's garment, and she was immediately healed of the flow of blood (Mt 9:18–26). The hemorrhaging woman is a type of the Church of the gentiles. What does it mean to touch the garment, except to have faith in the Incarnation? For the garment of the Lord is the flesh of Jesus Christ. But we go no further than touching the hem of the garment, since we are unable to understand the fullness of the mystery.[33] Whence the one [John the Baptist], the greatest of those born of women (Mt 11:11), proclaimed he was unworthy to loosen the laces of His sandals (Lk 3:16). The Church of the gentiles, then, robs the kingdom of heaven by the easy path of faith, because they snatched that blessing promised for so long to the Synagogue, as long as she obeyed the word spoken "all nations shall be blessed in your seed" (Gn 12:3).

The Magdalene robbed it with her sorrow for her sins and by her wailing aloud. For there was a sinner in the city, possessed by seven demons, who washed with her tears the feet of the Savior and dried them with her hair. She has chosen the better part and it will not be taken from her (Lk 7:36–50; 12: 38–42).[34]

What violence is greater than that of one who does not have the right of inheritance claiming a part thereof? What violence is more serious than that which afflicts and torments the body under the guidance of reason? What plunder is greater than for earth to conquer heaven? What thief is more dishonest than he

---

32 Yet notice how merchants and workers are to be saved, by ceasing those very labors.

33 Sicard makes elegant theological and exegetical points throughout, a delight to his listeners, in addition to the life being written in fine Latin.

34 Here Sicard makes the classic allusion. Church tradition since Gregory the Great had conflated Mary of Bethany, Mary Magdalene, and the "sinner in the city." This identification only began to unravel in the sixteenth century.

who mounts the sanctuary of heaven, from which he was barred because of lack of merit? Of this robbery the Lord spoke "From the time of John the Baptist the kingdom of heaven has suffered violence and men of violence take it by force" (Mt 11:12).[35]

Fourth Reading

For Zacchaeus, justified in name and in deed, conducted business, for he made restitution according to the law that [stipulated the restitution of what] he had taken and to donate half of the remainder to the poor, he merited to host the God of the kingdom of heaven and heard that salvation had come into his house (Lk 19:1–9).[36] Also Joseph, in purchasing the shroud in which the body of Christ was wrapped, obtained a pure heart, by which he had acquired faith in the passion and the eternal inheritance (Mt 27:57–61). Our Master, inviting us to this exchange says, "Make friends for yourselves of the mammon of iniquity, so that, when it fails, they may receive you into the eternal tabernacle" (Lk 16:9). And in another passage, "Sell all that you have, and give it to the poor, and you will have treasure in heaven" (Lk 18:22).

Making use of this profitable exchange, in which sterility is changed into fertility, heaviness made light, temporal into eternal, the multitude of believers who had but one heart and soul and held all things in common. For in laying their possessions at the feet of the Apostles, they obtained a place in the land of the living (Ac 4:32–35).[37] Yet these for that reason are called saints, who left the snares of the world, and followed the Lord, the same who promised them a hundredfold reward and life eternal (Mt 19:27–30).

---

35 Sicard makes a delightful interpretation of a difficult passage; Omobono and the rest of the gentiles are "Holy robbers", and they mount up to heaven by the easy path of faith (as opposed to the laborious application of the Jewish law).

36 Another opening for merchants. Zacchaeus made restitution and gave to the poor, but did not divest himself wholly, and yet "salvation has come" to his house.

37 Here is a repetition of the Patristic interpretation of "treasure in heaven."

For only the poor and the weak, the blind and the lame are compelled to the supper of the Lord, yet they who are oppressed by the narrowness of material goods, are weakened in body and deprived of any allurement of the world (Lk 14:21–23). For he who quickly turns to the Lord will not discover enticing things in this world through which to find pleasure.

Fifth reading

Oh theft, Oh blessed robbery! Oh commerce of noble violence! Blessed Omobono stole the kingdom of heaven by faith! He robbed it by penance, he purchased it with alms. Called through grace, he answered with the obedience of faith and a good life, though he was carried by violence in the midst of tribulation.[38] For he was a faithful Catholic, he loved the Christian religion and he despised heretical depravity, he was grieved by sin and by conversions that were delayed.[39] He forgot his house and the house of his father, and forgetting the past, reached out to the future (Php 3:13).[40]

He was the merciful father of the poor (Jb 29:16) and always attentive to paupers, for which he took necessities from himself and gave it to those who are the family of the Savior.[41] He was a storehouse of gifts and was pleasing to many on account of the abundance of his giving. On many occasions of tribulation he was

---

38 Sicard may be getting carried away on a Semipelagian course, which he only just saves by "Called through grace." It seems more likely that he is enjoying the transposition of his merchant metaphors.

39 Now begins an analysis of the particular elements of holiness detected in Omobono. First of all one must be orthodox.

40 Though we later see that this is somewhat misleading, yet still a traditional category of holiness had been a spurning of earthly ties. "If anyone comes to me and does not hate his own father and mother and wife and children and brothers and sisters, yes, and even his own life, he cannot be my disciple" (Lk 14:26).

41 Sicard follows the line set down by Ambrose, the poor are the specially favored of God, thus creating solidarity in the Christian community, and providing a path to justification for the rich.

tried like gold in the furnace (Wis 3:6). He was made strong in patience, humble in heart, meek in works, upright in both facets of man [bodily and spiritual], constant in prayer, in the midst of a sinful people (Php 2:15) he was like a hermit in solitude.

Why elaborate more? He was a sober man, dealt fairly with his neighbors, lived devoutly before God.[42] Girt with these spiritual flowers, fragrant with this scent (Song 1:3), he entered into the way of all flesh (Gn 6:13), and passed to the Lord.

Sixth reading

When the hour came to hasten on his pilgrimage to the Father's house, the race to the finish line (Php 3:14), from the Church Militant to the Church Triumphant, from the sufferings of the world to the glory of paradise, at his accustomed time in the morning he went to the church, that he might quickly come to heaven. Awaiting the end of the night, praying according to his custom until six in the morning, from the start of Mass he prostrated himself, hands and knees to the earth before the standard of the cross,[43] meditating how the price of our redemption was paid on the cross so that Christ, who through this standard rose gloriously, might make Omobono worthy of eternal glory through faith in Him. The soldier prostrated himself before the King, the servant before the Lord, the accused before the Judge, the one needing salvation before the Savior. Praying, he lowered himself; stretched on the ground, he prayed prostrate; the sun that rises from the east saw the supplicant, who expired while the *Gloria* was being sung; [at the same time] the Lord glorified him.

Yet as he was known to be devout, he expired without manifesting any sign of his passing, but appeared to remain on the

---

42 Through the commonplaces one thing comes out clearly: Omobono was a good citizen and a good neighbor.
43 One should remember that rubrics for the laity are a very recent innovation in Catholicism, and that pews had not yet been invented. The Church nave was a busy place with people performing various devotions or attending to less exalted matters.

ground in prayer, as if he still lived, and his soul was taken like a sparrow (Ps, 123:7; Mt 10:29) and, freed from the body, was again clothed in the attire of blessedness, receiving the crown of glory in the kingdom. But when he did not arise for the Gospel—like a soldier girded for war—the bystanders at last understood that he had died.[44] Immediately he was lifted up, bathed, and his funeral rites celebrated on 13 November.[45]

But the Lord did not wish that such a venerable man be buried like other men, since the life of such is so worthy of veneration. For truly the magnitude of his faith, as the Lord bore witness, was also as great as a grain of mustard seed (Mt 17:19), which would be able to move a mountain (Mt 21:21). He magnified him through innumerable miracles. For here the multitude of people came, here came many who were sick, and having made vows, miracles followed, and were freed if they fulfilled their promises.[46]

Therefore, brethren, let us who have known the faith and life of Saint Omobono, celebrate him with devout solemnity. Following his example let us hold the Catholic faith complete and intact, using our goods with sobriety, treating our neighbors with charity, and adoring God without idolatry.[47]

---

44 A somewhat humorous story. Omobono, known for his exceptional piety and devotional eccentricities, was basically ignored by his neighbors during the *Gloria*, the Collect, the Epistle, the Gradual, and the Alleluia. Given that these would have taken at least five minutes, I am not sure exactly how people were certain he expired during the *Gloria*.
45 A quick funeral indeed if it all happened that same day. One wonders about the reason for haste. I would propose it was the eagerness of the Church to maintain possession of the saint's body by a quick interment.
46 Spontaneous public cult is the key to ecclesial veneration. One thinks of the chants of "Santo subito" (Sainthood now!) at the funeral of John Paul II.
47 Sicard gives a brief exhortation connecting Omobono's holiness to the members of the church. This is important in an age which is transitioning from seeing saints as unrepeatable miracles of God's grace to those to imitate as examples of virtue.

With the aid of our Lord Jesus Christ, who with the Father and the Holy Spirit lives and reigns forever and ever. Amen.

Seventh Reading

God is wondrous, who marvelously works in all things, and still more marvelously in those events which occur outside the natural course of things, so that the faith and upright lives of the saints might be for the succeeding generations a motive for always living righteously, and are strengthened with deeds rare among men, which do not happen contrary to nature, always obedient to her creator, but rather beyond nature, which is not able to do these things by her own power.[48] For one must have faith in those things which are not seen, nor does one acquire merit from things which are demonstrable by reason (Heb 11:1). Faith requires firmness in the face of appearances, so that its sharp edge might be honed with merits, toward those invisible things that profit unto salvation.

For this reason at the origins of the infant Church, so that faith might be born in her, the Most High worked miracles among the faithful. Yet now in this world grown old and decrepit, in which faith has become tepid, in which wickedness abounds, and in which the charity of many has grown cold,[49] the infinite goodness of God has renewed the working of miracles, so that faith newly born, thus nourished, may grow strong. Also uncertain is the life of the saints, for the wolf can dress in sheep's clothing and often he whose life is believed to be spotless, lives in wantonness like a swine. Further one is able to know a tree by its fruits (Mt 7:15–20), yet no one knows where it falls except He who is able to read hearts. Where the tree falls, there it remains. For this reason, to establish the uprightness of a life, the Most High must make it

---

48 Here the bishop offers an excellent scholastic analysis of the nature of miracles.

49 This is a common medieval trope regarding the "last age" of the world. It is rich with both apocalyptic overtones as well as moral calls to reform.

shine by miracles.⁵⁰ Sometimes, however, even through miracles we are fooled by fake righteousness, because the father of lies (Jn 8:44) is able to mimic the fruits of truth and the son of darkness is able to transform himself into an angel of light. So the magicians of Pharaoh, it is read, were able once or twice to make null with their prodigies the miracles worked by Moses (Ex 7: 14–26; 8:1–11). Often then miracles come not by a person's merit, but through the efficacy of names and sacred things, as is read of the exorcists of the Pharisees and of the daughters of Philip (Acts 16:16–24; 19:11–16). Even false apostles cast out demons in the name of Jesus Christ, of which it was spoken "In your name we prophesied, expelled demons, and we did mighty works," to whom the Lord made answer, "I do not know you, depart from me, you workers of iniquity" (Mt 7:22–23).

What is more wondrous than when bread is transformed into flesh, and wine into blood?⁵¹ And this the priests do today, though they are unworthy in merit, they nevertheless do so by the power of the sacrament.⁵² Also the Antichrist will perform wonders at the end of the world so that, insofar as he is able, he might drag the faithful to him (Mt 24:24; Rev 13:11–18). Therefore neither the first without the second, nor the second without the third. But if there is found the Catholic faith and a virtuous life, which is confirmed by the subsequent testimony of miracles, indeed where these three witnesses of holiness are, there remains

---

50   Here we have the first commentary on Innocent's requirement for both virtue and miracles, evidence that *COS* is composed after the canonization bull. Alternately we may here see the source of Innocent's own meditations.
51   Here Sicard offers a well-trodden clerical sentiment that, no matter what miracles occur in the world, the miracle of the Mass is the greatest of all. Clergy continue to occupy the leadership caste in Christian society.
52   Here anti-Donatist sentiments are reiterated, refuting some that had been repeated by some Gregorian reformers, and passed on to contemporary heretics. Clergy, even when sinful, retained their authority and ability to perform sacraments.

no ambiguity.⁵³ Because we have written briefly of the life of blessed Omobono, now we will move on to describe his miracles.

Eighth Reading

The Lord, who gives sight to the blind and who lifts up the downtrodden (Ps 145:8), who opens the eyes of those born blind (Jn 9:1–35), and straightens the knees of the paralytic (Mt 9:1–9), and promised His followers that they would be able to do similar things (Mt 10:1) through the intercession of blessed Omobono. He restored sight to the blind and raised many who were cast down. For instance, one such wonder regarded a man nearly blinded from the bright flash of a heavenly body. Another was brought to blindness by painful and congenital whitening of the pupil, but—calling upon the name of this saint—both recovered the use of their eyes and the clarity of sight. Furthermore, many others who were blind, some partially, some completely, one for two years, and still another completely blind for seven years, by the invocation of the protection of this holy man, and since the light of faith had been born in their hearts, so also obtained the light of vision for their bodies.⁵⁴

Many other sick people were cured by the intercession of the most holy Omobono, among which were those afflicted by fistulas and gout, some were paralyzed, others suffered wounds, some who for various reasons had injured their limbs or were horribly deformed in the face, or were paralyzed in their hands or arms, or suffered from sciatica or arthritis in the neck, shoulders, or sides, or had broken or deformed legs or feet.

Not only momentary diseases [were cured], but congenital ones or those inflicted by some accident, or other, chronic,

---

53 Indeed, the author elaborates on Innocent, turning his two requirements into three, by adding faithful orthodoxy to the mix of holiness and virtues.
54 Sicard is strutting a bit for his listeners here, who will be impressed with the biblical citations, that are then connected to actual stories, and are wrapped up with a moral ending.

persistent cases, and those which had been despaired of by doctors. Some of the sick came carried on litters, some came with uncertain steps aided by walking staffs and, healed, they returned home under their own power, giving thanks to God and the saint. Others, lacking the strength of life, were completely healed. That being the case, we shall proceed by giving some details of a few episodes.[55]

A woman, up to that time, had been completely deformed for a long period, so much so that her knees were bent to her mouth. Even so, they carried her to the tomb of the saint in a basket, while unbelievers mocked her and those who carried her, but placing her before the tomb, in the sight of the wondering crowd, she arose, and stood before the multitude on her feet without difficulty and without support, and immediately went before the people, giving thanks. For health, which was granted by the command of the Lord, continually gives strength. Again, a man who had his ring finger contracted for seven years and another with a lump on his knee, so that his knees and hands were restricted in movement, such that it was not possible to move them, both made their vows, and both were freed by the merits of that holy man.

Ninth Reading

The Lord, Who has created the mouth of man that he might speak of the wonders of God, Who is the key Who when He opens, no one may close, and when He closes, none may open (Is 22:22; Rev 3:7), Who sealed the incredulous mouth of Zechariah and Who opened to those who have faith in Him (Lk 1:20), through the merits of the most holy Omobono, has loosened the tongues of the mute and has shut the mouths of the insolent.[56]

---

55 It is significant that Omobono is presented as a healer of bodies for several reasons. First it dovetails with his antiheretical presentation. The dead saint's body heals broken, material bodies. It also restricts his cultic identity, by focusing on certain types of miracles over others.

56 This parallel is found in many saints' lives. God gives grace to the mute and silences the unbeliever. This also defuses cultic opposition, as the mockers of the paralyzed woman are made silent in the previous story.

For one such, who spoke ill of these miracles, became mute, but in sorrow of conscience and having made a vow to God in his heart, his mouth was opened, since he had shame and did penance. Another, wounded in the neck in the battle for Jerusalem,[57] was without speech for ten years, and many others who suddenly lost the power of speech, made vows, had faith and were restored to speech. But what more can be said? Let us turn now to those who recovered who had been deprived by nature itself. A certain youth of eighteen years had been mute since birth. Through a vow uttered by his parents to the saint, he began to enjoy the power to speak, a thing alien to him and he returned home full of joy. Another youth also mute from birth, through the merits of most blessed Omobono, recovered his speech and equally began to praise God in a marvelous manner.

First Conclusion

In addition, a 10-year-old boy, blind and mute from birth, through vows made by his parents, recovered sight and speech, and began to praise and glorify God.

Second Conclusion

Also, an 8-year-old boy, blind and mute from birth, thanks to vows made by his parents, recovered the free gift of sight and speech. Hearing of the large number of miracles and of their magnitude, many crowds of sick people came that they might receive healing of every type of illness. Indeed, a woman who labored under an intolerable disease, and had been despaired of by the physicians[58] had a vision and heard a voice imploring her to invoke this man of God and his prayers, that his prayers would be answered by Him. She invoked him and was immediately

---

57   The siege of Jerusalem in 1187 which resulted in the permanent loss of the city to the Crusaders.

58   This remains today a key element in miracle stories for those presented for canonization. A panel of medical experts must certify a miracle as medically inexplicable.

healed. Also, some children, brought near to death by the course of nature, through the prayers of their parents were immediately returned to full health.

Also many who were tormented by unclean spirits were liberated. Among these that should not be left in obscurity was the fact that, before the death of the holy man, a demon who had been afflicting the body of a woman of Bergamo, when asked who among the saints was able to cast him out, replied "Omobono of Cremona." But no one was able to understand him, since no one spoke of this most holy man, for he was little noticed by men and avoided all appearance of vainglory. But after the death of the servant of God, her parents came to know of his miracles of exorcism, and she was brought to the tomb of the saint and she was immediately delivered from the demon.

In addition to this, every day the sick frequently present themselves before the tomb of the saint in faith and receive the gift of healing.

With the help of our Lord Jesus Christ, Who with the Father and the Holy Spirit, lives and reigns, God, forever and ever. Amen.

Quoniam Historiae

Scholars speculate that this life was written between 1230 and 1240. This life indicates a marked shift from the liturgical, theological, and stylistically elevated tenor of COS. It is here that we begin to see a profound change. Even at the beginning of this text we see that its anonymous author is interested in augmenting COS. Indeed, he considers that the older, liturgical life does not get the story straight.

While most scholars consider the author to be a member of the clergy, perhaps from the cathedral chapter,[59] it is possible that a layman wrote this vita, for it presents Omobono more clearly as he was during his lifetime. For instance, this text stresses his family life, which was left out entirely in the earlier COS. It also underscores his merchant past. From this life we garner most of the historical information that we possess on the merchant saint. Here we receive his birthyear—1117— as well as a specification of the fifty years he spent as an active businessman, from 1132 to 1182. The last fifteen years of his life were spent as a lay penitent.

For the first time we meet his wife and discover that he had two children, one of whom was named Monaco. His family does not always come off very well in the stories, yet this only underscores Omobono's holiness. We get details of his economic activity as well, including the fact that he was solidly in the middle class, neither too rich nor too poor. He also is reported as owning his family's townhouse in the "New City" as well as a small but productive vineyard outside the walls.

Piazzi notes that this life stands as a mean between COS and LA. While it does not employ marriage and work as devices for Omobono's acquisition of holiness, nonetheless they are present. What was absent in the earlier life constitutes new material for lay meditation, including the increasing concern with stories that will underscore that Omobono is a man to be imitated by the new middle classes. It paves the way for

---

59   Vauchez is of this opinion, id., *S. Homebon*, 20.

LA later in the century, in which the merchant life and the family are both presented, at long last, as paths to the acquisition of virtue and holiness.

1. Since the author of this biography [COS], whether out of negligence or ignorance, and because some facts were not known before the canonization, omitted things worthy of glory, and these things I have added and written for the devotion of those who wish to follow in his path, beginning with fasting.[60]
2. For blessed Omobono fasted for the whole of the Lent of the Lord, and on the four sets of Ember days[61] went even without any cooked food.[62] On Good Friday he fasted on bread and water, during the Lent of Pentecost he fasted on four days, and he spent the Lent of St. Martin like that of the Lent of the Lord, and fasted on all the Fridays and Saturdays of the year.[63] On

---

60 The author subtly indicates the unsuitability of the previous life, particularly for those who "wish to follow in his path." This is a totally new tack, moving from COS which emphasizes the deeds and grace of God present in Omobono's life, to the more prosaic details of a fellow townsman who made good.
61 These are the traditional three days of fasting—Wednesday, Friday, and Saturday—that mark each of the four seasons of the year. Dating from the early Church, these were maintained until 1965, and are still marked in the calendar of the preconciliar rite.
62 Fasting was a key part of penitential life. In addition to being a fundamental foundation of communal Christian identity and solidarity, the penitent could use fasting as a readily available means of sanctification, no matter what one's state in life was. It was also a private penance that would not inconvenience family or community. There are other meanings as well. It was a way to assert power over one's body, leading to the promotion of a correct ordering of the soul. It could also, in a very minor sense, be an economic benefit, one which tended towards the greater comfort of one's other family members and of the poor.
63 The author is discussing the normal Lenten period before Easter, but also a period of fasting following Pentecost, which draws the Easter season to a close, and the traditional fast from St. Martin's day (11 November) until Christmas, a more extensive Advent sea-

the vigils of the saints, which the Holy Church observes, he fasted without cooked food, giving his portion to the poor.[64] On other days he consumed bread, wine, meat, and fish.[65] He abstained from meat only four days of the week, not ever dining more than twice on the same day. He did not mitigate his fasting for any motive whatsoever, be it work or sickness.[66]

3. Every week he confessed his sins to the priest of his church.[67] If he was in the city, he never missed the Offices of the Church for any cause. For it often happened that he was going to his vineyard and praying there and applied the discipline to himself, sometimes clothed, sometimes disrobed.[68] And while he

---

son practiced by monastic orders and in some distinct rites of the Church (such as the Ambrosian).

64 The pittance is the smaller meal to be taken on fast days, less than the one normal meal. It was also common that the vigils of great feasts would be days of fasting. The cycle of feast and fast was critical in premodern Christianity, for one's celebration of a great feast was heightened by the self-denial of the day before. Dim shades of this remain in the Good Friday fast and the great feast of Easter.

65 In other words, he had a normal diet most of the time. He ate as was proper to his station and, in particular, he ate meat. This was a pointed challenge to the heretics of the time who, because of their anti-materialism, were vegetarians. One could say that eating meat may itself have been a holy act in Omobono's case. St. Francis did something similar, in that he told his brothers to eat what was put before them, including meat.

66 All Christians fasted, but the key is that Omobono went above and beyond what was required, and entered into heroic virtue, both by the extent of his fasts and by his refusal to mitigate them for work or sickness.

67 Another heroic act, quite uncommon at the time. In fact, it would not be until Lateran IV in 1215 that the Church would even prescribe just one confession *per year* as a minimum.

68 The "discipline" was a common penitential practice, still used in limited form in some religious orders. It was a small whip to mortify the flesh. He did this privately so as not to cause comment. It is important to note that medieval Christians did not use the discipline because they hated their bodies, but rather 1) to unite their sufferings with the sufferings of Christ, and 2) in order to bring the rebel-

worked with his hands, when he heard the sound of the bell for Terce, Sext, or None, or for Vespers, he ceased to work and hurried to his devotions and supplications in his vineyard.

4. But since the devil was displeased and despised this and other of his works, that devil came to him with a vast array of unclean spirits, that they might torment him, and they lunged at him, one after another, pounding him like a ball, saying "If you do not cease the works you do, I will consign you to death!" To which the blessed Omobono responded, "You may kill the body, but you are not able to kill the soul."[69] Then, after thus being tormented, he returned to his home and remained in his bed, half-dead, for two or three days. And even though he had been scourged and frightened, he not only continued to participate in the Offices of the Church, but after he had regained his strength, he returned to his vineyard.[70] There he prayed, and he was often lashed and tempted by the evil spirits. Yet he was like a cornerstone (Ps 117:22), persevering in faith and good works, blessing the name of the Lord in all his tribulations and adversities.

5. After having proven his patience, he was visited by the Archangel Michael, whom the blessed Omobono beseeched, saying, "Lord, do not permit me anymore to be tormented by demons."[71] The angel gave him a staff to defend himself against the unclean spirits, "Take this staff, and from now on

---

lious desires of the body into proper hierarchical order with reason and Divine commands. Fasting was one path, useful against gluttony; the discipline was generally used to quiet sexual desires.

69 It is a commonplace in saints' stories that the devil particularly hates holy men and women and will especially work to torment them.

70 Here Omobono demonstrates heroic fortitude. He returns to his place of work even though he had an encounter with demons there. It is interesting that the demons tormented him in his vineyard, rather than at his home or in church.

71 Omobono has passed the trial and is rewarded by God who hears the prayers of the saints. Similar is the story of St. Thomas Aquinas and his temptations against chastity and who, after overcoming them, was delivered from further disturbances of the same kind.

have no fear, because I will be with you." Then he returned home rejoicing, and his family saw him so happy that he did not wish to eat. His wife asked him, "My husband, I pray you, tell me why you formerly returned from the vineyard sad, but now are so happy." He confided it to her with her promise to keep it secret, the man of God did not tell her where he left the staff.[72] Regarding this, after the death of Saint Omobono, a possessed person was brought in front of his tomb and was questioned in the presence of witnesses. He was questioned by the son of blessed Omobono, named Monaco, whether he had known Saint Omobono during his life. The demon answered, "I knew him and I saw him." And Monaco said, "Where did you see him?" "In the vineyard." And Monaco said, "What did you seek in his vineyard?" The devil replied, "I wanted to injure him, but I was unable." And he said, "Why were you unable?" The devil answered, "Because Michael was with him, and gave him a staff to defend himself." And he asked the devil what became of the staff, where it was located, but the devil was unable to point it out.[73]

6. He was most generous in almsgiving, and he gave to the poor a portion of his own food, retaining for himself only a modest amount. And I am not forgetting to say that when his family ate meat, and he, according to his spiritual discipline, ate as if it were Lent, he gave the portion of meat that was due to him to the poor. For this his family often complained and so he would then take the smallest piece. They also complained when he gave his portion to the poor, keeping for himself only a small amount, as I said above. Therefore his son or another family member would cut his meat as a precaution, but

---

72 In this version of Omobono's story, his wife is a concerned spouse, who is also his confidante.

73 This is an odd story. Why is it Omobono's son who is questioning the possessed man in front of the tomb? Is Monaco interested in his Father's relics? The story is unclear, but the implication is that even the demons testify to the holiness of Omobono.

blessed Omobono, no less cunning, secreted the meat away under his plate or in a napkin, or in his lap or under his arm, so that when he arose from supper, he was able to give the poor of Christ something to eat.[74] He snatched bread, wine, meat, coins and anything that would be of use to the poor and the sick. And when his family learned of this, they put the bread, wine, meat, and similar things under lock and key. But the holy thief stole the key nonetheless, so that he might succor the poor with what had been hidden.[75]

7. He freely visited the sick and the imprisoned and zealously brought them things from his own stores. He gave the poor his clothing, and his family complained loudly about this. And so, they began to watch him as a precaution, and to pretend that he had been robbed. One day he was going through his vineyard and, finding a poor unclothed man, he covered him in his cloak and sent him on his way. Returning home without his cloak, he came to a guesthouse and took another in exchange from one of the guests. When his family saw him clothed in a cloak not his own, they asked him, "Where is your cloak?" Apologizing, he blamed thieves.[76]

8. He mortified his flesh for the love of God and afflicted himself by means of a *cilice* under his clothing, bound tightly around the bare flesh of his hips and legs, a band of rough cloth, around

---

74 This is quite a funny section, the "holy thief" gives his meat to the poor, so they give him a smaller portion. He secrets this away as well, so that his own family resorts to cutting his meat.

75 Again, quite a funny section. Here we see a disparity in conceptions of ownership. His family members consider their larder to be the possession of the household, but Omobono, who has provided them with food with his own labors, is forced to steal from himself, in order to give his excess to the poor. His concerns elide with Patristic commentary that the excess of the rich is the property of the poor.

76 One gets the sense in this story that Omobono is being run down by his family, who resort to lying to neighbors to defend his piety. In the end, Omobono unfortunately lies himself, in order to bring peace to his family, an uncharacteristic admission of a character flaw in a saint's life.

which his flesh swelled and became infected.[77] Hearkening to the advice of the priests, he observed their counsels.[78]

9. He was a simple and God-fearing man. He wished to harm no creature of God. For once when he encountered a bird of the air in the street in which he walked, he did not wish to disturb it and passed to the other side.[79]

10. He was a great man of prayer both inside and outside of Church, while walking, sitting, in vigils, or sleeping. For in walking he prayed so intensely that often his prayer would prevent his hearing the greetings of the people.[80] And he also prayed while sleeping, as often those present would witness. At times he was angry with his family, but immediately a penitential sorrow filled him, and he wept bitterly.[81]

11. He was a merchant, but before that he had been a tailor.[82] He

---

[77] The hair shirt or *cilice* was a favorite penitential practice. The wearer could wear it in complete privacy, while outwardly conforming to normal attire. The hair shirt would irritate the skin, causing nearly constant inconvenience to its bearer, and reminding him of his penitential duties. The wearing of a hair shirt was considered nearly irrefutable evidence of sanctity, for example the discovery of one on Thomas Becket's body after his murder was the catalyst for his spontaneous and universal cult.

[78] The hagiography is constantly concerned to note Omobono's submission and obedience to his spiritual superiors; it was the key that separated heretics from the orthodox laity.

[79] A charming story that recalls St. Francis' solicitude for animals, it is here told of Omobono's heroic gentleness, all the more astonishing because tenderness for animals was not a component of premodern people's worldviews.

[80] This detail may suggest a lack of neighborliness on Omobono's part, however that would not be quite consonant with the rest of his story.

[81] This document is precious because it shows the humanity of the saint. Even this holy man became upset with his family, particularly one that was so spiritually tone-deaf. However, he overcame this by heroic patience and immediately regretted his anger and did penance.

[82] Here we get an interesting detail about his particular line of work, and one that would influence his cult well into the future. It also implies that he was a successful tailor, and that he moved from there

was tall in stature, thin in body, dark in complexion, and he lived nearly eighty years, for fifty years he lived in the world, and around fifteen years he lived a spiritual life, and now lives forever in Christ. He slept on a feather bed, wore linen and black lamb's wool, he avoided colorful fabrics, and wore the dark cloth of Bergamo.[83]

12. He would always arise after midnight for Matins and he often pestered his priests, by making a racket to get them to awaken for the hour.[84] He enjoyed solitude, being a man of few words and not a preacher. If men wished him to preach or to recount some of his good deeds, he briefly gave them satisfaction, "My dear brethren, I have not studied and I do not know how to preach, so I can conclude quickly, 'what you do not wish for yourselves, do not do to others'" (Mt 7:12).[85]

13. He lived humbly with his wife in the world, and he had a few children with her; after her death he lived for another ten years, and he had no other. His wife prophesied of him, saying to her son, "Remember, son, that you will see many crowds come to venerate your father and if they knew him like I knew him, they would have venerated him even when he was alive. You desire goods and hoard the riches of the

---

to a larger and more profitable business, building upon his success. Omobono was apparently something of an entrepreneur.

83 These details, along with others in this life, underscore one clear fact: in the eyes of the author of *QH* Omobono did *not* leave the world; he acquired holiness within his family and within his business practices. While much of his piety remained traditional, yet it was achieved within a wholly new context and the implications would become clear in *LA*.

84 Another humorous episode, Omobono the pious layman makes life difficult for his good, but tired priests. Indeed, the holiness of layman is made a goad for the clergy, something that would not have made it into *COS*.

85 Omobono, a man of few words, distills the gospel itself into his one pious sermon, for indeed, his life is sermon enough to others.

world, oh Son, and your father dispersed them and left you poor, but later you will be made even richer."[86]

And let these things suffice about his conduct and life.

[Appendix of Miracles found in one manuscript, Munich, Bayerische Staatsbibliothek, lat. 434, ff. 262$^{r\text{-}v}$.]

1. Almighty God showed to the holy man already mentioned, how much the soul is blackened by money, for he had earned a great amount of money while engaged in his business. While he was counting it one evening, his hands became so blackened that he was unable to cleanse them in any way. Early the next morning he went to that experienced man of God, the priest and confessor Osberto, told him what happened, and received from him that wholesome advice, "Go and give your wealth to the poor, then wash your hands and they will return to their original condition, and you will understand that the soul is blackened by the heaping up of money, and that by giving it to the poor you will build up a treasure in heaven (Mt 19:21) and the water of grace will purify the soul." Having followed this advice, his hands immediately required their original coloration.
2. The man of God always showed himself generous in almsgiving. One day when his wife was making a pie for dinner, poor people clustered about and humbly requested food. Omobono, knowing his wife was not at home, shared the pie among twelve poor people and then put the lid back on the pot, as if the pie was still cooking. After the meal, he went into the church and devoted himself to prayer that he who had satisfied the poor, might not be the victim of his wife's anger. He remained there for a long while, until his sons called him to supper. He refused to go saying, "Children, go and eat," as

---

86 A final, touching scene where his wife finally comes to the realization of the quality of the spouse that she has had.

if he wanted to compensate for the meal he offered to the poor by his absence, saying "I have already eaten." For he feared his wife would be wrathful for his distribution of the pie to the poor. But his good Lord, who does not desert his saints in adversity and who gives to all in abundance, so that they are fitted for all things, and not wanting His servant to suffer the reproaches and insults of his wife, glorified His saint by willing to restore to his whole house a heavenly gift. Whence, finally arising from prayer at the importunings of his children, he went home for dinner. And when he had said the blessing, his wife lifted the cover of the pot and found a whole pie and presented to Blessed Omobono the half which was to feed the family. Seeing this, the holy man blessed God, who is wonderful in His works, and with great joy, related to the family how he had fed twelve paupers with the pie and then had replaced the cover on the pot, and how he had not dared come to the table for fear of his wife, and had now received this heavenly pie which had been given by God for his own nourishment and maintenance, as well as that of his household.

3. Another time, when the vines were to be dressed, and blessed Omobono, dear to God, employed more workers than he was able to feed at mealtimes. He filled large vessels with wine and took them to the vineyard. On his way he met a crowd of poor people who said they were thirsty and begged him in Christ's name to give them something to drink. Filled with devotion to Him who poured out His blood as the price of our salvation, and then gave it to us to drink, he gifted to them all the wine that he carried. After they emptied the vessels, he returned home. There he refilled them a second time, but having encountered other thirsty poor people, he gave them this wine in the name of Christ. Once again, he returned home, so as not to suffer the reproaches of his wife, he refilled them with water and carried them to the workers. Yet he did not dare to ask them to come and drink as was his custom. After leaving the vessels, he left with an embarrassed and downcast countenance to another part of the field. The workers approached

and drank. "O Brethren! Here is a new vintage from Cana in Galilee!" They drank, as at the wedding supper where the water turned into a delicious wine, and the guests were astonished and delighted. In the same way these workers, in drinking, tasted the water transformed into delightful wine, which filled the heart of each man with joy, and exulting, they exclaimed, "Lord Omobono, come here and drink with us in the name of God, this wine of delectable taste and such sweetness, with such a fragrant bouquet. Really it is an exalted donor that we owe this to today." He returned with a pleasant and joyful face and replied, "Men, do not be impatient, for the wine which you drink has been given to us by God." Then the laborers were even more amazed, and they demanded that he drink with them. And when the new "headwaiter" (Jn 2:9) tasted the wine, or rather the water changed to wine, and knew that it had been water, he said to them "My children, praise God for His marvels, who has changed water into wine by His power. And do not tell anyone what you have heard until this mortal body—here he was speaking of himself—is freed from its chains." Then, raising his hands to heaven, said, "I praise you, Lord Christ, you who changed water into wine, renewing for us the wonder you did in Cana, teach us to honor You always, you the Lord who has prepared this for us."

4. In the night after the death of the holy man, two waxen candles appeared on his tomb as a divine sign descending from heaven. Many worthy people saw this with their bodily eyes, and heard the voices of angels, singing from on high, "Come, dear Omobono, you who fought faithfully in the combats of charity and who has conquered the world, the flesh, and the devil, and who now shines in glory!"

5. When messengers from Cremona travelled to the most holy Pope Innocent to obtain the canonization of the illustrious Omobono, glorified by his life and miracles, in the course of the night, the holy pope himself had a vision of a venerable person appearing to him, whom he saw solemnly distinguished with the title of "Saint."

Sources for the Life of Omobono

LABENTIBUS ANNIS[87]

In this final medieval life we see Omobono as the fully formed lay-merchant saint of Cremona. This was written in the latter third of the 1200s, and certainly before 1301. By this time the medieval commercial revolution was reaching its zenith. Papal-imperial disputes had quieted down and peace brought with it the growth of prosperity.

Omobono appears in this life as a fully formed lay saint. His family name is identified, and his social origin is made clear. The keys to holiness in this effort are his anti-heretical activities and charitable works, both insofar as they are especially proper to the laity. Put another way however, this life presents Omobono as the height of neighborliness and civic participation. Omobono the saint is Omobono the perfect citizen.

It is here for the first time that we have a recognition of the holiness of Omobono during his time as a merchant, becoming well known for his honesty and virtue long before his penitential conversion. However, the presentation of his family takes a darker turn here. His wife becomes a nearly unbearable burden on him and seeks to thwart his path to sanctity by every conceivable method.

This life has also experienced cross-fertilization from the currents of sanctity that started with Omobono's own canonization, and then accelerated and matured during the century of mendicant holiness, with the exaltation of many members of the Franciscan and Dominican orders. This includes greater reporting of the process of conversion of a saint, as well as an increasing emphasis on miracles performed during a saint's life.

---

87 Diana Webb has produced a good translation of this life in her work. I have consulted it, but made my own from Piazzi's edition, supplemented by his Italian translation, and Vauchez's French translation.

All of this however is set within the context of Omobono's charitable penitence, and within the ambit of the civic associations of medieval Cremona.

1. With 1197 years since the Incarnation having elapsed, when the city of Cremona had been utterly blinded by the grave deceits of the heretics, which even often cut the souls of good men like thorns, God raised a rose from among the thorns, which by the sweetness of its fragrance might draw not only the city of Cremona but also the whole surrounding area from the foul smell of sins to the sweet savor of virtue, toward a blessed and upright life in the awareness of their Creator,[88] and that the errors which seduce the vain thoughts of nearly all men might be repudiated. Some at that time and in that same city, near the basilica of that famous confessor Egidio, the citizens had created a modest neighborhood, both by citizens moving there, and by the construction of buildings.[89]
2. In that place, among fellow citizens and their families, from the middle class called the *popolo*, lived a certain family called the Tucenghi, which for long years had lived by the profession of merchants and also the craft of making clothes, those whom we are accustomed to call "tailors" in the vulgar tongue. From this family of the Tucenghi came an old man who lived with his wife by the fruit of his labors, living in a home that formerly had been owned by his ancestors. To this house was also added a small piece of land not far from the city walls, which was sufficient to provide the family with food.[90] To this man's wife was born a son, who, hoping in the future good of his name, called him Omobono. Nor was it an empty or meaningless name in his case.

---

88 An allusion to the anti-materialist dualism of the Cathars.
89 This is the "New" City of the middle classes.
90 Many details about Omobono's social situation: he was firmly of the middle class, the only son and heir of an older couple, who possessed a townhouse and a vineyard.

3. Nor was he less good in reality than he was in name. This Omobono occupied himself in the work of his parents, becoming expert in the mercantile arts which, nevertheless, though it rarely happened [in that line of work], he was able to observe honesty and justice in business.[91] Yet while still young, he had already earned the esteem of his fellow citizens by his virtues, and by the will of his parents he was joined in marriage with a wife who was a virgin of marriageable age.[92] He lived with his wife for many years with his father, remaining in all things obedient to his parents. On the day of his father's death, and by the effect of the law, he came into governance of his own goods,[93] he began to consider how brief was the time of man on earth, and how deceitful was the world, and how ephemeral its goods, and that nothing was more holy than to do that which the gospel bears witness to, "But lay up for yourselves treasures in heaven, where neither rust nor moth consumes" (Mt 6:20).

4. Therefore he considered these thoughts for some days, and because of this, his formerly calloused preoccupation with increasing his wealth began to cool, and he began no longer to follow his associates, nor to do his job with his usual craftsmanship.[94] He was already earnest in frequenting churches, and was attentive to his prayers and fasts, and that which by his labors the wealth he earned he gave with his own hands

---

91 The old prejudices and commonplaces break through here as well.
92 He was humbly subject to his parents, following their will in his labors and in his marriage, again emphasizing that he followed the normal path of a medieval Italian.
93 In European families in the early modern period, one usually did not come into full adult authority until the death of one's father. It was a commonplace that transitional life changes provoked spiritual crises in the lives of saints: death of parents, adolescence, marriage, and the like.
94 Pious thoughts affect the work of Omobono, including a suggestion that his work may have suffered from his new spiritual preoccupations.

to the destitute and poor of Christ, to the sick he gave aid and pious offerings to those in need. Also, he assisted the afflicted by good works and advice, and he threw himself so wholly into the works of mercy that Omobono was commonly called "Father of the Poor."[95]

5. Still, when his wife, seeing his conduct so changed and having left his accustomed labor and trade, and had given himself over to a life in contempt of the men of the world, she became very agitated, saying, "At one time you were a prudent man, Omobono, yet now you have become mad, since you neither attend to work or trade, whereby you used to live honorably, but you have abandoned them to waste all our goods on destitute people, from whom we cannot anticipate even the least service!"[96] And she poured many other insults and abuses against the holy man. These he bore with patience, declaring to her that the goods of the earth were fleeting, just like dripping water and that he was a happy man who gathered treasure in heaven by assisting the poor of Christ. Often afflicted by various temptations on the part of his wife, he always triumphed with patience and humility.[97]

---

95 Vauchez suggests that this title is key. He does not become poor but becomes "Father of the poor." In terms of premodern social structure, Omobono becomes the great and magnanimous patron, whose clients are the poor. His wealth enables him to continue his magnanimity and retain his position as patron.

96 The problem with Omobono's new patronage, from his wife's perspective, is that his new clients cannot return the normative service that would be expected from the associates of a great magnate. Of course, Omobono knows that this service will be transmuted into heavenly glory. His wife cannot understand this higher "patronage."

97 Omobono's family becomes a particular burden in this *vita*. This is another commonplace in saints' lives. Holiness is so individual a gift of grace, that often the greatest persecution comes from those closest in relation. This was a theme repeated in all the mendicant hagiography of the thirteenth century, in Francis, Thomas Aquinas, Clare, and Peter of Verona in particular.

Sources for the Life of Omobono

6. Moreover it was the custom of this holy man to go to his church every night, that there he might participate in the office of Matins. A certain priest named Osberto, who then was rector of the church, a good and god-fearing man himself, when he saw Omobono's devotion, each night when he sounded the bell for Matins, came so that he might open the church door and let him into the church. One time when Omobono had come before the sounding of the bell and had stood for some time outside the church, the doors of the church, by the will of God, were opened by themselves in the sight of the saint of God.[98] When the priest saw him standing in the church he marveled, asking who had given him admittance, he said, "I found the church doors open." And yet the priest knew that he had closed the doors himself the previous evening. After a few days the same thing happened, and the doors stood open again, his having arrived before the hour of Matins. From this the priest understood that this was a work of God, and that he was in the presence of a holy man, since later in the twenty-six years that the priest was rector of the church, it happened again many times, just as recounted above.[99]

7. The saint of God continued to observe the canonical hours, so that he was always present for Matins,[100] yet he did not

---

98 This *vita* emphasizes miracles worked in life; not only will the man of God not be denied access to the Church, the place of liturgical, hierarchical worship is emphasized. It was not enough to pray privately; Omobono had to attend the Divine Office.

99 Osberto, the key witness in the canonization testimony, again here is underscored as the point man for identifying Omobono's sanctity and undergirding his relationship to the institutional Church.

100 It should be emphasized that the Divine Office was not simply clerical at this time. The Offices of the Church were celebrated widely, and certain hours were very popular with the laity, notably Vespers and, in Dominican churches, Compline. Pious laity such as Omobono would also have participated in Matins. Indeed, the way that medievals kept time was to the bells marking the hours of the Church day; it was deeply embedded in society.

leave when it was finished, but awaited the break of day and the hour of Mass, remaining before an ancient cross, praying without ceasing, often remaining with his whole body prostrate on the ground in contemplation.[101] One day, during a period of famine, the baker carried to the house of the saint a certain amount of bread, as was his custom, and many poor and needy people, knowing this was the bread of Omobono, the "Father of the Poor," followed the baker to the house of the man of God. Finding him, they begged that he might distribute it to them as alms, as was his custom.

8. He consented to them, because his wife would not be able to weigh them since she was then out, so he distributed the greater part to them.[102] His wife having returned, and the hour of dinner having arrived, she went to the bread bin and found two types of bread there. As much bread as Omobono had given away, she found well-made bread of incomparable goodness, together with that which remained. His wife asked him how they came to be there, but the saint also marveled, seeing it was the work of God, revealed it to the serving girl, who had seen what had happened, but the saint constrained her to tell no one. What happened with the bread, also happened to the wine.[103]

9. Indeed when he was pruning in a small vineyard, which he had alone kept for his own provision and for that of many poor people, after having sold his other possessions and distributed the profits to the poor, and was carrying a vessel of wine to the workers, but meeting some poor people, they

---

101 Physical prostration was once a much more common posture in liturgical and paraliturgical settings.

102 Omobono certainly fulfills the biblical injunction about giving alms, "do not let your left hand know what your right hand is doing." (Mt 6:3)

103 Bread and wine were, and remain, the staples of the Mediterranean diet, the two most important items in the family larder. This is probably a doublet with the pie miracle of QH.

begged him to give them a drink.[104] Having given it to them, it was nearly empty of wine. He did not dare return home to refill it, fearful of his wife's abuse. So he filled it with water, and made the sign of the cross over it, closed it, and carried it to the workers.[105] These, when they had tasted, perceived that it was delightful and precious wine, different than any wine they knew from the region, and they asked from whence he got it, since they had never drunk anything so good.[106] The man of God hearing this, thinking they were mocking him, tasted it himself and knowing it to be a work of God, gave copious thanks. Certain people having seen him putting water in the vessel, and knowing this, later recounted this marvelous miracle.

10. He showed forth many other signs of his sanctity while he yet lived, but many more after his death. The perfidy and disbelief of many heretics were confounded by the signs, power, and words of the man of God, and they were converted.[107]

Dedicating himself to these practices, to self-deprivations, and to works of mercy, though he had already entered the decline of his life, a certain Ides of November[108] (13 November) the day on which is celebrated the famous confessor San Brizio, he was present for Matins, he was healthy and quiet of heart. After the Office he began as usual to kneel before the cross, in his accustomed place where he remained until the

---

104 An incidental aside that Omobono is an employer, though perhaps these were seasonal workers for pruning or harvesting.
105 Making the sign of the cross over one's food or drink was formerly much more common, and not restricted to priestly blessings; indeed such lay practices continued long in many areas of Christianity as one can see in Dostoevsky's novels.
106 Italians of any social class know good wine when they drink it; their taste buds are here used as evidence of a divine miracle.
107 Miracles and sanctity were the two necessary elements to defeat heresy.
108 The old Roman calendrical system was used for an extremely long time in the Western world.

start of Mass. When the priest began the *Gloria in excelsis Deo*, he prostrated himself before the cross; a soldier before the King, a servant before the Lord (*COS*, 6), and, extending his arms in the form of a cross, and without any movement or sign that he was dying, stretching himself out in reverence to God, he gave up his soul to the Creator.

11. No one was aware of his passing except when the time for the reading of the Gospel had come. When he did not arise, they thought that he was asleep, whence, coming to rouse him, they saw that his body was lifeless. Immediately the glorious body was lifted up, was washed, and prepared for burial with solemn funeral rites. The poor, hearing that their father had died, came weeping to his funeral, for Omobono, the "Father of the Poor," was dead. And behold, that while they were coming to the place of his burial, an uncountable number of great miracles shone forth from God for His holy one.[109] Among the poor were some who were lame who came to mourn their benefactor; they were healed, and their legs and feet were restored to strength.

12. The blind received sight, the deformed were raised to full stature, and those afflicted by various infirmities were cured. Whence, his fame having spread, and many people blind for many years came from the surrounding regions, and those afflicted by other infirmities, were restored to health at the tomb which was built in the church of Sant' Egidio. Many paralyzed and crippled were cured. Many who were crippled and shriveled were restored to health. Many hastened there carrying the sick on litters and stretchers, and those who were able came themselves, hastening on staffs. All of these God healed through the invocation of His saints, and by his intercession.[110]

---

109 Public sanctity begins with popular cult confirmed by miracles.
110 Such tableaus are common throughout Christianity and can still be witnessed particularly at great Marian shrines, where sometimes whole walls of cast-off crutches are constructed, and mountains of

13. One woman who had been so constricted [in body] that her face touched her knees, caused herself to be carried in on a stretcher. Many mocked her, thinking she would never be able to be healed. However, when she was placed before the tomb, and having prayed, arose healthy and upright, giving thanks to God (*COS*, 8). As the news of the miracles spread, a certain one began to say foolish things about the saint. Immediately his tongue was swollen by the will of God so that he couldn't speak, but, fearing for his life, he repented in his heart, and having made a vow to God, was immediately healed (*COS*, 9).[111] Also many born mute, their parents having sworn vows to God, were restored to the use of their tongues through his intercession.
14. He also miraculously cured one who had been born blind and mute (*COS*, 9). Many possessed people were healed. Before his death, a demon had been tormenting a certain girl from Bergamo.[112] When he was compelled with many oaths and exorcisms, the demon said that he would never leave, unless he be expelled by Omobono of Cremona. The parents were not able to understand who this Omobono might be and thought the spirit deranged. Yet when she was conducted to the tomb with devotion, she was healed on the spot (*COS*, 9).
15. There was another demoniac woman, yet some declared that she was not possessed, so secretly they brought holy water

---

silver "ex voto" offerings line the walls. Premodern people expected nothing less than miracles, and often reported receiving them. We should not forget that in these days of "imitative sainthood," that the saint is glorified and magnified by God through the working of miracles.

111 Not all miracles are positive. This is a common type called an "aggression" or "chastisement" miracle. The dumb speak by the grace of God and the merit of the saint, but the impious are punished by losing the use of the organ whereby they derided God and the saint.

112 Only about 50 miles from Cremona, this story emphasizes both the local nature of Omobono's cult, and its spread to other cities of Lombardy.

and plain water, and in a pyx put one consecrated host and in another an unconsecrated one. They first sprinkled water on her that was unblessed, but she showed no effect, but stayed quiet. When she was sprinkled with holy water, immediately she was horrified and began to yell, and it happened similarly with the hosts (QP, 4).

16. When they understood that she was possessed, they led her before the tomb of the saint with devotion, and she was healed there.[113] These and many other miracles were seen by the lord Bishop of Cremona and many of the wise men of the city; they decided to send a tally of these miracles to the Supreme Pontiff, so that, having investigated them, he might see if this man of God merited to be canonized, and inscribed in the catalogue of the saints.

17. For this reason they sent Bishop Sicardo with many ambassadors to Rome to Pope Innocent IV.[114] Having heard and examined all these things, saying that he had dreamed the previous day that he was canonizing a certain man from Cremona,[115] by Bulls and Apostolic letters he canonized Saint Omobono with full solemnity. Given at the Lateran in the first year of his pontificate, this bull is preserved in the sacristy of the cathedral of Cremona, with the help of our Lord Jesus Christ. Praise be to God. Amen.

---

113 The conducting of the possessed into the presence of a saint's tomb was very common, including physically restraining them there until they were healed by the saint.
114 An error for Innocent III (1198–1216).
115 An interesting comment, perhaps redolent of similar dreams attributed to Innocent III regarding Sts. Francis and Dominic.

The Church and archeological area of Sant' Omonbono, dedicated to the saint in Rome at the steps of the Capitol Hill. It was the center of his devotion in the eternal city and the home of the Tailors' Guild who annually celebrated him as their patron.

An altar painting offered by a merchant saved from a storm dedicated to Saint Nicholas and Sant'Omobono in the Basilica di Santa Maria Assunta in Afri in Abruzzo.

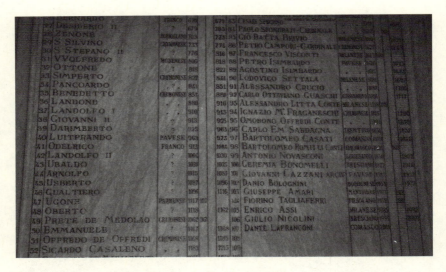

The list of Bishops of Cremona, including Sicard, the promoter of Omobono's cult in the city and in the Church, inside the magnificent Romanesque Cathedral of the city. Omobono would have seen it being constructed and consecrated during his lifetime, a symbol of the prosperity and devotion of the city.

The entrance into the martyrium of the patron saints of the city below the high altar. It says, "Here your holy patrons and co-citizens have altars for tombs, you who are about to come to venerate their relics, shall imitate their examples."

The relics of Sant' Omobono, covered with silver and dressed in the robes of a noble merchant of the city.

A depiction of Omobono on the right with his traditional moneybag giving alms, and a later saint, Facio of Cremona, a lay silversmith.

Statue of Omobono on the facade of the 1000-year-old Church of Sant' Egidio, later co-entitled to the new saint as well. He is clearly depicted as a lay saint with a moneybag as his iconographical symbol. The Church is only a few blocks from the beautiful cathedral.

A 17th century statue of Sant' Omobono in his parish church, depicted as in his role as 'Father of the Poor.'

The crucifix that Omobono regularly prostrated himself in front of, and at whose foot he was found on the day of his death in 1197 during Mass.

The original burial site of Sant' Omobono under the altar of his parish Church, later moved to the Cathedral of Cremona.

The facade of Sant' Omobono's parish church in his neighborhood.

The facade of the mighty Romanesque Cathedral, built in the 12th century. Cremona, the city of Omobono, Monteverdi, and Stradivarius, is located an easy day trip from many of the main tourist cities of northern Italy. It is pristine and undervisited, with marvelous Lombard-Emilian cuisine.

Chapter 4
THE CULT OF OMOBONO AND THE MEDIEVAL SYNTHESIS

Devotion to Omobono was exceptionally strong in Cremona, though it spread more slowly elsewhere. Over the course of the thirteenth century Omobono's cult began to take on different meanings, some of which can be traced in the unfolding of his various "lives." He began to inspire charitable efforts as well as the creation of pious confraternities. He became established as the communal patron of his city, an honor that remains to the present day. That said though, devotion to him did not become generally diffused throughout the Christian world. To say that, however, belies his significance, one that goes far beyond mere enthusiasm for his cult. His canonization propelled the recognition of the merchant life—and attendant issues regarding the middle class—to the center of the Church's thinking. While there were many moving parts that went into this revolution in Christian thought, Omobono's elevation was a crystallizing element. He inspired other lay saints in Italy, and paved the way for an increasing appreciation of the lay state and the value of labor, which would see its trajectory rise dramatically in the coming centuries. The recognition of lay Christianity as a force for good and holiness would mature over the years, through St. Francis de Sales in the seventeenth century, and come to fruition in movements like *Opus Dei* and the teachings of the Second Vatican Council in the twentieth. Before analyzing these developments, though, one should trace the evolution of Omobono's own cult, and from there a foundation can be laid that will support later investigations of the changes in Church practice and theory.

The Cult of St. Omobono

It seems that Bishop Sicard's Latin liturgical life did not gain much of a following among the laity. Indeed, during the thirteenth century there was significant pushback against its presentation of the virtues of the saint. Its clericalist vision of holiness was largely restricted to the Latin-speaking elite, usually only read on Omobono's 13 November feast during the night watch of Matins. It contained all of the traditional imprecations against the merchant life.[1] Merchants were false and greedy, and their only hope lay in the utter abandonment of trade for a life of intense penance for their past exploitative mercantile sins. In this Sicard was in accord with the tenor of an earlier age, typified by Honorius of Autun (1080–1154) a popular clerical writer. He had written regarding the question "have merchants any hope?" To this he responded: "Very little. For nearly everything they have, they acquired by frauds, perjuries, and avarice. Of these it is spoken, 'Those who trust in a multitude of riches, shall be like sheep appointed for the fire, death shall be their shepherd' (Ps 48[49]:14)."[2] Sicard's work sees lay holiness solely through this lens.[3] In *COS* there is no space for work, no mention of the saint's wife or his family, nor does it bear any witness to his civic participation. Yet Sicard's traditionalism was beginning to ring hollow. The platitudes of the agricultural/clerical past had no appeal to the new generations of pious, urban, middle-class Christians. Indeed, even within the Church a new appreciation of the life of the market was beginning to make itself felt, albeit very slowly. It is unlikely that Sicard's life had much of an effect on the development of the popular cult of Omobono as a fellow townsman, neighbor, and "Father of the Poor." Indeed, it may even be possible that Sicard wrote this life to appeal to those of the "Old" City, the more established episcopal-clerical-noble axis that had dominated Italian life until the dawn of the 1100s, while publicly he embraced the cult of Omobono of the "New" City, and preached veneration of the popular saint to the people. Perhaps this tactic was also a result of Sicard's policy of conciliation.

The Cult of Omobono and the Medieval Synthesis

We have already studied the cultic origins of Omobono devotion. The poor surged into his funeral and immediately miracles began to multiply: a classic medieval case of spontaneous recognition of holiness, one repeated with many saints all over Christendom. Sicard's public oversight of the cult was masterful. Any bishop who can simply travel to Rome with a dossier and a few witnesses and effect a canonization was surely exceptional. This is why I propose that he was skillfully able to manage the balance between interests in the town. Indeed, his public translation of Omobono's relics on 25 June 1202 demonstrated that he was a master *impresario* and effective Church leader. Earlier, in 1196, Sicard had translated the remains of Sant' Imerio (an obscure bishop of the 500s and another communal patron) to the Cathedral. To the relics of Imerio Sicard would add another prize, increasing the prestige of the mother church. Omobono's body was taken from the Church of Sant' Egidio in the heart of the "New" town and conducted to the cultic center of the city, the Cathedral. Sicard deftly managed the cult so as to present Omobono not as the saint of a faction, but as an intercessor and defender of the whole *comune*.[4] While underscoring the unity of the city, Sicard also positioned himself as its leader, sanctioned by the holiness of Omobono, now in possession of two saints at the heart of the mother church. Sant' Egidio was not left bereft of relics however, for it retained the crucifix before which Omobono prayed and died, and it became a secondary site of veneration and pilgrimage. It seems Sant' Egidio continued to grow and a new church was built in 1245.[5] Until 1521 the administration of this new church was managed through a cooperation of canons and a group of laity. It was for this church that the two statues that now stand on the facade of the church of Sant' Omobono were carved, certainly before 1230, one of Egidio and the other of Omobono, now iconographically classified as a layman and a merchant by his possession of a tunic and a purse, giving alms to the poor. Indeed it is probable that this statue had a far greater effect of the public perception of Omobono than on the rarefied Latin prayers of *COS*. Omobono was publicly displayed proudly as both a layman and a man of means. He had mounted not only the ladder of salvation, but had even achieved public sanctity in the Christian Church in his own lay state of life. Here, carved in stone, was a revolutionary sentiment.

Sicard's death in 1215 meant that the primary promoter of the cult was gone. Unfortunately, his carefully balanced maintenance of civil peace did not outlive him. With the rise of the German Emperor Frederick II (r. 1220–1250), Cremona again became a center of pro-imperial sentiment, in general favoring the old nobility against the civil democracy and proto-capitalism of the merchants. This conflict, commencing in 1228, led to the dominance of the Ghibelline forces (nominally pro-imperial and anti-papal) until the fall of Uberto Pallavicini in 1266. This provided a smoke screen for heresy, and a Cathar "bishop" was at liberty to reside in the city until around 1270.[6] While all this probably had no effect on the celebration of Omobono's cult as a civic patron, it also meant that there was little opportunity to spread his reputation abroad. There is some evidence that his cult had begun a tentative expansion. We have already seen the episode of the miracle at Bergamo, indicating an incipient cult outside of the city of its origin. While Vauchez has suggested that the cult may have had a temporary efflorescence that later faded, he also offers evidence of continuing interest. In 1245 the Dominican Bartolomeo da Trento wrote a compilation of saints' lives and miracle stories. He included several paragraphs on Omobono. Bartolomeo gives a rather standard list of virtues, underscores the saint's obedience to the Church, and reported on his penitential activities. He also testifies regarding Omobono's pious death. While it tells us no new information about the saint, it is significant for two reasons. In the first place it attests to interest in Omobono in the wider world, and his inclusion in a popular compilation by a well-travelled Mendicant friar shows that the saint's cult was being successfully deployed, though on a small scale. Further, it is evidence for continued cultic influence in his home town. Bartolomeo, interestingly, reports that Omobono had become a specialist in the freeing of captives and prisoners, many of whom left their chains at his tomb as *ex votos*.[7] Yet the *vitae* of Omobono, as we have seen previously, were chafing against the restrictions that restrained the search for mercantile holiness, and his cult began to parallel larger trends in the broader medieval society.

NEW ATTITUDES

The Church could not fail to notice the astonishing new wealth coursing through high medieval society. The successful and burgeoning cities were difficult to fit in the traditional agrarian models used during the previous half-millennium. In addition, the intellectuals of the Church were confronted with a tradition that was ambivalent at best to such developments. At worst, the long course of Christian thought at times displayed an attitude seemingly inimical to the merchant life and to the development of a positive attitude toward market forces. The infamous *Opus imperfectum in Matthaeum,* an Arian work falsely attributed to St. John Chrysostom, unfortunately influenced the Christian tradition with its wholesale condemnation of the merchant life.[8] Its proscriptions had even been incorporated into the normative collection of Canon law under Gratian and into the standard theology textbook of Peter Lombard. Even at the turn of the 1200s, churchmen were still strongly rooted in this venerable line of thought. Robert of Courçon (d. 1219)—a cardinal and associate of Innocent III and an astute diplomat who implemented reforms and oversaw the academic life of the University of Paris—was strongly in this camp. Taking his cue from Gratian, he repeatedly underlines the grave responsibilities of wealth: "Feed him who is dying of hunger . . . if he is not fed, you have killed him."[9] Robert takes this to its logical conclusion. The rich man must impoverish himself, for if any man dies of hunger while the wealthy person is still in a state of surplus, the rich man is guilty of murder.[10] Robert stops only at suicide; a person may not divest himself of the necessities for his own bodily life. This is not exactly a ringing endorsement of careful and prudent shepherding of surplus! Robert clearly approves of the canonical dictum (erroneously attributed to St. Clement of Rome) that the origin of wickedness was the first time the distinction between "mine" and "yours" was uttered.[11] The authorities weighed heavily upon medieval thinkers, with Gratian and Peter Lombard repeating a tradition that stretched back into antiquity. The very weight of such serious magisterial declarations demanded an exceedingly high burden of proof to challenge them. Clearly heavy lifting had to be done to clear such impediments from the road to fruitful development.

Answers began to arrive from two directions, from the ground up (as in the case of Omobono) and from the top down. The papacy was at the forefront of such developments, and began to address the problems that started to arise. Innocent III was a willing innovator, already demonstrated in his rapid canonization of Omobono. He recognized the deficiencies in previous attempts to address problems related to increasing wealth and heretical critiques. Perceptively he was aware that the two often went hand in hand. Many heretics professed a poverty that attempted to hearken back to the example of the Apostles, thus implicitly (sometimes explicitly) implicating the Church in corruption due to its possessionate nature. Churchmen saw that these heretics were especially popular among the rising urban gentry. While few in the new middle class became active heretics, many were certainly supportive of and sympathetic to the ministry of the unorthodox preachers. This is aptly demonstrated by the ready welcome many itinerant heretics found in the cities, and the ease with which they acquired the material necessities for their lives. Indeed, at first medieval heresy was most popular in the regions that were most concentrated into new urban agglomerations, and those that were most wealthy. Some have suggested that this rising tide of support for lives of voluntary poverty was directly proportioned to Christian guilt about the accumulation of wealth.[12] Providing material support to the "good men" who lived lives in imitation of the Apostles was a relief valve for releasing pent up anxieties about greed and avarice, criticisms of which ran exceptionally deep in the consciences of Christians. Giving to the holy poor was seen as a better investment than providing more gilding for an already rich Church. But such sentiments did not always dovetail with heresy. Pious lay people such as Omobono found many ways to support and defend the new urban poor and to engage in charitable activity that steered well clear of heterodoxy. Many paths existed to aid the indigent within the context of the Church itself. It was Innocent's genius to direct these real anxieties and preexistent lay piety into channels that would serve for charitable relief as well as forging a tool to combat heresy.

For this reason Innocent created a plan that would attack heresy on many fronts. In the first place he deployed his canonized saints against heretics, continuing a tack he had begun with the elevation of Omobono himself. All the later saints of his papacy would be directed against heretical activity, even though they may have never confronted it during their lives.[13] The saints would serve as the heavenly vanguard in the struggle against contemporary heterodoxies. Further, the pope encouraged those who wished to profess obedience to the institutional Church the opportunity to continue their practices of wandering poverty. This was exemplified in the case of the Waldensian preacher Durand of Huesca, who was reconciled to the Church and who, with his group, became known as the Poor Catholics.[14] They in turn returned to do battle with the Cathars and other unconverted Waldensians, a clear case of Innocent using poverty as a means of combatting heresy. He had also approved other lay groups that were dedicated to poverty and preaching repentance, such as the Humiliati of northern Italy.[15] But Innocent knew that the majority of the laity could not live lives of wandering preaching, and somehow there needed to be a way to steer their charitable impulses toward the support of groups that would answer the spiritual challenges of the time, while eschewing heretical tendencies. He discovered these in the founders of the mendicant movements.

Francis and Dominic, each in his own way, were the culmination of several centuries of meditations regarding the relative places of wealth, poverty, preaching, and orthodoxy in the life of Christendom. When the wandering tramp from Assisi was presented before the papal court with his small coterie of followers in 1208, Innocent saw the opportunity to direct them into the lay movements of piety and repentance that he had been busily approving and sending forth for years.[16] While the mission to preach came as a shock to Francis (1181/1182–1226), Innocent knew what he was doing. No more would the mistakes made with Waldo of Lyons plague the Church. Innocent brilliantly affirmed the Minorites' lay piety and, through their obedience to the hierarchy, made them into a weapon in the hands of the orthodox. Innocent insisted that they be aggregated to the institutional Church by taking orders, which in turn gave them license to preach. Francis had wanted to live with his small band, working with their hands, and living out his radical vision of the Gospel. The pope had changed the direction of his life utterly, and in so doing had markedly altered the history of Christianity. It is not known with certainty whether Francis ever met the pope again, nor if Innocent foresaw the astonishing growth and glories of the Franciscan order, yet it is certain that the mendicant group played a role in papal policy, a testament to Innocent's foresight in channeling the streams of lay piety into something at the same time fruitful and fully orthodox.

For Francis, individual poverty played a role in his self-conception, but was really in service of his broad programme of *minoritas* (comprehensive humility in all things). His vision was well rounded, and beyond poverty it included manual labor and reverence for the priests of the Church. The son of wealthy, middle-class parents, he abandoned his life of comfort in Assisi in order to become a lay penitent. While later reimaginings of Francis attempt to make him into some sort of proto-socialist, what he was really interested in was the radical following of Christ, in a similar way as those wandering preachers of the centuries before him. Francis situated poverty in terms of the typical medieval lay penitence of the time. He focused on the correct reception and celebration of the sacraments, he embraced almsgiving and works of penance, and he emphasized that manual labor was to be required for his brotherhood (mendicancy—or the practice of begging—was not initially used as a category of holiness).[17] So Francis himself did not fixate on poverty as a spiritual idol, though many of his later followers would fall into this trap. Rather the poor man of Assisi sought in all aspects of his life to live in humility. Francis was not a revolutionary, but rather embodied the culmination of all of the tendencies of lay piety up to his own time. Further than that, his life was a canticle to the goodness of the material world, and an implicit refutation of the aggressively anti-incarnational Cathars. Support of the Franciscan way of life would fulfill lay desires while at the same time combatting heresy. All of the good components of Waldo of Lyons and the penitential preachers of the twelfth century would find their completion in Francis and his brothers.

In addition Francis had neither rural nor aristocratic roots. He was a son of the city, a child of the bourgeois middle class, one of the new number of ambitious merchants. His business, however, was spiritual rather than temporal and, fulfilling as he did the fundamental spiritual needs of the age, he found himself inundated by followers. Indeed, Francis exhibited in his life one of the essential strengths of the middle class, channeled in the direction of holiness: Francis was a spiritual entrepreneur. The Franciscans drew their strength from the bourgeoisie, both in affiliations to the order and in a multitude of material offerings that enabled the Franciscans to grow, mature, and expand. Bequests to these voluntary poor flowed to the brethren, and they began a ministry in the urban centers of Italy and beyond, distinguishing themselves from the older orders who sought refuge in remote and rural locations. Here indeed was the truly innovative development, an urban religious order for an urban populace, both filled with the same spiritual aspirations and dedicated to the perpetuation of Christian charity and orthodoxy in a new and challenging environment. Such an alliance would lead eventually to the destruction of medieval heresies then abroad in Europe, while inculcating a new respect for bourgeois spirituality within the medieval church.

Dominic (1170–1221) followed a similar path. Likely descending from petty nobility or the more prominent bourgeoisie in

Castile, he became a cathedral canon in Osma. While this was a traditional position in the Church, Dominic learned to yearn for more. He followed his bishop, Diego, on missions of preaching and penitence in Provence, which kindled in him a fervent zeal for souls. He founded his order to be a band of preaching brothers, freed by mobility from attachments and the profession of individual poverty. Their aim was the salvation of souls, by means of the best preparation for preaching and disputation available. For this reason they gathered around the intellectual centers of Christendom, the famous universities. There they became educated and developed into the intellectual leaders of the orthodox Church. Yet they too followed a path similar to the Franciscans, for they pursued souls in the cities and established their convents and bases of preaching there. Ministering to the new urban concentrations brought the nascent orders popularity and wealth, providing an orthodox outlet for the material guilt of the laity, and focusing on them devotions that were far removed from heresy. The Dominicans provided powerful, charismatic, and educated preachers who marshalled the strength of the laity in favor of charity and shielded them from heresy. Their education was a prescient complement to the rising literacy and sophistication of the urban Christians. From the generosity of the merchant laity, mighty edifices were reared in these new cities, Franciscan and Dominican convents that today stand as testimonies to the glories of the two orders and to the charitable almsgiving of the middle-class faithful. One only need think of Santa Maria Novella and Santa Croce in Florence in order to witness this marvelous symbiosis of piety and poverty.

The success of the mendicant orders presaged a significant development in the medieval intellectual world. Never before had a religious order been "unmoored" from the convent, free to preach and wander, to beg and to exhort. The idea of apostolic preachers sanctioned by the Church was an astonishing novelty. United to hierarchical Christianity, these elite bands were the complement of a newly resurgent lay piety that would revolutionize the image of Christian holiness. They would form an interdependent relationship with the rising middle class, an alliance that would endure through the Middle Ages. Lay people affiliated themselves with what would eventually become mendicant third orders; they funded their churches and convents and requested burial inside them. They went to the friars for confession and advice. In turn it would be the thinkers of the mendicant orders who would pave the way for a wholesale reappraisal of the principles and practices of the bourgeois life, not out of a sense of self-justification, but of a real product of genuine social and doctrinal development. The unexpected covenant between the voluntary poor and the affluent men and women who supported them cleared a path for the reconsideration of the place of money, the merchant, and the lay person in the context of Christian holiness and the life of the Church.

Urban Catholicism was then developing apace. Merchant and mendicant together formed a significant partnership that harnessed the newfound wealth both to the good of the earthly community and toward the end of eternal salvation. The begging orders had provided a new way for the faithful to lay up "treasure in heaven." The urban setting had brought into relief for the first time a new class of the poor, hitherto nearly invisible in the self-sufficient and close-knit agrarian villages of early medieval Europe. The Commercial Revolution brought wealth and opportunity, but the concentration of riches in cities also laid bare the relative disparities of rich and poor as never before. These involuntary poor strained the resources of traditional Church charity. This was a problem that elicited strong feelings. Those who had become voluntarily poor—the Mendicants—were making a spiritual sacrifice and were doing good, and because of that merited sustenance. The involuntary poor, however, aroused some suspicion, in particular those who would not work. While Christianity had always defended the poor, it had also attacked indolence from the beginning. "If a man will not work, let him not eat," insisted the Apostle (2 Thess 3:10). The code of Justinian had forbidden able-bodied men to beg. Johannes Teutonicus (d. 1245), a prominent canonist of the thirteenth century, declared that someone who was capable of work and still accepted public assistance should be treated as a criminal.[18] Even St. Bonaventure, the Franciscan *par excellence*, was clear. "All able poor who lack means of subsistence should take up some manual or corporal labor."[19] Of course these sentiments exempted women and children, as well as the old and infirm, all of whom were the proper candidates for charity. What it does affirm, however, is a valorization of labor and the dignity that it provides. Such sentiments would accelerate with the birth of the humanist movement in Italy, and would inform modern Catholic ideas concerning the sanctifying power of work. Further than this, involuntary poverty was no ticket to heaven. Indeed it was a spiritual danger. It could lead to the desperation of immoral occupations and become a fount of envy and resentment. The thirteenth-century poet Jean de Meun was reflective of these conclusions. "Poverty is worse than death," he contended, "for she torments and gnaws at the soul and body, and not just for an hour but as long as they dwell together, and brings them not only to condemnation but also to larceny and perjury and many other difficulties."[20] These were not novel attitudes, indeed they had long pedigrees, but they came to be more visible as the issue of involuntary poverty came out into the open.

In spite of these negative approaches toward the new poor, the constant theme of solidarity and charity emerged. The old idea of the providential dispensation and division of rich and poor, while it did little to change structures, allowed the floodgates of charity to open. The poor were ordained by God so that the rich might be saved through enacting charity, and the indigent through humility. Inequality meant that humans needed each other; equality could lead to an absurd individualism that could destroy charity and fellow-feeling. Giordano of Pisa, an eminent Dominican preacher at the turn of the fourteenth century, summed up this position when he said, "Why are the poor given their station in life? So that the rich might earn eternal life through them."[21] The alms of the rising wealthy more than met this challenge, and new confraternities and mutual-assistance groups arose to meet these new demands head-on. The mendicant orders began to coopt traditional lay penitential piety, and over the course of the thirteenth century aligned that devotion according to what would later be known as the third orders. These groups would mature over the course of time, moving from affiliated lay *conversi*, who lived lives of penitence attached to the monasteries as lay brothers or lay sisters, into members of the laity who continued to live with their families and who maintained their secular ties to the business world. In this way the mendicant third orders and confraternities modeled the new type of lay piety of which Omobono was the precursor. Here was a way to live out holiness in association with the mendicant orders, joined to their spirituality, and under their supervision. By doing this the laity not only adhered to religious orthodoxy, but put to use the mighty force of common Christian religiosity and penitence, to the end of making the lay state a vehicle for holiness going into the future. In order to understand these developments in the world of the medieval cities, we need to turn to the intellectual evolution occurring among the thinkers of Christendom.

NEW INTELLECTUAL DEVELOPMENTS

Like Francis of Assisi, many of the thinkers who propelled scholastic thought in the twelfth and thirteenth centuries came from the rising bourgeoisie. They had come of age in the bustling towns, and had familiar concourse with the merchants and entrepreneurs then proliferating all over Europe and the Mediterranean world. This familiarity brought with it the material for a reconsideration and a reorientation of emphasis in the Christian tradition. For the first time we see the theories and practices of "white-collar" work developing. What was difficult for people to get their minds around was how such work was to be valued. How could one assess the productive capacity of a scholar or a lawyer, or even a clerk who merely changed figures on a piece of paper? Regarding the laboring and artisan classes, such a valuation was simple. They produced goods and sold them, but it was not clear just exactly what the rapidly growing bourgeoisie actually made. A merchant merely bought goods and then sold them for a higher price. Where was the social utility of that transaction? Was it not a bare grasping for wealth? Before there could be a sophisticated morality of the market, the thinkers of the Church had to understand what exactly a complex market economy was.

We have already met some of the members of the school of Master Peter the Chanter (d. 1197).[22] His student Robert of Courçon was a major figure at the University of Paris. Peter was a bridge between the worlds of early and mature Scholasticism, and his comprehensive biblical commentaries and manuals for preaching broke new ground in the assessment of contemporary moral problems. Another of his students, Thomas of Chobham (d. ca. 1235), carried Peter's work into the rapidly developing field of confessional guides. Private, auricular confession had been developing for over half-a-millennium, but with the declaration of the Lateran Council of 1215, it was made into a yearly requirement for all Catholics. With this decision came the proliferation of "field guides" for confessors.[23] Aside from traditional and perennial moral problems, confessors also faced new issues on the ground, among which was guilt concerning rising wealth and various market practices. Indeed, Thomas of Chobham repeats traditional nostrums about the dangers of commerce, but is the first to qualify them with more extensive analysis. Merchants are entitled to a profit not because they buy cheap and sell dear, but because they take needed products from areas of plenty to areas of scarcity. Therein lies expense and risk. A merchant is fully able to recoup that without sin. If he improves the product in any way, he also is to receive legitimate compensation for it. As long as the merchant did not taint the goods or sell with fraud, then his conduct was without sin. Thomas also recognizes conditions of scarcity, which would suggest a consideration of a market-based price rather than an inherent one. While this does not seem like a terribly large step, Thomas is really the first medieval to recognize the social utility of the market. In reality, Thomas made merchants subject to the same considerations as artisans. In collapsing these categories he removed the stigma from the merchants, and added them to a category of workers whose labors were sanctioned by the Christian tradition. This was the first intellectual step in a development that immediately began to gather steam.[24]

It was the Dominicans who promoted the reappraisal of the bourgeois life. These friars themselves were mostly drawn from the rapidly expanding middle classes and drew their generous donors from the burghers of medieval Europe. As such they brought with them a mercantile vocabulary and mindset. Their fourth General, Humbert of Romans, flatly declared that the Order of Preachers should be like merchants, whose profit in this case would be not money, but souls. The famous Dominican preacher, Aldobrandino Cavalcanti, called Christ "the good merchant" in two sermons.[25] These friars strongly established themselves in the urban universities of Europe in their first generation and, following the death of Francis, they were followed immediately by the entrance of the Franciscan Minorites into the academic life.[26] They too shared a mercantile mindset. Francis had been a merchant who traded earthly for heavenly traffic; he had become a "merchant for souls." The Franciscan Gilbert of Tournai preached "Christ comes like a merchant to do business."[27] The dynamism of these new orders provided both intellectual and spiritual leaven for thirteenth-century Christendom and, drawn as they were from the towns and families of the solid middle class, they were at the vanguard of developments in economic thought. Quickly they mounted academic chairs at prestigious universities such as Paris and Oxford, gained the trust of the papacy, and began to be appointed to significant offices such as inquisitor, bishop, and even cardinal. All of the Dominicans and Franciscans who attained such lofty offices were guaranteed to have had excellent university educations, and as such were from the rising intellectual elite, and began to process the tradition using their new insights.

One of the most famous of these early mendicant theologians was Hugh of St. Cher (ca. 1195–1263). Already a Parisian Master at the time of his reception into the Dominicans in 1225, he rose quickly through the ranks, becoming one of the most influential professors and administrators of the order. At last he was promoted to the office of cardinal in 1244, becoming an intimate associate of several popes and using his clout to shepherd his order into maturity. His efforts on the streamlining of biblical study were among the most audacious and exceptional academic works of the Middle Ages, providing a corrected Vulgate along with a concordance and exhaustive commentaries, tools that would prove invaluable for the progress of Christian theology. These works gave him ample space for considerations of the biblical injunctions on wealth. In commenting on the famous passage "You cannot serve both God and Mammon" (Mt 6:24), Hugh first sticks to the traditional reading. The love of God necessitates the hatred of riches. Yet Hugh stresses that Christ uses the word "serve" and not "have." The man of greed "serves" riches, and for that reason despises God. Yet the rich man who is not a slave to his riches, who does not "serve" them but merely "has" them in order that he might use them well, commits no sin.[28] Yet Hugh does not focus solely on the rich. The majority of people in his society were not well off, and this presented them with their own sets of temptations. Riches unburden the bearer from being overly solicitous about material needs. Proceeding from his own experiences as a member of the *voluntary* poor, he counsels the involuntary poor not to give too much thought to jealousy or the building of earthly riches. Hugh then strikes a balance in which he recognizes the difference between the issues facing the different social orders, and opens a window for the reappreciation of riches.

It was during this period that Aristotle was beginning to filter back into the consciousness of the West. Lost for centuries, the commentaries of the Philosopher had returned by a circuitous route from the Greeks through the Syrians to the Arabs, and then back into the Latin West in the Iberian peninsula. Aristotle's *Politics* and his *Nichomachean Ethics* provided new grist for the analysis of economic exchange. As we have seen in the first chapter, Aristotle could be just as censorious about greed and the merchant life as the most trenchant Father of the Church. Yet Aristotle was not bound by the weight of revelation, and couched his criticisms in rational argument. That these so often dovetailed with Christian analysis was the wedge in the door for the Greek thinker. Yet the Philosopher went further, and painted the picture of man as a naturally social animal, making interaction and exchange constituent characteristics of humanity as such. This naturalistic vision of social harmony intrigued the scholastic thinkers, particularly the urban mendicants, for it was a vision of humanity in its original state, governed by natural law, bounded by the irrational defects of avarice and fraud. It was a vision consonant with a Christian appraisal of society, albeit with a bit more optimism about the human condition than had existed in the past. Such considerations began to be seen with Robert Grosseteste's commentary on the *Ethics*, in the Summa of the Franciscan Alexander of Hales, and in the copious commentaries of St. Albert the Great. Indeed, Albert adapted Hugh's commentary on Matthew and fused it with an Aristotelian position. He noted that in the *Ethics* Aristotle had commented that the virtuous life required a modest amount of material means; it was nearly impossible for the indigent man to live the life of goodness envisioned by the Philosopher.[29] Albert said that while the tradition had aptly discerned the evils that could come from riches, one had also to be wary of excessive (and involuntary) poverty, which could seriously hinder the pursuit of happiness. This became such a commonplace that it even filtered down into popular literature by the end of the century in the *Roman de la Rose*: "The soul can be just as thoroughly ruined by excessive poverty as by excessive wealth; both wound with equal severity."[30]

Of further concern was Aristotle's outlining of the Magnanimous Man and the virtue of liberality, two ideas which, of all the classical virtues, were the most difficult to fit within the Christian system of humility and charity. For the Greek thinker these virtues were impossible without the guarantee of private property. Aristotle had demanded a "mean of sufficiency" for the virtuous man, and had rejected Plato's suggestion of communism in all things (including of women and children). If liberality was a genuine virtue, then such a virtue demanded something to be liberal with, i.e., one's own possessions (since one could not justly alienate the property of another). Thus private property was demanded as a condition of virtue itself. Aristotle had argued that private property reduced dissension, particularly between those who worked hard and those who did not. In that sense private property promotes peace and social harmony. In addition Aristotle noted that people take better care of their own goods than goods owned in common (one might consider the relative care one expends on a rental car versus one's own automobile). He also indicates that the possession of one's own goods brings pleasure, and that it makes possible the aforementioned virtue of liberality.[31] Albert takes these contentions head-on. In the first place he transmutes the virtue of liberality into the theological virtue of Christian charity. In one sense this is logical, for it implies giving of excess to those in need, but Albert never quite squares the circle. Aristotle had stated that magnanimity was a virtue that one is supposed to be seen practicing in order to become a great man. Even so, this tension was on the side of humility rather than in the fundamental area of giving of excess.

Of greater moment for Albert was the Philosopher's contention that private property brought peace. As we saw before, this seemed to be the exact opposite of earlier patristic and medieval arguments that it was private property that itself introduced dissention in the community. Albert reframes the question away from sinful acquisitiveness and puts it in terms of the virtue of justice. The hard worker has earned his fair wage, the lazy man has not. In a situation of communism the slothful man will get as much as the hard worker, which is a violation of the virtue of justice. Albert has turned the appeal to sinfulness on its head. The hard worker is not desirous of his wage out of the greed of appropriation; rather he is entitled to it as a basic requirement of justice. This undercuts the older appeals to universal greed and discord, and situates private property as a natural good flowing from the virtue of justice itself. Deftly, the Dominican thinker has oriented property not as a lamentable result of original sin, but has situated it as a natural precondition of the life of man in society. Albert is also wholly behind Aristotle's argument from productivity. The man who works his own land uses it better and generates more production than those who hold land in common. While Albert retains the maxim that in necessity all things are common, he allows the retention and use of private property precisely because of the current condition of humanity, and to provide for one's own family and for the poor. Albert had fully accepted that sentiment of Aristotle that liberality is the virtue that respects the mean as regards wealth. He also appeals to the tradition of the religious life, familiar to most in the context of chastity. Christ has sanctified marriage, but has *counseled* chastity. There is no obligation to remain celibate, but to choose to do so for the sake of the kingdom is counselled as a more perfect path. Albert speaks similarly regarding possessions. The giving of all one possesses to follow Christ is not a commandment, but a counsel of greater perfection. Private possessions are a natural good—they are not evil—but abandoning them for Christ is a better way. Albert also recognizes that different states of life require different amounts of material goods. The more socially significant one is, the more goods one may legitimately possess in order to fulfill the state in life that God has allotted to them. Albert condemns merchants nowhere in his works. He accepts the Aristotelian position that exchange produces social goods, and is necessary to human activity, and so *ipso facto* cannot be an evil. Evil comes from the intentionality of perjury or fraud, which can happen in many areas of human life, and not just business. All in all, Albert uses the rediscovery of Aristotle to reorient the whole tradition, preserving the vital insights of the past but plotting them on a new chart, using the rational observations of the Philosopher not only to undergird Christian teaching, but to give it a depth it had not had before.[32]

Tradition had held since the beginning that riches were distinct from one's use of them, and one's motives in doing so. However such a distinction had occasionally been rather hazy and indistinct, with some more puritanical and hyperbolic voices putting them all in the same boat. Riches *could* be used badly, therefore eschew riches altogether. Similar sentiments could be found in the *Contemptus Mundi* tradition rooted in monasticism (contempt for the world, so as to focus on spiritual things). There were temptations in human sexuality; better to avoid it altogether. Because of this, the distinctions had not always been clearly reinforced. Enthusiasm sometimes trumped logic. However, the incarnational center of Christianity always held: riches and bodies were goods, creations by God in the material world, they could not be wholly rejected. Rather it was the Christian's mission in the world rightly to order good things in their relationship to God. The Scholastic period was the age of distinctions. St. Thomas Aquinas strongly reaffirmed Aristotle's concept "Sapientis est ordinare" or "the office of the wise man is to order things." The distinction between possession and use had to be underscored and brought into relief. This renewed emphasis on distinctions, particularly as they applied to moral theology, was partly a result of the increasing frequency of auricular confessions. As seen above, this led to the birth of a extremely popular literary form known as confessional manuals, in which priests were advised how to handle sins confessed to them, in order to give suitable penances for the good of the spiritual life of the penitent. These demanded not only knowledge of the moral teachings of the Church, but an appreciation of the subjective conditions necessary for the committing of sin. It was relatively easy to specify as sins serious matters such as murder, adultery, and the like, but once subjective conditions were added such as force, fear, and revenge all of a sudden the moral calculus became much more complex. Canonists and pastors had begun in earnest to develop one of the most significant shifts in ethics: the centrality of intention.

Gratian had applied a heavy-handed definition of the merchant life: those who "bought cheaply and sold at a high price." He condemned this as shameful.[33] Framed in such terms it was difficult to separate the possession of riches from any conceivably good intention. Later Decretist commentators, notably Huguccio (d. 1210), penetrated more deeply into the question than Gratian's cursory overview (though Huguccio had the benefit of having another 60 years of medieval proto-capitalism to consider).[34] There were actually justifiable reasons that a merchant might buy low and sell high. If he added his labor to the price, that was legitimate. If he applied his craftsmanship in transforming the good to be sold, that too was acceptable. It was the intention that made the transaction evil or honorable, rather than the transaction itself. If the merchant was motivated by greed, then such an intention poisoned the transaction and made it sinful on his part. If however the merchant conducted the transaction with a view to a reasonable profit for supporting himself and his family, then such an intention was good. Huguccio had made a critical transition, drawing into sharp relief the distinction between trade itself and the intention in carrying it out. The effort to legitimize trade as an honorable course of action was gathering speed.[35] The thirteenth century had become the "Golden Age of intentionality" in ethical thought. New ideas that would encourage the recognition of the bourgeois life were coming to bear fruit. For the first time mixing one's labor into the product, either by transport, risk, or craftsmanship, came to be seen as legitimate grounds for profit. Perhaps even more significant for the future was the rising idea of the social utility of the merchant, and the benefit of such men to the state. The bourgeoisie were not merely to be tolerated, for in reality they actively promoted the common good of the community.[36] St. Thomas summarizes this transition well. While he makes deference to the earlier tradition which had viewed trading with suspicion, he went on:

> Gain, which is the end of trading—though not implying by its nature anything virtuous or necessary—does not in itself connote anything sinful or contrary to virtue: wherefore nothing prevents gain from being directed to some necessary or even virtuous end, and thus trading becomes lawful. Thus, for instance, a man may intend the moderate gain that he seeks to acquire by trading for the upkeep of his household, or for the

> assistance of the needy: or again, a man may take to trade for some public advantage, for instance, lest his country lack the necessaries of life, and seek gain, not as an end, but as payment for his labor.[37]

Thomas had distilled the developing line of reasoning by clearly drawing the distinction that had sometimes eluded thinkers in the past. Trade was neither inherently evil nor an unadulterated good. Rather trading was morally neutral; intention determined its ethical value. When intention was taken into account, trading could become necessary, good, virtuous, and even—as in the case of St. Omobono—a path to holiness itself.

DOCTRINES IN DEVELOPMENT

In order for this reappraisal to take place, the scholastics had to take a closer look at both moral theology and the nascent science of economics. Following Aristotle, they knew that first one had to come to proper definitions about the subjects in question. As a result there were several doctrines that had to undergo a period of examination so that they could usefully be inserted into a new Christian theology of the market, one that would undergird the developments then transpiring. Two of the most frequently cited examples that purport to show the "backwardness" of the medieval period in economic thought are the intertwined concepts of *Just Price* and the problem of usury. It had been suggested in the past that just price theory implied that there was a "natural price" for all material goods, which could not be increased without incurring sin. If a merchant attempted to increase his profit through a premium over this "natural price" then he was guilty of fraud and avarice. Economic historians have demonstrated how much more complex the medieval attitude was. It was as simple as saying that the current market price in the local market, in the absence of force and fraud, was the just price.[38] This price had to also be the common price, that is it was not privately fixed for the benefit of a few, but had to be the price that would be charged to people in general. This is where the "just" part of the price came in. Justice was the correct determination of the market price in such conditions. On this the mendicant theologians Alexander of Hales, Albert, and Thomas all agreed.[39]

All of the thirteenth-century thinkers agreed that such a price must be fixed by an *unconstrained* market. They were particularly concerned with the danger of monopolies, which unbalanced the just and natural market price considerably. In this they stood within a hallowed tradition of condemnation, stretching back to Aristotle and the Roman Law. Alexander of Hales even argued that monopolists be expelled from the Church, because of the grave injustices that they introduced into the common good. Albert the Great condemns monopolists precisely because they disturb the natural equilibrium by creating conditions of artificial scarcity.[40] Yet at the same time these thinkers were not advocates of an unfettered *laissez-faire* system. Deeply embedded in the medieval culture was the idea of guilds, consisting of men of a single profession banding together to assure quality, training, and the security of the members. Such a medieval solution prevented the rampant avarice of monopolism, while at the same time assuring the dignity and common good of the artisan workers themselves. It should be remembered that the goal of Catholic economic thought has always been fundamentally rooted in the dignity of human persons, rather than in the utter freedom of exchange.

One of the most mature exponents of this developing tradition was Giles of Lessines, O.P. (d. ca. 1304). More than any other mendicant author, he emphasizes the necessity of free agreement in the reaching of justice in bargaining. He rooted this in human freedom, in the implications of the possession of a thing, and in one's ability to alienate it without interference.[41] In this sense freedom was not the end, but the necessary precondition for the market to effect justice. Yet even at this extreme, all of our authors insist on the commonality of property in times of need. Thomas Aquinas stressed that it is no sin for a starving man to steal bread, no matter what the market conditions. Nor was there to be gouging. Demanding a pearl for the basic necessities of life was avarice of the most sinful kind. As always the standard was the dignity of the human person, a free individual essentially embedded in numerous communities.

The second key doctrine that had to develop was the teaching on usury, far more ingrained in the mind of the Western world than the concept of just price. As seen previously, usury was universally excoriated by not only the three monotheistic traditions, but also by the pagan philosophical schools. Aristotle's concept of money as a dead thing which could in no way reproduce itself burrowed deeply into the Christian worldview. The rhetoric against usury was unabated throughout even the thirteenth and fourteenth centuries, even as economic and ethical thought was beginning to make provision for it in a limited way. Though popularly condemned, thoughtful scholastics had begun a reconsideration of the nature and practices regarding money-changing and usury. In the first place money-changing was increasingly necessary in a society rapidly becoming prosperous and involved in carrying goods over great distances and across borders. In itself, people began to make distinctions between necessary money-changing with a legitimate fee appended, and exorbitant charges whereby moneychangers took unfair advantage of travelers.[42] Once again a distinction had made the difference; the socially useful moneychanger who made a legitimate profit was different from the exploiting huckster. Money-changing, though, was much easier to integrate into Christian ethics than usury, or the charging of interest for loans.

As before, scholastic distinctions began to change the way intellectuals thought about the nature of interest. Previously thinkers had speculated that the usurer attempted to sell time itself, a possession he did not own. However as the Middle Ages progressed the idea of a limited ownership of time, as measured by money, began to be permitted. Money lent could be considered like any other product. The lender experienced loss of use of that sum of money, and so in a certain sense alienated a certain period of time. He was legitimately entitled to indemnification for the use of that money that he had lost. Money was not begetting more money—

the core of sinful usury—but the loss of the use of that money was being justly recognized, and a fair approximation of its value could be agreed upon as a use fee. Later it was also admitted that the lender incurred serious risk in the lending of money. There was a genuine possibility that the debtor would be unable to repay the debt. Sometimes whole investments would have to be written off. The lender was thus entitled in justice to indemnify himself against this type of risk (it is not coincidental that it was at the same time that the birth of the insurance industry was occurring). There were now two titles to profit on moneylending, opening a chink in the armor of the blanket teaching against usury. A final development was in the idea of labor. The older model of usury was colored by the accusation that the lender expended no labor, and yet earned a profit, using a sterile thing to earn money unnaturally. As the thirteenth century progressed, scholars began to accept the conception that possibility of labor was extended to the debtor by the activity of lender. In reality labor was being made possible, and the loss of use and the risk run by the lender entailed a real type of labor transfer, which itself was able to be subject to some type of legitimate and just remuneration.[43] In the end, much like moneylending, the existing, concrete practices of lending with interest began to weigh heavily on theoretical appreciations of it. The rapid advance of Europe in the proto-capitalist period would have been impossible without the extension of credit and the lending of money, as indeed any complex economy is dependent upon it. It was the sophisticated distinctions that enabled the scholastics to differentiate sinful usury from the practices that could not only be tolerated, but could even perhaps be morally praiseworthy because of their contribution to social harmony and economic prosperity. As Odd Langholm, the authority on medieval economics, describes at the end of his chapter on the subject, "what is permitted for the sake of the common good, will lose the stigma of individual evil."[44] Indeed by end of the medieval period, it was ironically the Franciscans themselves, so long dedicated to individual poverty, who provided the essential practical breakthrough. Recognizing the benefits that accrued to the wealthy by the availability of credit, they decided that the poor should have similar aids. To that end they set up institutions that went under the name *Monte di Pietà* (mounts of piety). These provided pawnbroking services, along with small loans to the less advantaged. Seen in this light the modest interest rates charged were seen fundamentally as a benefit to the borrower rather than to the lender, and so would not fall under the prohibition of usury. In that sense the Church itself became one of the primary lenders in the Western world. Truly there had been a revolution in the nature and understanding of usury.[45]

The Franciscan foundation of the *Montes Pietatis* is especially unexpected considering the history of their own order. Founded by Francis as an expression of *minoritas* or absolute humility, it was intimately related with the profession of not only individual poverty but of common indigence. While for Francis this was merely an outward indicator of his own piety, for later generations of Minorites it became a neuralgic issue of epic proportions. In the hundred years after Francis' death, debates about poverty churned through the order. The vast majority followed the counsels of the saintly but rational Bonaventure, who realized that in an order made up of thousands of men, absolute communal poverty was an impossible ideal. Because of this the papacy permitted them to retain use of all of the houses and churches to which they were attached. This was a betrayal of the vision of Francis for some of the more puritanical members of his order. They demanded absolute poverty to such a degree that they ran the risk of identifying it with holiness itself.[46] This position outraged many of the secular clergy and, while the majority of the mendicants moved away from the radicals, still the controversy forced the Preachers and the Minorites to assess their position more clearly. This drove them to a deeper consideration of the nature and morality of property itself.

The radical critique of wealth and property put forward by the Spirituals drove the university masters into defending the natural goodness of both. Further, in their haste to free themselves from the shadow of a group increasingly seen as heretical, the Dominicans and Franciscans were forced to come to terms with the morality of possessions. In the first place, they condemned absolute communal poverty, particularly as it related to salvation. The Franciscan puritans came dangerously close to denying the possibility for salvation to anyone who had even a moderate amount of wealth. In time Pope John XXII (r. 1316–1334) was even pushed to define dogmatically that Christ and the Apostles held goods in common and were not practitioners of absolute poverty. As always it was distinctions that saved the scholastics. Evangelical poverty was a counsel of perfection, and not a commandment. If it were a commandment, how few indeed would be saved! Therefore the possession of property was a good, even if it were a less perfect choice than voluntary poverty. It was St. Thomas who, as happened so often, provided the balanced solution to the problem.[47] In the first place he saw correctly that both wealth and poverty were means, and not ends in themselves. Poverty is counseled by the Apostle as the means for seeking perfection, but even voluntary poverty can be evil if it is not subordinated to the end of holiness and instead becomes itself a cause of spiritual pride (as in the case of the radical Franciscans). In a certain sense poverty is bad, first because involuntary poverty can lead to vices such as avarice and envy, but further because poverty can impede the genuine goods that wealth can provide, such as providing for one's family and for the poor. As Thomas says:

> And since neither riches, nor poverty, nor any external thing is in itself man's good, but they are only so as they are ordered to the good of reason, nothing prevents a vice from arising out of any of them, when they do not come within man's use in accord with the rule of reason. Yet they are not to be judged evil in themselves; rather, the use of them may be evil.[48]

Poverty and wealth are then means to achieve the ends dictated by reason and subordinated to the purpose of human life, which is happiness in God. So then Thomas recognizes goodness within a hierarchy, the person who can use goods well has ordered them and himself rightly. He goes further on the offensive against the Spiritual ideas in the *Summa theologiae*:

> The vow of obedience is the chief of the three religious vows . . . because by the vow of obedience man offers God something greater, namely his own will; for this is of more account than his own body, which he offers God by continence, and than external things, which he offers God by the vow of poverty.[49]

Again Thomas has ordered things according to their proper relationship to God. Obedience deals with the highest part of man, and is to be ranked higher than poverty, which merely deals with material externals. St. Francis himself would seem to have agreed, since for him poverty was always the means to his most valued possession: *minoritas* or humility.

Later Mendicants of both orders followed this middle path blazed by St. Thomas. One of his Dominican confreres, John of Paris (d. 1306), makes a decisive move in the history of property. Known as a partisan of the French king in his quarrels with the pope, John offers a spirited defense of the natural right to private property. In order to undermine papal arguments of universal dominion, John argues that laymen had acquired just and real title to their own properties by their "skill, labor, and industry." By virtue of that the lay owner has acquired actual dominion over such property, and in light of that—underscored by natural justice—it could not be taken from him by either king or pope. Yet John moderates this seemingly absolutist principle by declaring that sometimes property is acquired unjustly, or that disputes about it can arise. For this reason civil authorities have been established for just adjudication. Further than that, if a man sets his own private good against the good of the community, the leader of the community is empowered to effect a just balance between common good and private possession. Hence, while people have a natural title to the property, their rights over it are not absolute. Their title cannot be taken away indiscriminately since they hold the property by virtue of natural justice, yet they are still bound to use their property in such a way that it is useful to the common weal when necessity demands it.[50] John justifies this in a traditional way, by declaring all property common by nature, yet justly divided by civil law. Interestingly he does not make reference to the division of property as descending from Original Sin. Duns Scotus (d. 1308), one of the most brilliant (but problematic) Franciscan thinkers, continued along this line of thought. Scotus is one of the fundamental theorists of *voluntarism*, which roots law and morality in the free will of the lawmaker. While this has significant consequences for ethical theory, what interests us is that Scotus imports it into the philosophy of property. He refuses to accept Thomas's argument that private property is a rational augmentation of the natural law, flowing from natural justice. Scotus, perhaps drawing from his Franciscan formation, does not root private property in either revelation or in natural law. Scotus instead roots private property solely in the civil law mediated by the lawgiver in any society. This has the effect of totally severing private property from moral considerations deeper than the mere obedience of the civil law. Property thus becomes not natural but volitional, based only on existing legal orders. This development places a wedge in the Christian theory of property, which will only widen with time, creating a virtual declaration of independence of property, and which would result in modern conceptions of property law as mere bundles of rights conceded by authority. Those evolutions however were yet far in the future. The significant thing here is that for both Thomas and Scotus, the concept of property had been transformed. It was not evil in itself, nor even a lamentable consequence of sin; instead it formed the bases of a functioning social order and, as such, could be the basis of social and even moral goods.

When all of these new developments are taken together, what we are presented with is a new direction in the relationship between the Church and wealth. The rise of the merchant class, the rediscovery of Aristotle, and the challenge of Spiritual Franciscanism had all done their part to promote this transformation. Confronted by the anti-material heresy of the Cathars the Church—as she had done since the beginning—ringingly affirmed the goodness of the natural world. In spite of their love of poverty, the orthodoxy of the mendicants drove them to affirm this position so deeply embedded in Christian history. By making careful distinctions when confronted with new problems, the scholastics were able to make the tradition flower once again, using the insights of the past as a way to understand the present. Henry of Ghent, an opponent of Thomas, had positively affirmed the role of wealth, in particular for those who have the care of communities. Much as turning the other cheek was a heroic counsel of *individual* virtue (i.e., I cannot make anyone else turn their cheek to unjust violence), so too was wealth a necessary concomitant to political and family life. Henry asserts that to give away wealth meant for the support of one's family is actively sinful (a lesson Peter Waldo had learned the hard way). Even an individual could not alienate so much property as to endanger his own bodily life. Property then was not only necessary, it was a positive good.[51] Henry also lionizes the means by which the wealthy contribute to society; for by their labor, ingenuity, and skill they provide products otherwise unobtainable. The merchant's activity is not purely selfish but, in the absence of fraud and force, is a real moral good. The rehabilitation of the bourgeois life, as a result of these and similar meditations, began to acquire steam around the year 1300. Omobono had shown how a merchant could achieve the heights of holiness; it remained to create a general rule to demonstrate how businessmen could be saved.

Omobono's case had indeed been extraordinary, but in light of the developing tradition a way had to be pioneered to make the extraordinary ordinary. Given the foregoing meditations one begins to see evidence of evolution in the common teaching about access to salvation then being deployed throughout the Church. Preachers began to employ these themes in their sermons to urban audiences. While not failing to mention the dangers associated with wealth, men including Giordano of Pisa preached that we know wealth is a good, since there were many wealthy saints, both in the scriptures and in the history of the Church. Indeed they used their wealth in such a rightly ordered way that he even suggested that the more wealthy they became, the nearer they came to heaven. Rightly used, wealth was a path to holiness.[52] Peter John Olivi (1248–1298) was one of the most plainspoken in his rehabilitation of the bourgeois state. This is particularly ironic because after his death Olivi's cult became something of a *cause célèbre* for the radical Spiritual Franciscans. Olivi directly challenges pseudo-Chrysostom, the source of so much anti-merchant rhetoric. The profession of being a merchant and the business of the market are in no way evil, but rather neutral. He admits that there are many sins that are proximate to the marketplace, such as fraud, lying, and greed. But these are merely conditions which color a neutral transaction as evil. In the absence of these, and in the legitimate desire to support one's family, the Church, the poor, and to uphold the state, the condition of the businessman is a good one. As a result, Christian merchants existed in a state of sanctifying grace, unless they themselves interposed some sin due to a meretricious transaction.[53] Olivi even justifies higher salaries for "white-collar" work even though it necessitates less physical labor. Their offices require industry and wisdom, and are usually the result of extensive apprenticeship or expensive education. The intellect is of higher value than the body. It is their expertise in management and production that entitles them to a higher wage, and thus their greater importance to the community as a whole. They are entitled to bear their office with the dignity which their profession commands.[54] Scotus is in complete agreement with this reasoning. The merchant serves the state with honesty and is of great benefit to his society, because of the knowledge and expertise he brings to bear. Scotus permits him in justice to receive even more in compensation than that necessary to support his family. The common good provided by merchants to a state was being increasingly recognized, and this service came to be seen as compatible with a life that could eventually end in eternal salvation in heaven.

The benefits of trade were beginning to be seen across Europe, and as had happened throughout its history the Church brought this new class of trader within its ambit. While it is true that simple necessity drove this evolution, it went deeper than that. The beneficial side of business came to be understood more thoroughly, while the ancient objections to the bourgeois life began to be broken down by the careful and wise distinctions of the scholastic thinkers. This trajectory, which the Church was able to hold together in the premodern period, later went off in quite a different direction. Indeed the utility of free exchange could come to displace the personal considerations of dignity in such a system. Morality could become subordinated to economics when free exchange came to be seen not as a means to human flourishing, but as an end in itself. This result can be seen in the economics of some radical forms of modern classical liberalism. The medieval Church did not intend such a result. Rather the free exchange of goods was to be conducted within an atmosphere that prioritized human dignity and that underscored interpersonal relations. For the medieval Church, freedom and ethical obligation were not opposed, but rather the Church began to stress human freedom as propaedeutic to virtue, the means and foundation for truly moral actions. Freedom was not the end of the transaction, but the means whereby it could become morally good. The end result was the vision of a new Christian moral economy. Property was common at the time of creation, but in time became divided. Such a division was good and useful. Merchants opened themselves to new types of temptations, but temptations can be found in any area of Christian life. Money, property, wealth, and business are morally neutral, and can be turned either to good or evil by method and intention. Finally, good merchants could have solid hope of salvation, guided by their exemplar, St. Omobono of Cremona.

Omobono's Later Medieval Cult

While the movement to place the bourgeois at the heart of the Church was much broader and deeper than the cult of the Cremonese saint, still Omobono's modest cult flourished. His canonization had opened the door for a reconsideration of many issues. It resulted in the slow recognition of lay sanctity. In the century after Omobono's death, lay saints were discerned throughout Italy and, later, all of Europe. This led to significant public devotion and, eventually, ecclesiastical recognition.[55] This increased perception of lay holiness was contemporary with a number of developments too numerous to go into in detail. The first was a nascent acceptance of the possibility of holiness within the married life. While marriage had always been considered an objectively less perfect way of life, its fundamental goodness was stressed against the anti-materialist Cathars, and in so doing opened the door for a reconsideration of the possibilities of holiness available to those in the honorable estate of Christian marriage. In addition the old lay emphasis on penance, while it endured throughout the Middle Ages, was also evolving into more active forms of piety and good works. As the Mendicants had moved from contemplation to action, so did lay piety begin to stress the corporal works of mercy, and the increasing wealth of the middle class enabled them to start and sponsor innumerable charitable enterprises. These included hospitals, orphanages, leprosaria, and even pious confraternities to bury the indigent dead. Indeed the confraternity became the locus *par excellence* for lay piety. It was the creation of entirely new communities, dedicated to pious works under the protection of some patron saint. It was these confraternities, which numbered in the hundreds all over Europe, which became the engines of charity that channeled the wealth of the Middle Ages into charitable activity, taking care of the poor, the sick, and any in need. These confraternities were a prime example of the positive ends of community in a justly ordered economic system, from the perspective of the Church. They provided solidarity and civic unity, joining the whole of the community in the great project of charity and salvation.

Omobono's cult proved a microcosm of these changes. After the defeat of the imperial forces in Italy in by 1266, some modicum of normality began to return to Cremona. Coming under the sway of the papacy once more, a series of bishops worked to re-order Church life in the diocese. In 1298, Bishop Rainerio di Casole held a diocesan synod in which the remembrance of

Omobono and Imerio was made obligatory at Vespers in all churches. This was another gesture of unity, foregrounding the two patron saints of the city, intended to encourage peace between the factions that had for so long been at loggerheads. In 1310 a statue of Omobono attributed to Marco Romano was erected in the Cathedral. Omobono was depicted not as a lay penitent, but in the garb of a successful merchant, and with his usual iconography holding a purse of money. Omobono was recognized as a civil patron as well, with a painting of him installed in the *palazzo communale* by the 1270s. He was included in the 1339 statues as a communal patron, with a law stipulating that offerings from the city be presented at his tomb every feast day, among which was the offering of a massive candle. In 1355 Pope Benedict XII conceded an indulgence of 40 days to those who visited the tomb of Omobono with pious intentions. This was perhaps in preparation for the elevation of Omobono's relics in 1356 by Bishop Ugolino into a new tomb, during which his remains were exposed to public veneration. During this period Omobono's home church of Sant' Egidio was finally co-entitled in his name. These events presaged a serious upswing in Omobono's local popularity.[56]

The very next year one of the most significant moments in the cult's history occurred: the foundation of the Consortium (*Consorzio*) of Saint Omobono. This was centered at the church of Sant' Egidio and Sant' Omobono, where a group of canons organized the parochial administration, while a group of laymen directed by a leader called a *minister* was in charge of the distribution of alms to pilgrims and the poor.[57] The confraternity was called to model Saint Omobono as a pattern of lay Christian life, both in matters of charity and in his opposition to heresy. They were to say five *Paters* and five *Aves* each day for the living and the dead, and were recommended to attend the canonical hours. Each Sunday they were to give an offering at their parish church according to their means, and at least once a week to offer alms to the poor in honor of God and the saint. The third Sunday every month they were to meet to have Mass at

Omobono's tomb and to offer alms. They were required to say extra prayers for the dead of the confraternity and to attend their funerals. Finally they were charged to fast on the vigil of Omobono (a common practice of saintly devotion). The *Consorzio* was particularly entrusted with distributing bread to the needy, a function it followed for the next 430 years, until it was suppressed by the Austrian Emperor Joseph II in 1786, during a period of serious anticlericalism and state interference in the affairs of the Church.

The extension of devotion to Omobono outside of Cremona developed slowly and unevenly. An interesting early example is a mosaic of the saint in the famous basilica of San Marco. Venice was one of the most powerful mercantile cities in the world. We know that a copy of his *vita* was kept in the library of St. Mark's. It is certainly possible that the merchant-saint's cult made inroads into the great trading city on the Adriatic. There is some evidence of liturgical remembrance in Verona and Milan around the year 1300, however the historical animosity between Cremona and the Lombard capital made it difficult for Omobono devotion to take deep root there. As Vauchez says, "it seems that Omobono, until the end of the 1300s, remained principally the saint of Cremona and of its people."[58] Yet a change took place around 1400. The guilds of the tailors (*sartori*) around Europe began to adopt Omobono as a patron. The final shift from lay penitent to active merchant saint had transpired. In Modena, Venice, and Bologna Omobono was adopted as a patron or co-patron of the professional guilds. In 1566 the cult of Omobono the tailor reached Rome and in 1573 the old church of Santa Maria in Portico was rededicated to Saint Omobono. Before the Reformation, Omobono as a patron of the guilds had even spread beyond the Alps, to French- and German-speaking areas. Emblematic of this shift is the prayer sung together by the Roman tailors' guild while on procession:

> O glorious Protector,
> Who, with needle and thimble,

> Worked as a tailor,
> Give us always good work
> We all pray together as one!
> Help us to earn our wages well
> With our work!
> Give of your graces
> O holiest Omobono.[59]

The change had been effected, and the evolution was complete. No longer was Omobono to be viewed through the older models of lay penitence and clericalization that we witnessed in his earlier lives, but now he lived as a fully-formed lay saint in the hearts of Christians, earning his keep as a businessman in piety and faithfulness. The changes that the canonization of Omobono had betokened had come full circle. The business of the market now had been plotted on the Christian map. The life of the laity, of the merchant, and the market—now within the ambit of Christian ethics—had indeed become a path to sanctity and holiness.

CHAPTER 4 ENDNOTES

1. See Giacomo Todeschini, "Linguiaggi economici ed ecclesiologia fra XI e XII secolo: dai *Libelli de lite al Decretum Gratiani*," in *Medioevo, Mezzogiorno,Mediterraneo: Studi in onore di M. Del Treppo*. Ed. G. Rossetti and G. Vitolo (Naples, 2000): 59–87.
2. Honorius Augustodensis, *Elucidarium* L. II. n 35, Cfr. André Vauchez, *Omobono di Cremona* (1197): *laico e santo: profilo storico* (Cremona: Nuova editrice cremonese, 2001), 28, n 31.
3. This is more than understandable, as Sicard was a product of a previous generation, and had other good intentions in mind as he promoted the cult.
4. Translation of relics recorded in *Supplementum Annalium Cremonensium (Ad annum 1202)* in Monumenta Germaniae Historica, Scriptores 31 (Hannover, 1903), 187. Also reprinted in Vauchez, *Omobono*, 114.
5. G. Voltini, "La prima chiesa di sant' Omobono: architettura e fonti storiche, " in *Omobono. La figura del santo nell'iconografia, secoli XIII–*

XIX. Ed. P. Bonometti (Cremona, 1999): 130–40.
6 See Antonio Rigon, "Religiosità dei laici a Cremona al tempo di Federico II," in *Cremona, città imperiale. Nell'VIII centenario della nascita di Federico. Atti del convegno internazionale di studi* (Cremona, 1999): 193–203. Cfr. Vauchez, *S. Homebon*, 40.
7 Bartolomeo da Trento, *Liber epilogorum in vitis sanctorum*, ed. Emore Paoli, (Florence: SISMEL, 2000), 83, reprinted in Vauchez, *Omobono*, 114. *Ex votos* are a token of piety, usually in the form of some offering left at a shrine in thanksgiving for favors granted. These can come in many forms, for example small silver hearts that decorate the shrines of Italian saints.
8 Indeed this is the book that St. Thomas famously declared that he would rather have in its integrity, than the whole city of Paris. Erasmus established it to be an Arian forgery in the 1530s, not before it had spent centuries as a source of theological authority. While the medievals were aware of its theological deficiency, the authority of the attribution to Chrysostom of the non-Arian parts was decisive. In fact the achievement of the Church in overcoming this work's condemnation of the market makes the creativity of the Middle Ages even more impressive.
9 Gratian, *Decretum*, I, D. 86, c. 21.
10 Cf. Odd Langholm, *Economics in the Medieval Schools* (Leiden: Brill, 1992), 42.
11 Gratian, *Decretum* II, 12, 1, 2.
12 See especially Lester Little, *Religious Poverty and the Profit Economy* (Ithaca, NY: Cornell University Press, 1978).
13 This pattern would continue in canonizations for the rest of the thirteenth century; all canonization bulls reference the fight against heresy.
14 For Durand, see: Richard Rouse and Mary Rouse, "The Schools and the Waldensians: A New Work by Durand of Huesca," in *Christendom and its Discontents*, eds. S. L. Waugh and P. D. Diehl (Cambridge, 1996), 86–111; and, Christine Thouzellier, *Une Somme anti-Cathare. Le 'Liber contra manicheos' de Durand de Huesca*, Spicilegium sacrum Lovaniense 32 (Louvain, 1964).
15 See Frances Andrews, *The Early Humiliati* (Cambridge: Cambridge University Press, 1999).
16 For Francis, see Augustine Thompson, O.P. *Francis of Assisi: A New Biography* (Ithaca, NY: Cornell University Press, 2012); see also, André Vauchez, *Francis of Assisi: The Life and Afterlife of a Medieval Saint*, trans. Michael F. Cusato (New Haven: Yale University Press, 2012).

17 See the essays in: *The Origin, Development, and Refinement of Medieval Religious Mendicancies*, ed. Donald S. Prudlo (Boston and Leiden: Brill, 2011).
18 Brian Tierney, *Medieval Poor Law* (Berkeley, CA: University of California Press, 1959), 58.
19 St. Bonaventure, *De Perfectione Evangelium*, 2.3, cf. Langholm, *Economics*, 159.
20 Jean de Meun, *Roman de la Rose*, lines 8107–111, cf. Wood, *Medieval Economic Thought*, 46.
21 Giordano of Pisa, cf. Diana Wood, *Medieval Economic Thought*, 43.
22 J. W. Baldwin, *Masters, Princes and Merchants: The Social Views of Peter the Chanter and His Circle*, 2 vols. (Princeton: Princeton University Press, 1970).
23 Leonard Boyle is the key figure for studying this genre. See the overview of his work in Joseph Goering, "Leonard E. Boyle And The Invention Of Pastoralia," in *A Companion to Pastoral Care in the Late Middle Ages (1200–1500)*, (Leiden, The Netherlands: Brill, 2010), 7–20.
24 See Thomas of Chobham, *Summa Confessorum*, 6.4.10, cf. Langholm, *Economics in the Medieval Schools*, 55.
25 Cfr. F. N. M. Diekstra, "The Language of the Marketplace in the Sermons of Robert de Sorbon (1201–1274)" *Forschungen zur Theologie und Philosophie des Mittelalters* 75.2 (2008): 348.
26 The classic history of the medieval universities is: Hastings Rashdall, *The Universities of Europe in the Middle Ages*, updated by F. M. Powicke, 3 vols (Oxford: Oxford University Press, 1936).
27 Cfr. Caroline Astrid Bruzelius, *Preaching, Building, and Burying: Friars and the Medieval City* (New Haven, CT: Yale University Press, 2014), 127.
28 Hugh, *Postilla in Mattaeum*, cf. Langholm, *Economics in the Medieval Schools*, 100.
29 Aristotle, *Ethics*, 1.8.
30 Jean de Meun, *Roman de la Rose*, cf. Diana Wood, *Medieval Economic Thought*, 51.
31 For an introduction to the difficulties surrounding the virtue of magnanimity in the medieval world, see: René Antoine Gauthier, *Magnanimité: l'idéal de la grandeur dans la philosophie païenne et dans la théologie chrétienne* (Paris: J. Vrin, 1951).
32 Langholm, *Economics in the Medieval Schools*, 172–75.
33 Gratian, *Decretum*, D. 88, c. 12.
34 Study of Huguccio, perhaps the most important of the decretists, is hampered in that there is still no edition of his massive commentary.

Wolfgang P. Müller, *Huguccio, the Life, Works, and Thought of a Twelfth-Century Jurist* (Washington, D.C.: Catholic University of America Press, 1994).

35 For commentary on Huguccio see: Wood, *Medieval Economic Thought*, 113.
36 One must be wary however of projecting too much into the future. This was not the Smithian "invisible hand." Rather the medieval merchant was coming to be seen as a coherent part of the fabric of the common good, which in the premodern world existed in a tense but real harmony with the good of individuals.
37 Thomas, *ST*, II-II, 77.4.
38 Raymond de Roover, "The Concept of the Just Price: Theory and Economic Policy," *Journal of Economic History* 18 (1958): 418–38, cf. Wood, *Medieval Economic Thought*, 135.
39 Langholm, *Economics in the Medieval Schools*, 202–05.
40 Wood, *Medieval Economic Thought*, 139.
41 Langholm, *Economics in the Medieval Schools*, 305.
42 Even today, airport money changers in Italy are called *ladri autorizzati*, "authorized thieves."
43 For this especially see Wood, *Medieval Economic Thought*, chapters 7 and 8.
44 Langholm, *Economics in the Medieval Schools*, 478.
45 For a substantive analysis see: John Noonan, *The Scholastic Analysis of Usury* (Cambridge, MA: Harvard University Press, 1957), especially when augmented by Langholm's study, passim.
46 The best account of this controversy is David Burr's, *The Spiritual Franciscans: From Protest to Persecution in the Century After Saint Francis* (University Park: Pennsylvania State University Press, 2001).
47 Indeed it was the same pope, John XXII, who canonized Thomas as a complement to his dogmatic definition on Christ's poverty. John was convinced that Thomas had achieved the correct doctrine on the matter.
48 Thomas Aquinas, *Summa contra gentiles*, III, 134, a. 6.
49 Thomas Aquinas, *ST*, II-II, q. 186, a. 8.
50 John of Paris is rightly recognized as one of the fundamental theorists of private property. Langholm, *Economics in the Medieval Schools*, 392–93.
51 Ibid., 251.
52 Ibid., 51.
53 Ibid., 355.
54 Ibid., 363.
55 For a consideration of these developments see: André Vauchez, *The*

Laity in the Middle Ages: Religious Beliefs and Devotional Practices, trans. Margery J. Schneider (South Bend, IN: University of Notre Dame Press, 1993), 51–84; and, Augustine Thompson, *Cities of God: The Religion of the Italian Communes, 1125–1325* (University Park, PA: Penn State Press, 2005), 179–234.

56 André Vauchez, *Omobono di Cremona (1197): laico e santo: profilo storico* (Cremona: Nuova Editrice Cremonese, 2001), 82–83.

57 It is possible that this group was in existence long before the formal foundation, since a similar group dedicated to the later lay saint, Facio of Cremona, was in existence before 1270. Ibid., 84–87.

58 Ibid., 95. For the later development of his cult, see Vauchez, *S. Homebon*, 50–60.

69 Ibid., 99–100.

Chapter 5
MERCHANTS ON PAGE AND STAGE: LITERARY REPRESENTATIONS AND THE CREATION OF STEREOTYPE

A Saint for Times of "Unremitting Transition"

On 24 June 1997, Pope John Paul II issued his apostolic blessing in a letter addressed to Giulio Nicolini, Bishop of Cremona.[1] In this letter, John Paul II briefly recounts the history of St. Omobono of Cremona, emphasizing that Omobono was "the first and only layman of the faithful, not to belong either to the nobility or to a royal or princely family, to be canonized during the Middle Ages." The letter, written in recognition of the "Year of St. Omobono," called by Bishop Nicolini and celebrated in Cremona from 13 November 1997 until 12 January 1999, is among the first modern Church documents to reference the merchant saint. John Paul correctly recognizes the "striking parallels" between twelfth-century Cremona and our contemporary world: "Although distant in time, Omobono does in fact figure as a saint for the Church and society of our time . . . because of the exemplary way this faithful layman worked and lived the Gospel perfection. The striking parallels with the demand of the present time give [this] celebration a profound sense of 'contemporaneity.'" Indeed, the profoundly complex economic and social changes faced by Omobono 800 years ago mirror our modern world in compelling, fascinating ways.

Our world seems marked by increasing disruption, dislocation, and disagreement. Although the blinding speed with which current technology develops has no genuine historical precursor, history is replete with examples of "paradigm shifts" and disruptions of large scale, including the printing press, the mechanical loom, the steam engine, hydraulics, and a host of other developments that anticipate digital photography, the smart phone, Uber, and other forms of "software substitution."[2] Chat GPT and other manifestations of AI will only speed up this disruption, eliminating millions of "human" jobs while creating largely unforeseen opportunities in the process. Each of these innovations produced winners and losers in the economy, especially when entire industries become redundant and then extinct. The printing press displaced the scribe, digital photography eliminated Kodak, and Netflix famously bankrupted Blockbuster.[3] Such moments produce obvious tensions and uncertainties, as traditional methods give way to new realities and the established order unravels, either at the margins or at the very center. As we have seen, Italy, and Europe in general, experienced many such disruptions in the Middle Ages, shrinking the distance between the world of St. Omobono and today. Pope St. John Paul II builds upon this observation.

Omobono sought to find integration between his professional and personal lives, a unity between the conventions of his trade and the teachings of his professed faith. The pope praises Omobono for the virtues he exemplifies to a modern or post-modern audience striving to find stability amid turbulence, including such obstacles (as we have seen) from his family circle, his parish, his work environment, and from the "market dynamics" inherent in the profession of a merchant. These market dynamics include the pressure of pricing and quality, supply and demand of labor and materials, and the injunction to treat people as ends and not simply as means to an end. The apostolic blessing concludes by noting that the turbulent times of the twelfth century serve as a precursor of sorts to our own time of disruption and change. According to the pope, the model provided by Omobono "is exactly what we need in the climate of unremitting transition that we are experiencing; we need it for developing the present positive premises and for responding to the serious challenges deriving from the profound crises of civilization and culture." According to the pope, the model presented by this holy layman makes clear that "sanctity is not reserved for some but proposed to everyone without distinction." In many ways, it is a stunning document and the reclamation of a history which began in 1197 and finds expression to this very day.

St. Omobono does indeed present a compelling model for today's lay merchant (and business professional, executive, entrepreneur, manager—anyone involved in the "world of work"), for all those people engaged in business and in the myriad manifestations of commerce and industry. It is a model worth recalling, especially for those who strive to find a balance between the often-conflicting dictates of the material and spiritual realms. As we have seen, for a variety of reasons, the veneration of Omobono never migrated far beyond Cremona or its environs; it certainly never made it to England, the United States, or the English-speaking world. In the absence of such a model, other representations of the merchant character in the English-speaking world appeared over the course of many centuries. A survey of these varied (but almost universally negative) representations will help place the life of St. Omobono in context, but also provide context to the words of St. Pope John Paul II.

The canonization of St. Omobono in 1197 remains a seminal, even if largely unrecognized in the English speaking world, event for the Church.[4] As a lay saint without ties to a religious or monastic community, Omobono developed his reputation for holiness outside of the traditional channels for personal sanctification. These lay saints were extremely uncommon and "were above all good neighbors, exceptional principally in the intensity with which they lived the common religiosity."[5] The bull of canonization (*QP*) places primary emphasis upon this personal holiness and the divine endorsement, both the "virtue of life and virtue of signs." Pope Innocent III especially cites Omobono's piety and his devotion to worship, prayer, almsgiving, the sacraments, and other Catholic practices almost to the complete omission of his life as a merchant. Yet in the years after 1197, new details emerged about Omobono and his reputation for honesty in the world of business, including heroic virtues that "saved him from the perverse and miserable practices of the market" and the pernicious effects of the world of commerce at large. To achieve such holiness, Omobono "did not frequent the company of worldly men, among whom he was distinguished like a lily among the thorns" (*QP*). He was, in other words, "in the world but not of the world." Even at this early date of pre-capitalist economics, the Church recognized a need to develop a "theology of work" and find models of virtue for the rapidly rising merchant class. According to Fr. Thompson, the early emphasis upon Omobono's "lay and civic-minded piety" also grew with later biographers to include his reputation for honesty in business, "thereby recapturing an aspect of his piety missed by the pontiff [Innocent III] but prized in the workaday world of the communes."[6] These workers now had a Christian model, one of their own, so to speak, to help them navigate the complexities of the merchant life. The emergence of "work from home" and "work from anywhere" in our post-Covid world makes this a more, not less, pressing issue. The very nature of work is under a massive, and potentially dire, redefinition.

Thus, this action, directed toward the world of commerce and entrepreneurial activity, sought to start an important conversation about the nexus between the worlds of commerce and faith. This conversation brought about, over the course of centuries, a more refined and nuanced understanding of the nobility of work and the virtues required for proper sanctification of one's working life. However, the effects of the canonization, while profound in Cremona and the surrounding communities, were not directly felt in Rome and certainly did not extend to the far reaches of Christendom. Yet the social disruption, the emerging economic and technological realities, and the rising merchant class were not confined to Lombardy and north-central Italy. These forces spread rapidly in Europe, creating new economic and political relationships, thus requiring new models for understanding this disruptive transition. Moreover, since any market can be subject to dishonesty and corruption ("the perverse and depraved practices of the market" noted above), the Church recognized the need for genuine human virtue to be part of that emerging economic system and the need to develop a morally sophisticated vocabulary for integrating work into the lexicon of the Church.

Twelfth-century Rome, especially the second half, experienced a time of abrupt economic change and disruption. The rise of the merchant and the merchant class upset traditional forms of economic stability and created opportunities for vast wealth creation and material consumption among the so-called middle class. According to Christopher Hibbert, during this time:

> In Roman society, a new force was developing, composed of craftsmen and skilled artisans, now organized into guilds, of entrepreneurs, financiers, and traders, of lawyers, lesser clergy, and officials employed in the administration of the Church.[7]

This new force was the merchant class—the very class in which Omobono flourished in Cremona. At this time, if one walked the myriad streets of Rome, or many cities throughout Italy, a vibrant, lively market would unfold. A wide variety of goods were available, as men sold straw hats and bedding, cobblers repaired and made shoes, fishmongers and fruit sellers shouted into the vast crowds trying to attract buyers. Booksellers and scribes offered reading materials (including popular guidebooks, of which a few examples still survive) to tourists traveling to the various pilgrim sites in the city. Organically and without central planning (absent even a clear animating principle), private enterprise emerged in a largely guild-regulated economy. More and more people arrived in the city, creating a need for additional goods and services, and merchants of various types and expertise quickly supplied that demand. During this century and beyond, the merchant class grew in size, scope, influence, and wealth. It was into this growing merchant class that Omobono was born and inhabited. Many of these merchants became leading figures in local and national affairs, often acquiring large fortunes and enormous power.

However, some of these merchants, it should be noted, were unscrupulous and acted without good faith or even a shred of honesty. Such unscrupulous behavior was often associated with merchants, almost from the time the merchant class appeared; as a result, literary representations often depict them as greedy, dishonest, narrow-minded, unintelligent, and even immoral. If Omobono's death represented "a spontaneous recognition of holiness," the frequent depictions of the merchant character inverted this ideal and rather created a near "spontaneous recognition for dishonesty and double-dealing." The notion of *caveat emptor* (buyer beware) operated in every transaction, and one needed to pay special care in the market to protect against the unscrupulous and greedy merchant. As we shall see, centuries of negativity reinforced this perception into a widely held reality for many social commentators and critics. The power of the stereotype runs deep and wide.

In the English-speaking world, the growth of the merchant class likewise flourished. The expansion of the merchant class, and its attendant increase in wealth and power, occurred largely outside of the Church. Although the communion of Saints was alive and well in England, the life of St. Omobono was largely unknown and the reputation of the merchant, as a social presence and a literary character, grew organically, in a secular fashion, apart from the conventions of martyrdom and hagiography. One notable exception exists: The Reverend Alban Butler (1711–1773) heroically chronicled hundreds and hundreds of *vitae* in his immense *The Lives of Saints*.[8] The sheer scale of Butler's work continues to impress, as his collections amount to over 1200 pages of two-column small type. The 1866 edition of *The Lives* contains an entry for St. Omobono. While Butler provides a decent narrative outline and makes some insightful commentary, the entry did not garner much attention in the English-speaking world. It spurred neither renewed academic nor popular interest. No churches or universities sought his patronage or his name; no academic scholarship or English language biography appeared.

Butler's entry does merit some attention, however, for the emphasis he places on the tension between the active (*negotium*) and contemplative (*otium*) life—the heroic struggle to live in the world but not be of the world. As we have seen, the early documents of St. Omobono's life all emphasize this negotiation in one way or another, and these documents stand, in the words of Doyno, as models of how deftly a saint had "lived an active life without falling victim to the secular world's temptations."[9] Butler begins with this insightful pronouncement: "All lawful secular professions have furnished heaven with saints, so that the slothful in all states may be without excuse." If a merchant such as Omobono can flourish and achieve sanctity, so can the reader.

Butler also echoes and even enhances the observations from the early documents of the Saint's life: "Trade is often looked upon as an occasion of too great [an] attachment to the things of this world, and of too eager a desire of gain; also of lying frauds, and injustice. That these are the vices of men, not the fault of the profession, is clear from the example of this and many other saints." Faithful, hard-working people of virtue do not grab the headlines in literature. The depiction of the humble, modest merchant character evolved in order to create more literary tension and provide dramatic contrasts. Over the course of centuries, the literary stereotype deepened to include a whole host of vices and deprivations. The primary critique of the merchant in the pre-industrial world (a preoccupation with business matters left little time for prayer, conversation, reflection, philosophy, or other aspects of the balanced, well-lived life), eventually took on a more sinister and immoral character. Instead of a naïve rube focused exclusively on commerce, the entrepreneur eventually became an active agent of immorality.

In literary terms, character implies a sketch of a personage who typifies some definite, essential quality. Character in this sense does not focus on the individual per se, but on collected, repeated, and recognizable behaviors and attitudes. Thus, authors tend to focus on a dominant trait or two, often at the expense of a more subtle rendering. If these traits are carried to an extreme, and thus resulting in caricature, the depiction will lose any authentic claim and become a mere shell of the actual person one hopes to portray. The author must, as a result, both capture the dominant trait without falling into cliché while at the same time avoid excessive distortion which can lead to the grotesque. If done well, the character receives depth and dimension.[10]

The depiction of the merchant character in English literature occurred over many centuries and in a wide variety of genres. As the following (largely chronological) survey will demonstrate, some clear generalizations manifest themselves: During this period, many authors displayed either indifference or hostility toward the merchant figure. The indifference, at first glance, might seem hard to measure. Given the vast literary output over the centuries, it would be reasonable to assume that literary characters engaged in business would appear frequently and in a variety of key situations, including roles of central importance in fiction. Yet the relative dearth of such representations suggests widespread indifference to the commercial side of life. Business (and by extension the entire world of commerce) generally did not compel poets, dramatists, artists, and novelists to explore the nature and function of the enterprise. Certainly such characters appear in fiction (as we shall see), but the regular, daily functions of business, including the account books, inventory control, pricing, strategy, sales, and marketing, hardly served as a rich source of raw material for compelling and poignant conflict. As such, merchants often exist, if they appear at all, as minor background figures of little interest and rather scant development. As such, the world of commerce and the quotidian activities of the merchant class generated rather limited interest.

When the merchant finally appears in literary texts, it is often with bias, even hostility, against those engaged in commerce and sales. While exceptions certainly exist, the depiction of the merchant character displays a remarkable consistency over the generations, indeed over the centuries. As seen in chapter 1, this bias stems from many factors, including scripture, experience, philosophy, and tradition. In reality, the practical demands of the merchant required intense focus on the world of work. The Church believed that the lure of worldliness and material wealth would infect many and lead them away from a robust inner life necessary for the pursuit of harmony and growth. As the *Quia Pietas* states, Omobono, this "holy man" deftly avoided these temptations and the subsequent contagion, as he "held himself aloof from the society of worldly men, among whom he bloomed like a lily among the thorns." In other words, total immersion in the commercial world often precludes personal holiness and the marketplace becomes a barrier, a real threat, to sanctity. In fact, most of the bull focuses on Omobono's individual piety and his participation in the daily life of the Church, allowing him to cultivate his devotion largely *in spite of* his profession. The document all but ignores his life as a merchant or entrepreneur. The subsequent documents, however, provide a fruitful account of the tensions inherent in trying to find a synthesis between the two worlds.

Labentibus Annis (*LA*) provides important details, including Omobono's family name (Tucenghi), his primary profession (a tailor, merchant, entrepreneur), station in life (of middling popular rank), and family status (married with children). The document provides other rich details. Omobono was a successful merchant, but after the death of his own father, and keenly reminded of the brevity of life, "his previous great occupation with increasing his fortune began to cool" and he began in earnest to distribute alms to the poor, giving his own material "wealth" to those in need. This transformation, however, worried his perturbed wife: "What madness has seized you Omobono?" She "poured out reproaches and insults" toward her husband and the home became rife with tension. Omobono had, in essence, suddenly departed from character (i.e., a total focus on business and the accumulation of wealth) and changed the script of his life (i.e., toward a more conspicuous inner life of piety and prayer). The model of heroic virtue does indeed require transformation within the individual and a corresponding commitment to stewardship to the external community. *LA* is thus a radical presentation and flies in the face of the typical, common behavior of the merchant class.

The merchant character presented in English literature both captures a reality and creates one. The literature clearly invokes commonly held assumptions and current reputations of the merchant. If the portrait did not have some genuine resemblance to actual merchants, the character would not be recognizable. But the very act of representation, of course, shaped and created the conventions of character—especially the outlandish qualities that lead directly to stereotyping. This occurs in all literary depictions of hundreds of characters, of course, including the ubiquitous students, lawyers, soldiers, doctors, clerics, but also the wise fool, the jealous husband, the clownish buffoon, the scheming villain, or the love-sick teenager. All types of literature develop stock characters and readers recognize these common depictions in order to examine departures and variations in representation. We can indeed find patterns in the depiction of the merchant character, and the patterns reveal an intriguing history. This survey does not profess to be a comprehensive and exhaustive coverage of all merchant characters in English fiction, as that would require a book itself. However, this overview will help illustrate the conventions of the merchant character and partly explain why the life of St. Omobono was almost universally neglected for the past 800 years.

"What a Notable Man"

The Canterbury Tales, written by Geoffrey Chaucer (c. 1343–1400) in the late fourteenth century, displays a remarkable panorama of English life. Although scores of manuscript versions and fragments survive, the first printed edition appeared in 1478, the famous text printed by William Caxton. Chaucer originally intended to tell 60 different tales, but he died before completing that ambitious task, and we have 24 stories totaling about 17,000 lines of verse. Chaucer himself was not a merchant, but he certainly worked among and with the emerging merchant class in his capacity as royal servant, diplomat, judge, member of parliament, and most especially in his role as a customs official collecting taxes at the port of London. In his profession, Chaucer would have interacted with merchants and traders on a daily basis, and his varied experience "explains the breadth of knowledge and the kind of temperament which made Chaucer one of the best recorders of the medieval world."[11] In this collection of tales, Chaucer presents a number of familiar character types traveling together to the tomb of St. Thomas Becket, the murdered archbishop of Canterbury.[12] Chaucer provides vivid descriptions of these pilgrims, including clerics (the monk, friar, pardoner, and summoner) and religious (the nun's priest and the prioress) as well as a knight, squire, miller, lawyer, franklin, and physician. Chaucer famously includes a wide "slice of life" from English society and provides details about their appearance, habits, clothing, and demeanor. The narrator largely avoids passing judgments on the characters, but rather compels the reader to discover the discrepancies and the ironies in each depiction. In the "General Prologue," for example, Chaucer describes the monk (a "sportive horseman") as one who spends much time outside (his skin was tanned) engaged in hunting and feasting. He disdains the Rule of St. Benedict and rather dedicates himself to earthly pleasures of food, drink, and clothing. He refuses to abide by communal life and possesses a pleasant and sanguine disposition. The narrator provides no overt censure for this obviously ironic departure from expectation and leaves it to the reader to detect the hypocrisy in the character. Clearly these depictions fall well outside of the hagiographical tradition and create delicious moments of irony, paradox, and ambiguity for the reader. Hence, Chaucer directs most of the satire at the clerical class.

In the *General Prologue*, Chaucer also includes a portrait of the Merchant with a "forked beard," an especially current fashion for facial hair, and the short description is worth recounting in full:

> He was dressed in an outfit of many colors, just like the players in the Mysteries, and rode on a high saddle

from which he looked down at me. He wore a Flemish hat of beaver, in the latest style, and a pair of elegant as well as expensive boots. When he expressed an opinion, he did so carefully and solemnly; he was always trying to weigh the likely profit to be gained from it. He commented, for example, that the sea between Holland and England should be defended at all costs. He was good at exchanging dealings, as you would expect, and in fact this worthy gentleman was canny in every respect. He was so dignified in his business, in his buyings and in his sellings, in his barterings and in his tradings, that no one would ever know if he was in debt or not. What a notable man! Funnily enough, I did not discover his name. I never bothered to ask him.[13]

Although a rather short description, the sketch itself provides an array of cultural stereotypes about the established merchant class. Chaucer here notices a manifest preoccupation with matters of commerce—the buying, selling, trading, and bartering. The merchant clearly personifies *negotium*—the active life of the world of commerce and industry. While necessary, *negotium* needs proper balance with *otium* (the philosophical reflection and contemplation about life and its proper meaning). Clearly the merchant places far too much emphasis on the external world and as a result sacrifices the interior or spiritual dimension of life. Business preoccupations, and a subsequent narrowness of life and mind, remain a prominent feature in most representations of the merchant character in literature. Thus, the world of business, and its many complications, has a limiting, confining effect on the mind and soul of the merchant. For Chaucer, the world of commerce is certainly not considered a morally or intellectually edifying endeavor.

We see this very sentiment in the vitae of Omobono. In the Second Reading from *Cum Orbita Solis*, the assertion of this theme appears. The document praises Omobono not only for his personal virtue, but for the model he provides others of the commercial class: "Pay attention that the Most High, through mercy alone, drew blessed Omobono to Himself, so that where sin has abounded, grace may have superabounded (Rm 5:20), *since it is difficult for one who practices business to divest himself of religious indifference"* (*COS* emphasis added). Business becomes such an all-consuming endeavor; one has little time to think or talk about anything else. As a result, religious indifference occurs from the very nature of commercial life—a spontaneous recognition of worldliness. According to the document, without heroic virtue and God's mercy, such a quest for individual holiness and sanctification would fail. The intense focus on business matters prevents one from fostering a rich inner life or attending to matters spiritual and not exclusively material. Chaucer's merchant fits this stereotype, for he always spoke carefully and solemnly, weighing the potential *profit* ("wynnyng") that might be gained or lost from any utterance.[14] The concern with profit thus colors all actions of the merchant and reduces him so much that he never reveals his proper name.

Chaucer's brief description also introduces the second primary stereotype employed by writers when depicting the merchant: The focus on the material, especially clothing and personal appearance. The emphasis on the material becomes abundantly clear in the merchant's dress: colorful outfits, expensive boots, and Flemish hats (in the latest style, of course). For such a "notable" man, the externals become an essential part of the occupation. His high saddle literally places him above the others, forcing the merchant to "look down" upon the world from his exalted position. The *appearance* of success takes precedence over actual success. According to the narrator, the merchant might be fully leveraged and even in great debt, but from external appearance alone, one could never tell. The emphasis upon the material requires some context, as materialism has always been considered an enemy to the cultivation of the spiritual. The Decalogue warns against the sinful nature of coveting a neighbor's goods and letting the material possessions have sway over the mind and soul. One must be in the world, not of the world, as the Gospel of John proclaims.[15] Even today, the phrase "keeping up with the Joneses" resonates with an anti-material message. In fact, merchants help fuel and satisfy these desires for material goods. In sharp contrast, Omobono does not wear expensive, fancy clothing (the hallmark of a tailor), but rather employs modest sartorial choices. The merchant of Cremona "wore linen and black lamb's wool, he avoided colorful fabrics, and wore the dark cloth of Bergamo." Omobono did not wear silk, satin, velvet, mink, ermine, gold, or any of the other conspicuous fashion statements so common among tailors and merchants, suggesting an unusual modesty and prudence.[16] In his deportment, he displayed a contra-conventional style and attitude toward fashion and material consumption.

Later in the poem, the Merchant has a Prologue to his own bawdy, randy tale. In his prologue, the Merchant rails against the institution of marriage and complains bitterly about his own wicked wife and her evil ways. He admits to "wailing" and "lamenting" his plight, despite being married only two months. The tale is about a sixty-year-old bachelor knight who decides to marry and takes a much younger wife ("she must be under the age of twenty"), only to be cuckolded by his own squire. The raunchy tale is replete with stock images, common biases, and outright chauvinism. It's also full of irony and satire, directed toward both men and women, both jealous husbands and amorous wives. Although it says little about merchants directly, we can infer from the tale that possessing property and a desire for an heir plays a primary role in the bachelor's decision to find a faithful wife who can care for him and "be a keeper of [his] worldly goods."[17] The young wife, May, does indeed betray her husband but her cleverness allows her to convince him otherwise. In the final analysis, the tale reveals little about the Merchant as a character per se, but his inclusion in the group clearly provides some indication of the status and prominence of the merchant in medieval England.

Despite the popularity of Omobono in Italy and the conspicuous rise of the merchant class in England in the decades and centuries after his death, the reputation of the saint never traveled across the English Channel and into the English-speaking world.

English Catholics at that time had a strong attraction to saints' lives. The early mystery and miracle plays often used saints' lives as raw material and these forms of drama actually served as a type of religious instruction for the illiterate and semi-literate. Peter Happe calls the plays "one of the chief glories of late medieval literature," and they surely exerted a tremendous influence on the culture, for "the plays were meant to celebrate the Christian story from the Creation to Doomsday, with two central peaks in the Nativity and the Passion of Christ."[18] In fact, according to Glynne Wickham, by the close of the eleventh century, "the idea of dramatic re-enactment of historical events as a normal adjunct of worship on major feast days had come to be widely accepted" in London.[19] The powerful presence of live actors on stage must have been a compelling sight to many thousands of spectators who saw re-enactments not only of the crucifixion but every major scene of Christ's life and the involvement of the saints. No play survives featuring St. Omobono.

In Elizabethan and Jacobean drama, the age of Shakespeare and his contemporaries, we tend not to find (for obvious reasons) extended discussions of saints and precise matters of religion on stage. A post-reformation England did not readily lend itself to robustly Catholic interests in public venues. To be sure, scores of plays examine the "supernatural" in various forms. Barbara Traister, for example, notes that "at least two dozen plays involving magicians, conjurors, and enchanters" survive and this suggests a compelling interest in matters spiritual but not formally religious.[20] The stories of the saints, once such a vibrant and essential part of the literary tradition, effectively ended with Henry VIII's break with Rome. As such, Catholic writers could not use the stage to introduce stories of heroic virtue in order to educate and entertain the faithful. According to Jose M. Ruano de la Haza, "hagiographical plays were an extremely popular form of theatrical entertainment in seventeenth-century Spain, with no real counterpart in seventeenth-century England."[21] This makes obvious sense, of course, on a number of levels. England experienced a massive shift in religious belief, practice, and sensibilities during the sixteenth century, moving away from the traditional Catholic practices toward a conspicuous Protestantism. This move entailed more than merely a refashioning or reconfiguration, but more accurately a wholesale rejection of many essential Catholic dogmas, doctrines, and popular pieties.[22] The pilgrimage site in Canterbury, for example, dedicated to the murdered Archbishop Thomas Becket almost immediately after his assassination in 1170, and venerated as a holy site, was destroyed by Royal Proclamation in 1538, when Henry VIII determined that Thomas Becket was to be "unsainted" and the shrine itself demolished. According to Robert Scully, the process was part of a larger effort to de-sanctify and de-sacramentalize the emergent Anglican faith.[23] All trappings of Catholicism needed to be erased or made palatable to Protestant sensibilities. This effort encountered many problems, resulting in a wide number of Protestant denominations.[24]

From the origins of English drama, the merchant character appeared on stage in a variety of forms. We find a "spice seller" (*unquentarius*) in *Quem Quaeritis*, among the earliest extant form of drama. The Mystery Plays (alluded to by Chaucer in his sketch of the Merchant) and the Miracle Plays both contained merchant characters, including one Aristorius Mercator, a Christian merchant who buys and sells merchandise all over the world, in *The Play of the Sacrament* (c. 1475–1500). Merchants also appeared in the *Chester Play* (c. 1475), where Jesus ejects the merchants from the temple. In both *Gentleness and Nobility* (c. 1519) and *The Play of the Weather* (1533) merchants defend their function as representatives of the commercial class. Louis B. Wright calls the merchant the "backbone" of English society and the new wealth allowed the merchant class both better educational opportunities and a public profile.[25] Even so, the merchant character rarely played a central role in the drama of the period and even less frequently served as an example of ethical and moral dignity. These plays, written and performed in Catholic England, did not seek to find a synthesis between the professional and sacred lives. The various Protestant Reformations obviously rendered any such attempts moot.[26]

Although large pockets of the population held onto their traditional religious practices for decades, England, by degrees, evolved into a largely Protestant country within a few generations.[27] By 1576, with the establishment of the first public theater in England, the Catholic hagiographical tradition on the English stage was, for all practical purposes, over. Public theaters became a distinctly secular endeavor, with tight controls over content and action. There was no space for a St. Omobono or his venerated merchant brothers to appear on stage, full of life and charity, striving to heal divisions within a community, before dying dramatically during Mass at the foot of the cross. Such moral edification would need to find expression in other quarters.

Even so, we still capture glimpses of Catholic religious practice and traditions on stage. Consider the writings of Shakespeare. Scholars warn against using Shakespeare as a "test case" for the entire English Renaissance and, true enough, he was one among many dramatists. But his range and influence on the English language remains unparalleled. According to Richard Lederer, Shakespeare used 20,128 basewords in his plays, narrative poems, and sonnets. For sake of comparison, Milton used about 10,000 words, Homer about 9,000, and the King James Bible about 8,000. Shakespeare was the first person known to have used about 1,700 of them. Thus he invented nearly 8.5% of his vocabulary. According to Lederer, "reading his works is like witnessing the birth of language itself."[28] As such, Shakespeare provides a useful point of departure for representations on the public stage.

Shakespeare necessarily avoided specific discussions of doctrine and dogma in his works; he was, after all, a dramatist and poet, not a theologian. If he was a Catholic, he was not free to be open and public with the expression of that creed and would have effaced any conspicuous doctrinal allegiance to the old faith.[29] Yet we still find poignant examples of the transcendent and sacramental in his plays. Weddings in Shakespeare, for example, tend toward the Catholic practice of the sacrament—as the language used suggests a holy covenant and not merely contract. Marriages in Shakespeare, for example, are completed in the presence of a priest and the blessings of the Church, as Friar Laurence famously exclaims in *Romeo and Juliet*: "Come, come with me, and we shall make short work, / For by your leaves, you shall not stay alone / Till Holy Church incorporate two into one" (2.5.35–37).[30] The comedy *Twelfth Night* provides a Catholic description of a wedding recently celebrated by an elderly priest. As the apex of comic confusion approaches, Olivia, secretly wed to Sebastian only hours prior, asks that priest to confirm the recent nuptials. The priest responds with a very Catholic description of the sacrament:

> A contract of eternal bond of love,
> Confirm'd by mutual joinder of your hands
> Attested by the holy close of lips,
> Strength'ned by interchangement of your rings,
> And all the ceremony of this compact
> Seal'd in my function, by my testimony;
> Since when, my watch hath told me, toward my grave
> I have travell'd but two hours. (5.1.156–63)

Shakespeare obviously drew upon Catholic wedding traditions and practices in his plays. But his knowledge of the "old faith" is more than examples of fossilized piety.

In *Hamlet* the dead King laments his early death at the hand of his brother. The late king rails against the injustice of the crime—a brother killing a brother—and the loss of life, crown, and wife. The king vividly recalls the heinous crime and the lethal potion dispatched into his ear, including "The leprous distilment, whose effect / Holds such an enmity with the blood of man" (1.5.64–65), leading to a sudden, violent death. But his deepest anger, despair even, results from his lack of spiritual preparation for death, including his failure to receive the three crucial sacraments considered essential for Catholics who desire a peaceful death and the promise of salvation: the Eucharist, Reconciliation, and Extreme Unction:

> Thus was I, sleeping, by a brother's hand
> Of Life, of crown, of queen, at once dispatch'd

> Cut off even in the blossoms of my sin,
> Unhous'led, disappointed, unanel'd,
> No reckoning made, but sent to my account
> With all my imperfections on my head.
> O horrible, O horrible, most horrible. (5.1.74–80)

The archaic language should not obscure the power of the words and the overwhelming sense of despair found in the loss of the sacraments. English dramatists largely refrained from frank and candid discussions of profound theological matters for obvious reasons, and such precise theological terminology occurs infrequently on the Renaissance stage. In fact, although Shakespeare used thousands and thousands of words in his corpus, he used the words *unhousled* (without the Eucharist), *disappointed* (without spiritual preparation, including a last confession of sins), and *unaneled* (with the anointing of the sick or Extreme Unction) only in this single instance. Rare indeed.

As a result of this lack of preparation, the ghost of Hamlet's father must pay a price, "doom'd for a certain term to walk the night / And for the day confin'd to fast in fires, / Till the foul crimes done in my days of nature, / Are burnt and purg'd away" (5.1.10–13). It takes very little imagination to conclude that the ghost speaks here of purgatory, a Catholic teaching passionately rejected by most Protestant theologians, in part, because the Bible contains no explicit mention of purgatory.[31] In spite of these rich passages and allusions, the vast majority of Elizabethan and Jacobean drama remains free from explicit and overt theological discussions and the tradition of hagiography on the English stage.

With one notable exception discussed below, Shakespeare largely avoids sustained representation of business and commerce in his plays. As a businessman himself (and one who speculated in commodities), Shakespeare created very few characters involved in the world of business. For example, in 2.1 of *The Comedy of Errors*, two minor characters (generally referred to as "First Merchant" and "Second Merchant") advance the plot in minor ways. The First Merchant reminds the audience of

Egeon's desperate plight and provides minor counsel to Antipholus, while the Second Merchant attempts to collect a debt from Angelo. In *Timon of Athens* (1.1), an unnamed Merchant converses with a Jeweler regarding Timon's generous nature and they try to devise ways to profit from it. Neither the merchant nor the jeweler shows any depth, and they exist as stock characters representative of greed and flattery—traits commonly associated with courtiers and upstarts. Shakespeare also used a generic tailor in *The Taming of the Shrew*. In 4.3 a tailor brings a beautiful gown to Katherina. Petruchio rejects the gown and rails against the innocent tailor for his insufficient efforts. The tailor attempts to defend himself before his hasty exit, but the character adds no real dimension or substance to the scene. These minor characters add some local color, of course, but rarely advance the plot in significant ways. Shakespeare was not alone in using figures from the world of commerce for characters on stage.

The Elizabethan and Jacobean stage frequently made use of this character, especially after 1600, when the merchant became a ubiquitous presence on stage. In his magisterial study, W. W. Greg lists 836 printed extant plays from *Fulgens and Lucrece* (ca. 1515) to *The Benefice* (1689).[32] This total does not include plays printed in Latin or the "lost plays" no longer extant. The surviving plays cover a wide range of genres and mixed genres, and they provide a remarkable catalogue of the various dramatic tastes and preoccupations of the writers and the audience. During these two centuries, England experienced remarkable growth and transformation in all aspects of life—political, religious, military, economic, domestic, and community. The stage in many ways anticipated and reflects this growing concern, as 95 separate plays contain a merchant character.[33] In other words, over 11% of all plays written during this remarkable period contain a commercial figure.

The above comment requires some context. Only a small number of characters appeared more frequently than merchants—including ship captains, maskers, officers, prisoners, shepherds, and soldiers. And this makes sense, as these generic characters are found in a wide variety of settings and genres. The merchant, on the other hand, appears mostly in "city plays" (a pastoral play, for example, exploring the richness of rural life in harmony with nature and animals, hardly represents an opportunity for a merchant character). Nonetheless, the merchant exists on stage in numbers greater than other recognizable characters, including barbers, beggars, bishops, cardinals, clowns, clerks, courtiers, doctors, generals, judges, lawyers, musicians, nurses, poets, sailors, scholars, usurers, and widows. Clearly, the merchant had become a ubiquitous presence both on and off the Renaissance stage.

Shakespeare examines the emergent role of commerce most directly in his famous play *The Merchant of Venice*. Although the moneylender Shylock attracts much of the critical focus, Antonio stands as the actual merchant in the title. His speaking role is rather modest (Portia, Shylock, and Bassanio all have more lines), but he serves as the catalyst for action. As the title character, he speaks the first lines in the play, as he famously describes his acute melancholy:

> In sooth, I know not why I am so sad;
> It wearies me, you say it wearies you;
> But how I caught it, found it, or came by it,
> What stuff 'tis made of, whereof it is born
> I am [yet] to learn. (1.1.1–5)

To this admission, his companion Salerio offers the obvious explanation: Antonio's mind is vexed, even tormented, because of pressing business concerns. Salerio employs common metaphors for the vexation caused by such commercial activity: "Your mind is tossing on the ocean, / There where your argosies [large merchant ships] with portly sail / Like signiors and rich burgers on the flood." Antonio's ships are so grand and stately (portly), that "they command the high seas" (1.1.7–10). Solanio, the other companion, provides a vivid account of the obvious preoccupation of the merchant and the hazards of the business enterprise:

> Believe me, sir, had I such venture forth,
> The better part of my affections would
> Be with my hopes abroad. I would be still
> Plucking the grass to know where sits the wind,
> Piring [peering] in maps for ports and piers and roads;
> And every object that might make me fear
> Misfortune to my ventures, out of doubt
> Would make me sad. (1.1.15–22)

In a few short lines, Shakespeare captures the central tensions facing the merchant class. Merchants must indeed spend the "better parts of their affections" in business-related activities, concerns, and pre-occupations. The merchant's life affords no opportunity for leisure and harmony. Antonio hardly relished life or has a tranquility of soul, but rather displays the merchant life as the "grindstone" mentioned in COS. Moreover, he has indeed fallen in the trap of the "snares of the world," a trap Omobono managed to escape. Yet the play thus raises the question: How can one both satisfy the needs of the market while also crafting a life with reflection, repose, and tranquility?

As shown in chapter 2, this type of unease—the incompatibility of the world of commerce and the world of tranquility—infects much commercial activity. According to the many theologians discussed above, these worldly concerns (and by extension, the worldly men of commerce) have a pernicious effect on an individual. As we shall see, once Antonio becomes fully immersed with loans, bonds, and lawsuits, he becomes trapped in a vicious cycle and nearly ends up dead. Refraining from this trap requires a special temperament and habituation to escape the corrupting influences of the world. Antonio, unlike Omobono, becomes ensnared in the deadly thorns and requires near divine intervention (in the form of Portia) to save him. Omobono achieved holiness, in part, from his refusal to engage fully in the affairs of worldly men; Antonio clearly failed in that regard.

Antonio however rejects these explanations of his melancholy, for he claims to be well-diversified and free from the uncertainties inherent in shipping and trade:

> Believe me, no. I thank my fortune for it,
> My ventures are not in one bottom trusted,
> Nor to one place; nor is my whole estate
> Upon the fortune of this present year.
> Therefore my merchandise makes me not sad. (1.1.41–45)[34]

For all his assurance about his personal prudence and financial solvency, Antonio tells a very different story to his dear friend Bassanio when he requests a loan to court the wealthy and beautiful Portia. When pressed for assistance, Antonio confesses that he is over-leveraged, and his current investments preclude any ready cash for Bassanio's immediate use: "Thou know'st all my fortunes are at sea; / Neither have I money nor commodity / To raise a present sum. Therefore go forth, / Try what my credit can in Venice do" (1.1.177–80). Antonio has every confidence that he will find a loan to assist his good friend in his quest, but his perilous financial condition and unease strike to the very heart of the stereotype of merchants. As seen in the *Canterbury Tales*, one cannot tell, from a glance, whether the merchant is successful or bankrupt. As a result, Antonio must project confidence and he willingly enjoins Bassanio to seek out a loan on his line of credit. This requires Bassanio to visit the famous Rialto.

The world of business and commerce in Venice took place in the Rialto, an area specifically mentioned by Shakespeare. According to Peter Ackroyd, the Rialto was the "power station" of Venice, "an island of money-making, from the highest to the lowest. It was a little Venice within the larger Venice, a vivid instance of the commercial life . . . with traders of every description."[35] By Shakespeare's time, the Rialto already enjoyed international fame as the center of the world of commerce and finance. William Goetzmann describes Venice as the epicenter of trading and finance, developing innovative financial instruments such as government bonds to help pay debt and finance government services.[36] As early as 1298, when Marco Polo was ransomed and returned to his home in Venice, the Rialto

> brought together shipping magnates, entrepreneurs, financiers, investors, speculators, bankers, borrowers, insurance agents, brokers, money changers, tax authorities, government inspectors, and even, perhaps, gossips, gamesters, spectators, and tourists to see the financial heart of the greatest commercial center in Europe.[37]

Shylock, as a moneylender, operates in this realm—the early modern version of the chaotic trading floors of Wall Street. After some discussion, Shylock agrees to offer the loan. Most of the scholarship regarding Shylock focuses on his Jewish religion and his status as a cultural outsider to the corridors of power in Venice. Yet in terms of the comedic genre, Shylock clearly fulfills a common role of "blocking character" or comic villain—the anti-comic spirit that stands as enemy to festivity, union, fertility, and renewal.[38] Shakespeare enriches the character in many ways and famously grants him a stirring monologue in 3.1.53–73 as he disrupts the stereotypes often found on the Elizabethan stage. But he clearly serves as a foil character to Antonio, as Shylock himself remarks in an aside very early in the play. His conspicuous animosity toward Antonio stems more from profession than from religion:

> How like a fawning publican he looks!
> I hate him for he is a Christian;
> But more, for [because] that in low simplicity
> He lends out money gratis, and brings down
> The rate of usance here with us in Italy. (1.3.41–45)

Religious tension, even outright hatred, obviously fuels Shylock's quest for revenge, but his primary complaint centers on Antonio's business practices and the lending of money without interest, thus reducing Shylock's own profits. The debate over the proper use of money dates from the time of Aristotle; clearly Shylock and Antonio have a very different understanding of the proper use of money. For Shylock, the accumulation of wealth is an end in and of itself. The purpose for lending money is to create more money to lend and to amass wealth. In fact, Shylock does not even enjoy spending the money on pleasures of food and material goods. His own daughter Jessica rails at this situation, claiming that "our house is a hell" (2.3.2), before she elopes with Lorenzo and freely converts to Christianity.

Antonio, on the other hand, views money as a means to an end: Money can purchase goods or services to enhance the ends of life. Moreover, Shylock makes money by making money—the unnatural use of money discussed by Aristotle and some of the Church Fathers (as discussed in chapter 1). Antonio, as a merchant, makes money by buying and selling things—material goods used in the service of life. Properly ordered and thus understood, the actions of the merchant in taking currency (passive, cold, inert, and lifeless) and turning it into material (food, clothing, shelter, among other things) are both licit and valid. His obvious flaws notwithstanding, magnanimity and generosity become his defining traits when dealing with money—as the means to an end rather than an end themselves.

Yet the tension between the two results, in part, from a fundamental difference in understanding the proper function of business. Shylock focuses on rules and the strict letter of the law. Shylock correctly argues that laws must be honored and allowing a breach of a valid contract violates the ethical norms of business. If Venice will abrogate such a valid contract simply to save Antonio, then Venice itself forfeits its claim to integrity, honesty, and pillar of proper commercial activity. Markets obviously require the rule of law and integrity in order to function properly. Shylock argues passionately for the full exercise of his bond: "If you deny me, fie upon your law! / There is no force in the decrees of Venice. / I stand for judgment. Answer—shall I have it?" (4.1.101–03). Antonio and his followers argue, on the other hand, for the spirit of the law—as they now possess the money required to pay off the bond many times over its face value: "I tender it for him in the court, / Yes, twice the sum. If that will not suffice, / I will be bound to pay it ten times o'er" (4.1.209–11). Bassanio and Antonio argue that the spirit of the contract is honored with this payment and that Shylock must accept the offer as fulfilling the contract. Markets and transactions often produced such varied opinions.

Portia, disguised as the learned doctor Balthazar, must arbitrate this disagreement. She reads the bond carefully, asking Antonio "Do you confess the bond?" Antonio does indeed confess the bond and the judge has no option but to rule in Shylock's favor. Of course, he soon learns that an entire and full confidence in the letter of the law presents unintended consequences. After Shylock rejects the spirit of the law and offering even the slightest mercy toward Antonio, the full force of the letter of the law becomes apparent. Shylock can indeed have his pound of flesh, but according to the literal reading of the law, he is not entitled to any blood. If he does shed "one drop of Christian blood," the bond is forfeit and the laws of Venice allow for the confiscation of all his material goods and the imposition of the death penalty. The letter of the law is a decent servant but a tyrannical master.

Yet Shakespeare also offers a possible solution to the "merchant's dilemma." The central tension in the play, it could be argued, concerns the letter vs. the spirit of the law. It's well understood that the rule of law and the honoring of contracts remains an essential feature of any market-based economy. Without the rule of law and the enforcement of contracts, any form of complex trade would be impossible. Commerce also needs capital in order for businesses to grow and expand. The Christian prohibition against lending money had by this time largely ended.[39] The play addresses each of these concerns and strives for a harmony, a unity, required of the comedic genre. Portia argues for the spirit of the law in her famous "the quality of mercy is not strained" monologue. Business transactions must combine the rule of law with the universal principle of mercy, a synthesis of prudence and charity.

We might even witness this same synthesis—the coming together of two disparate but ultimately compatible positions—in the life of Omobono. In the Bull of Canonization (*QP*), Innocent develops a new "theology of sainthood" by expressly requiring two distinct but related conditions—sanctity of life (as determined by the letter of the Decalogue) and supernatural signs (the spiritual endorsement of holiness). Innocent writes that "two things are necessary for one to be venerated as a saint in the Church Militant, namely a holy life and the power of miracles—namely works of piety in life and the sign of miracles after death, these are required." Shakespeare says much of the same thing—one must find a harmony between the letter and the spirit of the law. It's a lesson Shylock refuses to accept but one embraced by Antonio. The strict letter of the law allows Venice to confiscate 100% of Shylock's material possessions (fifty percent to Antonio and fifty percent to Venice) and sentences Shylock to death. After the sentence, Portia tells Shylock to "beg mercy of the Duke." But the Duke responds before any supplication and offers a new sentence, one governed by spiritual context: "That thou shall see the difference of our *spirit*, / I pardon thee thy life before thou ask it. / For half thy wealth, it is Antonio's / The other half comes to the general state, / Which humbleness may drive into a fine" (4.1.368–72). The wording of Antonio's response creates some ambiguity, but he too tempers the strict letter of the law with mercy, while allowing Shylock to keep some of his material possessions and then bequeath the rest of his estate to his daughter upon death. Antonio the merchant, like Omobono before him, plays a crucial role in this complex synthesis between spirit and letter of the law.

Christopher Marlowe produces a very different merchant character in *The Jew of Malta* (1589). Critics debate the scope of Marlowe's influence on Shakespeare and, more specifically, if and to what extent the villain Barabas ("a wealthy Jew") might have colored the depiction of Shylock.[40] Marlowe often lacks the subtlety of Shakespeare and the shocking treachery of Barabas displays little nuance or complexity. A figure of fantastic evil, Barabas is directly responsible for seven murders; he also poisons the water supply of an entire convent of nuns. He shows little remorse and no genuine sympathy for his victims' plight, rather reveling in the horror he creates. He is not a moneylender like Shylock, but a powerful and wealthy merchant. His economic success as a merchant stems, in large part, from his proficient employment of Machiavellian principles; this connection between wealth and duplicity, immorality, and treachery will become a lasting fixture in the stereotypes of merchant figures on page, stage, and screen.

The play famously begins with a prologue spoken by one "Machiavel," a clear reference to the teachings of Machiavelli, a name synonymous in the sixteenth century with evil, cunning, and amorality. The prologue defends many of the positions advocated by Machiavelli and utters shocking opinions to an Elizabethan audience ("I count religion but a childish toy, / And hold there is no sin but ignorance"). According to the prologue, the spirit of Machiavelli lives, alive and well, "beyond the Alps" and into France and even England. Machiavel the narrator prides himself on his reputation and brags that even those who profess to hate his "odious" teachings still follow his advice in order to advance politically and gain wealth: "Admired I am of those who hate me most. / Though some speak openly against my books, / Yet they will read me, and thereby attain / To Peter's chair" (Prologue, 9–12). Peter's chair, a clear reference to the papacy and the intrigues surrounding the papal office, registers the overt anti-Catholicism of Elizabethan England and establishes the cultural influence already exerted by Machiavelli within a couple of generations after his death. Machiavelli blatantly urged expediency and profit over and above morality and charity as the proper use and maintenance of power. This conflation of the merchant and Machiavelli will continue to resonate over the next 400 years.

The ghost of Machiavelli proudly boasts of his influence on Barabas and his ability to accumulate vast wealth:

But wither am I bound? I come not, I,
To read a lecture here in Britain,

> But to present the tragedy of a Jew,
> Who smiles to see how full his bags are crammed
> Which money was not got without my means. (28–32)

Significantly, Barabas accumulates his wealth not via lending money at interest, but rather secured through trade and enhanced by Machiavellian means. Barabas did not amass his wealth through usury—his accumulation of capital was not therefore unnatural, but it was excessive and exploitive. His wealth derives from trading spices, silks, cloth, oils, wines, and other valuable products, and exists as a legitimate practice, but a practice perverted by Machiavelli's teachings. While Shylock sees value in the money itself, the collection of the bond creates severe moral problems. Barabas, on the other hand, takes delight in his role as successful merchant, seeking solely to maximize his wealth. The conspicuous linking of wealth with Machiavelli will continue to color, directly or indirectly, nearly every presentation of the merchant character moving forward.

Barabas begins the play, alone, in his counting house, before heaps of gold, ruminating on the value of gold and precious stones. He grows weary of counting the enormous wealth and attributes his wealth in large measure to his Jewishness and the promised blessings to Abraham and his descendants as recorded in Genesis 15 and 17. The play moves away from the questions of trade and wealth and then verges into the realm of religious bigotry, deceit, and murder, but the conspicuous linking of Machiavelli with business success adds a significant dimension to the negative depiction of those engaged in business. For centuries, the name Machiavelli stood for treachery, cruelty, and deception of the highest order. In fact, within a very short time of his death in 1527, Machiavelli already had secured his infamous reputation. In 1559, the complete works of Machiavelli were placed on the *Index of Prohibited Books*, compiled by the Holy Inquisition in Rome, and the printing, purchasing, or reading of the text was considered a crime.[41] Although Machiavelli largely distrusted religion and had nothing good to say about Catholicism or the leaders of the Catholic Church, some Protestant reformers accused Machiavelli of being a Jesuit. Yet the Jesuit College in Bavaria publicly burned his books in 1615. For the Elizabethans in Shakespeare's England, Machiavelli was the consummate sinister Italian: spying, scheming, manipulating, and destroying.[42] The French King Henry IV, Oliver Cromwell, Frederick the Great, Napoleon, Hitler, Stalin, Mussolini, and Saddam Hussein were all compared to Machiavelli or influenced by his writings.

The Prince continues to sell thousands of copies each year, and, scores of books advocate a Machiavellian approach to business and entrepreneurship. It is, without hyperbole, among the most influential pieces of political science ever written. Clearly, Machiavelli asserted and continues to assert a spectacular influence over a very diverse audience. Yet this intense fascination with the modest book hardly engenders a uniform opinion about the actual meaning of the work. Although Machiavelli claimed in the dedication that he strove to be "absolutely plain" in his intended meaning, the renown social historian Sir Isaiah Berlin famously counted over twenty contending interpretations of *The Prince* published by scholars and critics.[43] Professor Angelo M. Codevilla, one of the many translators of *The Prince*, calls it "the fountainhead of modern political thought" and any computer search using the words "Machiavelli and politics" will generate thousands and thousands of references. Yet *The Prince*, written in the sixteenth century about politics for politicians long dead and largely forgotten, influences far more than statecraft.

Judging from the number of business books bearing his name, he may well be considered an important influence on modern business and economic practice as well. Considering the recent headlines and the spate of corporate scandals dominating the news cycles, the "ends justify the means" approach to profits continues to operate and these dictates often push individuals into reckless, illegal, and unethical behavior. Machiavelli always pays heed to the bottom line of acquiring and maintaining power; all decisions were filtered through this ultimate prism. Like the paradigm advocated by Milton Friedman (discussed in the next chapter), Machiavelli believed that each and every action needs to be considered on how it would impact the bottom line and only the bottom line of the ruler and the empire. Those actions beneficial to the regime and prince (and efficacious in increasing power) were praiseworthy; those that posed a possible threat needed to be eliminated. While Friedman asserted the importance of the rule of law and playing the game within the rules, Machiavelli believed the end always justified the means. In this way, Machiavelli composed one of the earliest SWOT exercises in history. He conducted his S (strengths), W (weaknesses), O (opportunities), and T (threats) analysis without the influence of sentiment or morality, and he presented the results of the analysis with all the confidence of the most highly paid consultant.

The esteemed political philosopher Leo Strauss created a minor tempest (as these things go) among academics with his 1958 book *Thoughts on Machiavelli*. The mild-mannered professor began his analysis with a striking claim: "We shall not shock anyone, we shall merely expose ourselves to good-natured or at any rate harmless ridicule, if we profess ourselves inclined to the old-fashioned and simple opinion according to which Machiavelli was a teacher of evil."[44] Strauss was immediately challenged by a wide variety of scholars and defenders of Machiavelli. Although the question still engenders some debate, the vast majority of my students do not agree with Strauss; most of them simply assert (or assume) that all politicians and capitalists follow Machiavelli's teachings: They simply accept at face value the premise that in the "real world" one must use every available means to get ahead and stay ahead and that the very system itself is "rigged" and those who profit do so by engaging in immoral behavior. In other words, Machiavelli just expresses the obvious facts of life—since the entire system is rigged, one must occasionally break the rules in order to get ahead. They believe that Machiavelli articulates the case for economic *realpolitik*, stating the way things actually work. My students are not alone in their defense of Machiavelli, of course, or in linking business success with Machiavellian practices.

A litany of books, in fact, endorse a proto-Machiavellian approach to business and industry today, and many more use Machiavelli as a point of reference. It is rather more surprising that these advocates employ him not only as a suitable model for business leadership and activity, but some actually *advocate* a clear emulation of Machiavellian principles. Alistair McAlpine writes about "the new Machiavelli" and the "art of politics in business."[45] McAlpine begins his book (recommended reading at some graduate business programs) with unstinting praise for Machiavelli ("a brilliant student of human nature") and then argues for a sanitized version of Machiavelli for leaders of business and industry. In 26 chapters, McAlpine explores topics such as "capturing a company," "stealing a business," and "rising to power." He places a premium on efficacy while extolling the virtue of profit-making and growth. Yet at times, McAlpine throws in empty pieties such as "good employers . . . strive to make their businesses into grander things than just vehicles for making money."[46] Machiavelli might disagree. Moreover, if one follows blindly the teaching and maxims of Machiavelli, little or no indication exists of how or what that "something grander" might be. Machiavelli offers no counsel and makes few recommendations about issues beyond power and the appearance of the continuation of that power. Virtue and the inner life receive short shrift in *The Prince*.

Michael A. Ledeen also believes that Machiavelli provides an excellent model for contemporary leaders. In fact, the subtitle of the book, "why Machiavelli's iron rules are as timely and important today as five centuries ago," urges a wider application of Machiavelli—not one confined to business but a conspicuous presence in the world of politics as well.[47] Ledeen seeks "to present the basic principles of the proper and successful use of power in language that contemporary leaders can understand, the better to advance the common good."[48] This is a noble aim and worthy project, yet it requires considerable mental gymnastics to bend Machiavelli and his teachings into a support for the "common good." For Machiavelli, the common good began and ended with the Prince and his hold on power. History provides ample evidence to suggest that what exists for the good of the prince alone (or the CEO and shareholders alone) is not always for the benefit of the common good; the largesse is not always shared between rulers and subjects, management and labor.

English Renaissance drama continued to depict the character of the merchant on stage right until the closing of the public theaters in 1642. According to Charlotte Coker Worley, the merchant character underwent a rather pronounced change from its early formation.[49] After 1603, the merchant is shown as "a social upstart, an extortionist, a usurer, a tyrant, and, at his lowest, a degenerate."[50] She argues (with mixed efficacy) that in Elizabethan England, merchant values of thrift, industry, honesty, and wealth were equated with Puritanism and generally praised and held in high esteem. As the tension between the Puritans and the theaters grew into outright hostility, the depictions on stage altered correspondingly. She cites plays from Thomas Deloney (*The Shoemaker's Holiday*) and Robert Greene (*George a Greene*) to show the positive depictions of the merchant class. But shortly a flood of negative characterizations written by Jonson (*Volpone*), Beaumont (*The Knight of the Burning Pestle*), Middleton (*A Chaste Maid in Cheapside*), and others appeared on the stage. By the time the theaters reopened in 1660, the largely negative stereotype of the merchant was fixed and surprisingly resilient.

This survey of merchant characters, not meant to be comprehensive but rather illustrative, expands in English fiction to include a wider scope of business activity—not simply the merchant or shop proprietor, but also industrial tycoons, magnates, managers, landowners, manufacturers, bankers, speculators, traders, and a host of related activities. Charles Dickens, among the most popular and beloved of the great Victorian novelists, combined fiction and social criticism in his novels, often focusing his attention on the poor and distressed. A prolific writer, Dickens (1812–1870) did not hesitate to criticize the exploitation he observed in England. Among his most famous works, *A Christmas Carol* tells the story of Ebeneezer Scrooge, a lonely miser in love with money and the accumulation of money as an end in itself. A moneylender by trade, Scrooge demands long hours and offers low pay, refusing to offer alms of any type, even during the Christmas season. With the help of the ghosts of Christmas Past, Present, and Future, Scrooge ultimately finds redemption and uses his resources with proper charity and stewardship. But the stereotype, indeed the very name Scrooge, became a vivid and powerful metaphor for the merchant or entrepreneurial class.[51]

THE MERCHANT IN AMERICA

In America, most serious literature stayed away from a close inspection of the business realm. One thinks of the splendid short story "Bartleby the Scrivener: A Story of Wall Street" by Herman Melville, an absurdist tale about a scribe who refuses to work and, finally, succumbs to death by starvation. While the work of a scrivener differs from a merchant in obvious ways, one can see parallels in the depiction of the corrosive impact of total work on the human soul and psyche. The scrivener was a professional copyist, and this required ample energy, talent, and fortitude. It did not require the business skills or leadership savvy of a merchant but does indeed serve as an apt metaphor for business alienation and the possible reduction of the human as a result of working drudgery.[52] In schools, an entire generation of students learned proper grammar, syntax, and style from the "McGuffey Readers," a series of primers used as textbooks for grades 1–6. Between 1836 (when first published) and 1960, scholars estimate that over 120 million "Readers" were published. It would be hard to overestimate the pedagogical influence of these texts, but also the emphasis upon salvation, righteousness, and piety in both personal and professional realms. In many of the issues, moral lessons emerged with a strongly Presbyterian flavor—thrift and industry will lead to virtue, salvation, and the Gospel of Wealth.

A related message can be seen in the famous "rags to riches" novels written by Horatio Alger (1832–1899). Alger was a prolific, even if mediocre, writer of young adult novels featuring boys who escaped the crushing impact of poverty not simply through hard work (although each protagonist displayed industry and enterprise) but generally as a result of bravery or honesty. The most successful book in the series, *Ragged Dick* (1868), became a foundational myth of the American spirit: In a land of opportunity, anyone can succeed if animated by virtue and the genuine desire for self-improvement. Thus, the industry required by business was a means to the end of middle-class comfort and stability, provided by Max Weber and his notion of the "Protestant work ethic" engendered by resiliency and fortitude.[53] These were not part of the fairy tale genre—no one married a prince, retired to a palace and lived happily ever after—but were grounded in a reality that allowed thousands of young people the opportunity to prosper and raise themselves into another station in life. Alger was far from a great prose stylist, and each book simply repeated the same themes over and over, changing only bare elements of plot, location, and character. But the basic plot line of "luck and pluck" (good fortune aided by grit) resonated with readers, for his books sold over 17,000,000 copies and presented the world of commerce and industry as an opportunity for advancement and self-improvement. However, the reading audience eventually tired of the redundancy and moved on to other types of fiction, as the unbridled optimism and confidence in economic stability faded. In fact, the world of commerce and the potential alienation in business was about to gain a leading man.

On 10 February 1949, Arthur Miller's play *The Death of a Salesman* debuted to critical and commercial success in New York City at the Morosco Theater. Perhaps the most biting and melancholic depiction of the world of commerce in modern literature, *The Death of a Salesman* continues to receive robust scholarly attention and numerous theatrical revivals. Miller's nuanced depiction of Willy, however, defies any monolithic critical pronouncement. Critics view Willy Loman, the play's protagonist, in a wide variety of ways: hero, coward, victim, dreamer, pathetic loser, deceiver, fatalist, enigma, minion, Luddite, lemming, and even tyrant.[54] Two things, however, are certain: Willy Loman is a salesman, and he is ill-suited for his job. The play uses the activity of sales, and by extension, the role of free market in commercial activity, as a backdrop for discussing significant social and psychological issues, including family, love, fidelity, betrayal, happiness, disillusionment, and the American dream. Although Miller, by his own admission, intended the play as a critique of the brutality of capitalism, the text itself hardly supports such an unmediated reading.[55] Not all characters in the play suffer from despair and alienation—many of them seem to navigate the world quite well.

The haunting drama maintains its power and poignancy to this day as it explores basic issues confronting people and families of all types. The play begins with an exhausted Willy, utterly deflated by life and overwhelmed with a sense of defeat and sadness—not unlike Antonio's lament that begins the *Merchant of Venice*. Linda, Willy's devoted wife, pleads with him to "rest your mind."[56] This comment registers a repeated theme found in "merchant depictions" from all periods—a belief that the overwhelming demands of business infect the mind and become all-consuming, leaving little space for reflection, tranquility, or *otium*. In fact, Willy displays a fanatical preoccupation with his career, sales, money, reputation, image, appearance, and all the external trapping of success and status. Linda Uranga observes this misplaced emphasis:

> Willy's decision to pursue capitalism's materialistic values is based on what wealth represents to him—being respect and "well-liked," which are merely exterior trappings that mask Willy's deeper emotional needs. . . . A free market holds few guarantees of financial security and no guarantees of emotional satisfaction. Brought on by his lack of introspection and ready acceptance of popular societal values, Willy mistakenly focuses on only one aspect of the human condition, the material.[57]

The play provides ample evidence to support such an argument. Willy's preoccupation with image, status, social standing, and popularity privileges the external trappings over the life of the mind. Using such externals as the only measure of success destroys not only Willy but perhaps the next generation of the Loman family as well. As the life of Omobono suggests, material accumulation by itself cannot produce contentment or tranquility.

Willy's son Biff keenly recognizes this misplaced attention and strongly desires to escape the legacy of futility and materialism associated in the play with the world of commerce. Early in the first act, Biff (who at 34 has never held a serious job and remains a drifter and petty thief) vents to his brother Happy:

> I spent six or seven years after high school trying to work myself up. Shipping clerk, salesman, business of one kind or another. And it's a measly manner of existence. To get on that subway on the hot mornings in summer. To devote your whole life to keeping stock, or making phone calls, or selling or buying. To suffer fifty weeks of the year for the sake of a two-week vacation . . . and always to have to get ahead of the next fella. And still—that's how you build a future.[58]

In terms of the proper understanding of career, work/life balance, charity, stewardship, and entrepreneurial drive, Biff's comments not only fall woefully short of the model offered by Omobono, but represent the nadir, even the death, of the American dream. Biff lacked the fortitude required by life (and the free economy) and, as a result, never managed to flourish in his career or in his own personal life. Ernest Hemingway once wrote that "the world breaks everybody and afterward many are strong in the broken places." The members of the Loman family never read Hemingway.

Biff's non-conformity does not find expression in the life of Willy: He tried, unsuccessfully, to be a salesman. He proudly points to the fact that he has spent the prime years of his adult life working for the Wagner family firm, selling the same line of products for nearly 34 years. Willy realizes, rather pathetically, that he has no natural skills for sales—he talks too much, he's fat, shabbily dressed, and "people don't seem to take to me."[59] His redemption, he believes, is the fidelity he shows to the firm and his loyalty ought to be returned: "You can't eat the orange and throw the peel away—a man is not a piece of fruit!"[60] But that's precisely what happens when we eat fruit—we throw away the peel. The painful discussion with Howard, his boss and the son of the founder, dramatizes his brutal descent. Here Willy humiliates himself, first by asking for a promotion from road sales to in-store sales, then being removed from salary to straight commission, and finally losing his job outright, ultimately breaking his spirit. Willy grovels and reflects on the nature of sales as a calling, a profession ("I realized that selling was the greatest career a man could want") until Howard tells him the hard, painful truth: "I don't want you to represent us. I've been meaning to tell you for a long time now."[61] It takes a short moment for the full weight of the words to sink in, for if Willy understands one thing, "business is business." At this point Willy finally understands his predicament: The market does not reward dreams and desires; it rewards hard work and talent.

Willy's downward spiral quickens, and he moves from despair, thoughts about suicide, to actually committing suicide for the $20,000 life insurance money. It's a painful story and many believe an accurate indictment of business, commerce, and the free market. For many, Willy is the victim, and he bears no responsibility for his failed life. In fact, Willy has become a metaphor for disillusionment in the commercial sphere, further propagating the stereotype of the evil machinations of the cold, unfeeling market. Generations of readers believe that the market not only created the shell of humanity called Willy Loman, but the essential nature of the market itself cannot be reconciled with individual dignity, a healthy interior life, material comfort, and human happiness. Critics see the "ruthless capitalism" in the play as a devastating critique of an entire economic system.[62] Since few critics see business as a morally serious or complex undertaking, they easily assign blame to the nameless and faceless tyranny of the market. Such reductive readings miss several important points. First, a few characters in the play seem to have navigated the complexities of the world in a successful and healthy way. Ben, Howard, Bernard, and Dave have far more success than Willy, and they all participate in the same economic system. Charley, the happy, prosperous neighbor, "functions well in the capitalistic system, [and] despite his evident success, he has not lost his capacity to feel, help, and sympathize with those who have not succeeded in it."[63] Such success obviously escapes Willy and his children, for they each lack the skills, virtues, and vocabulary necessary for such lasting success.

After the debut of this play, the depictions of merchants in serious literature morphed from the provincially small-minded person of business largely consumed with the mundane issues, then into the alienated, feeble salesman, and finally into the Machiavellian, immoral Wall Street dynamo. The entrepreneurial class, in this rendition, becomes the new villain, the personification of greed, gluttony, and avarice, one who lives a life of misguided debauchery, not concerned with basic morality, human dignity, and legal restrictions. The setting is almost always New York City—the epicenter of finance—and the antagonists are universally solipsistic and greedy. The characters become grotesque distortions of the free economy, rather than its natural projection or teleological end. In these cases, "Wall Street" stands as code word for a wide variety of careers covering the entire spectrum of finance and business. In the extended sense, Wall Street includes CEOs (and the entire C Suite in general), but also bankers (commercial and investment), bond traders and bond sellers, stockbrokers, government regulators, and an entire array of people involved in the vast financial network. Thus, "Wall Street" becomes a powerful metonym to cover a host of real and perceived sins, a convenient shorthand for anyone profiting from the free economy and private enterprise. In the hands of a talented writer, the excesses of Wall Street made for exciting, powerful copy. The curtain to this universe was vividly pulled back by a writer born and raised in Richmond, Virginia, worlds away from the financial epicenter of New York City.

Tom Wolfe's best-selling *The Bonfire of the Vanities* (1987) explores racial tension, social class, religious hypocrisy, and corrupt politics in a stark, unrelenting fashion.[64] Wolfe takes his title from the actual bonfires used to destroy the objects of vanity (including, but not limited to, fashion, art, make-up, playing cards, fiction, etc.), most famously led by the charismatic Dominican Girolano Savonarola in Florence in 1497.[65] Savonarola urges his followers to destroy all vain objects and the trappings of wealth and conspicuous consumption, any item that might lead to an occasion of sin or create a false idol.[66] But as Wolfe himself states, he also means another bonfire, a "corruption from within," a form of vanity where the inferno is internal and first destroys the soul and the conscience.[67] In the novel, this internal corruption touches everyone and spontaneously infects. Wolfe sets the novel in New York City, surely the most cosmopolitan city in America, the undisputed financial capital of the world, and ground zero for wealth and materialism such as expensive suits, sleek automobiles, world travel, and lurid excess. The protagonist, uber-successful bond trader Sherman McCoy, personifies the appalling excesses of Wall Street and amoral attitude of the successful.[68] Wolfe famously calls the men in the novel (and they are all men) "Masters of the Universe"—for they control the economic levers, and their wealth means that normal rules of morality, custom, and decency simply do not apply to them. These "masters," adeptly manipulate the levers of finance, perverting a free economy, and thus preventing it from functioning properly. But this manipulation, far from irregular, becomes a sign of grace among the initiated.

Sherman has his epiphany, and it does indeed sound like a religious experience, after a particularly lucrative trade. The name "Masters of the Universe" comes from a set of plastic dolls akin to rapacious superheroes:

> They were unusually vulgar, even for plastic toys. Yet one fine day, in a fit of euphoria, after he had picked up the telephone and taken an order for zero-coupon bonds

that had brought him a $50,000 commission, *just like that*, this very phrase bubbled up into his brain. On Wall Street he and a few others—how many?—three hundred, four hundred, five hundred?—had become precisely that . . . Masters of the Universe. There was . . . no limit whatsoever![69]

This monologue, an interior stream-of-consciousness, gives expression to sentiments McCoy would never utter out loud, granting them a measure of unmediated, unfiltered honesty, a stark contrast to the deceit, hypocrisy, and dishonesty of normal life. Using this attitude as fuel for his desires, Sherman justifies his mansion, his new Mercedes, his expensive clothing, and even his adulterous affair. Surely, as a Master of the Universe, his wife would not only understand but even encourage these endeavors. All he needed to do was *explain* it to her, to show her that he simply "deserves *more* from time to time, when the spirit moves [him]."[70] This sense of perverse entitlement results from wealth and the ability to manipulate the financial markets for personal gain. Thus, the Master of the Universe rules his empire from the 50th floor in the offices of Pierce and Pierce.

McCoy does indeed have a throne befitting a lord, the bond trading room, where the roars of profit "filled Sherman's soul with hope, confidence, esprit de corps, and righteousness."[71] Wolfe brilliantly captures the sights and sounds of privilege at Pierce and Pierce, the raw and unfettered warriors, the seekers of profit overcoming all obstacles; in doing so, he completes the vivid and powerful stereotype, full of bigotry and bias, directed toward an entire profession. The warped sense of morality saturates the novel, even in the descriptions of the office and the splendid, expensive decorations. Sherman's inflated sense of self masks significant insecurity, but his persona projects confidence, success, and power. Masters of the Universe did not and were not expected to observe conventional morality, especially in matters sexual:

> Technically, he had been unfaithful to his wife. Well sure
> ... but who could remain monogamous with this, this,
> this *tidal wave* of concupiscence rolling across the world?
> A Master of the Universe couldn't be a saint, after all ...
> It was unavoidable. You can't dodge snowflakes, and
> this was a blizzard! He had merely been caught at it, that
> was all, or halfway caught at it. It meant nothing. It had
> no moral dimension.[72]

Notice the assertion: The life of a successful Wall Street bond trader precludes a life of morality, let alone a quest for sanctity. The two activities—the active life of *negotium* and the contemplative life of *otium*—were, in the final analysis, simply impossible for Sherman McCoy to reconcile.

The depiction owes something to the concept of *ubermensch*, found in Friedrich Nietzsche's *Thus Spoke Zarathustra* or the related notion of "The Great Man Theory." Briefly considered, the *ubermensch*—the overman or superman—would not direct his intellect, powers, or vision to a future world (such as the Christian heaven), but rather focus on the present world and moving beyond the stale conventions of stale morality or polite civility, resulting in an effort to transcend and efface the limitations placed by society and religion.[73] The exalted man ought to act not according to social dictates, but rather the requirements of greatness. Sherman, the Wall Street *ubermensch*, has his own moral calculus, even if his wife fails to understand, yet alone appreciate, his significance, "moving the lever that moves the world was what he was doing"[74] and this, by extension, made him a god: "As the number one bond salesman, Sherman had no official rank. Nevertheless, he occupied a moral eminence."[75] The apotheosis of Sherman McCoy, the colossus astride the greatest financial city in the world, exists for a very brief time; his downfall is as quick as it is deep.

Sherman's meticulously created world crashes as lust, fear, and death combine on a dark street, late at night in the Bronx. At the end of the novel, Sherman exists only as a bitter, broken man—divorced, friendless, penniless, and on trial. His life, in utter ruins, reduced to a news story found (appropriately) on "page B1 of the Metropolitan News section of the New York Times." No longer front-page material, Sherman, the "patrician figure," now lives a greatly "diminished lifestyle" and rails against the tyranny of the corrupt legal system and calls himself a "professional defendant," a modern-day Sisyphus, punished by the gods for his crimes, sentenced to a life of perpetual struggle against an unyielding and impossible task. In a prophetic way, the ending resembles the lives of Jeff Skilling, Ken Lay, Michael Milken, Bernie Madoff, and scores of other wealthy, educated executives who ended up in jail for legal and moral transgressions. Thus, the novel resembles the "morality tale" genre, a genre used frequently in the Middles Ages, a time when gesture and symbol played a powerful role in the largely unlettered, illiterate world. Wolfe seems to imply that our own world resembles the Middle Ages, with a small number of lords exercising dominion over exploited serfs and vassals. In another sense, however, we might need such powerful symbols and images, for we no longer can read the laws of ethics, morality, stewardship, justice, decency, and prudence.[76] We have no modern-day Omobono to provide clarity in these complex times; we no longer have the credible examples of heroic virtue, for the sound and fury of excess does not allow us to differentiate between the noise and the signal.[77]

Michael Lewis's *Liar's Poker* (1989), an intelligent, funny, satirical, and unsettling memoir of his experiences as a bond salesman for Salomon Brothers, covers some of the exact ground tilled earlier by Wolfe, and thus both advanced the prevailing stereotype of Wall Street and added an additional dimension to the negative depictions.[78] Lewis graduated from Princeton with a degree in art history, but wanted a career on Wall Street (he thought) to learn more about economics and make some serious money. He accomplished one of those goals. Lewis crafts a tale, partly autobiographical, that depicts "Wall Street Culture" as not only infantile (some of the gambits seem more probable in a frat house rather than a bond trading desk at the venerable Salomon Brothers), but also hedonistic, greedy, duplicitous, and gluttonous. The widely admired training program designed by Salomon Brothers, ostensibly for hard-working and industrious college graduates, was far from refined or sophisticated, and it ironically helped perpetuate a culture of crass behavior—suitable for the Darwinian culture of the trading floor itself. The participants attended the most prestigious schools in the country, but the 127 neophytes of the class of 1985, especially the denizens of the back row, soon learned the realities of Wall Street:

> The firm's management created the training program, filled it to the brim, then walked away. In the ensuing anarchy the bad drove out the good, the big drove out the small, and the brawn drove out the brains. There was a single trait common to the denizens of the back row, though I doubt it ever occurred to anyone: They sensed that they needed to shed whatever refinements of personality and intellect they had brought with them to Salomon Brothers. This wasn't a conscious act, more like a reflex. They were victims of the myth, especially popular at Salomon Brothers, that a trader is a savage, and a great trader a great savage.[79]

The firm spent hundreds of thousands of dollars on the training program, inundating the class with speakers, presentations, and stories all geared toward the single aim of making money, quickly and in great quantities. The first part of the book provides a stinging assessment of this program and concludes that the very culture of the firm encouraged, in fact required a loss of refinement, compassion, or sophistication.

In the chapter called "Adult Education," Lewis describes the lessons gleaned from speaker after speaker, especially the bond traders—that rare species in which "fast brains" and "enormous stamina"[80] allowed them to hold dominion over entire departments. The traders required impressive market savvy, as they were closest to the money. Lewis soon realized he was not suited for the trading desk and became a bond salesman; this option required a different set of skills plus the chance for speedy promotion and generous bonuses. The exalted senior leaders who worked in bond sales, however, provided no model for Lewis, no pattern of how to be successful at work while cultivating a healthy mind or enlarging the scope of human experience. Those in sales "expressed no interests outside selling bonds, and they rarely referred to any life outside of Salomon Brothers. Their lives seemed to begin and end on the forty-first floor; and I began to wonder if I wasn't about to enter the Twilight Zone."[81]

Lewis punctuates his writing with humor and wry observations, and he certainly does not wear blinders. He offers occasional self-critique while tempering his account of the two years on the trading desk, only rarely letting his strain of self-righteousness shine through. He does not use the term "Masters of the Universe," but, in essence, he describes many of the same characteristics used by Wolfe in *The Bonfire of the Vanities*. Wolfe, in fact, spent time on this precise trading floor of Salomon Brothers as he researched his own book a few years prior. Lewis believes that financial incentives work, and the free economy thus creates not only markets for trading but also human behavior. In this particular market, ethics, morality, justice, decency, and charity played no role at all:

> Goodness was not taken into account on the trading floor. It was neither rewarded nor punished. It just was. Or it wasn't.... The place was governed by the simple understanding that the unbridled pursuit of perceived self-interest was healthy. Eat or be eaten.... The range of acceptable conduct within Salomon Brothers was wide indeed. It said something about the ability of the free market to mold people's behavior into socially acceptable patterns. For this was capitalism at its most raw, and it was self-destructive.[82]

According to Lewis, he never fully understood the bond market and, for that matter, nor did most of his colleagues, but he learned how to sell the products to equally ignorant buyers. Since he writes with humor and creativity, the transgressions appear, at first, as examples of isolated boorish behavior, but, taken together, present a strong and compelling critique of Wall Street. The characters have real names, but they also become character types themselves and generally help solidify the crass representation of those engaged in business and finance.

In many ways, Lewis's account is more devastating than Wolfe's. When writing fiction, authors often engage in creative license, adding, exaggerating, or enhancing character traits for effects; readers of fiction understand this freedom and make allowances for that authorial creativity. When confronting a character such as Sherman McCoy, the reader necessarily factors this fiction into the reading calculus. But when reading non-fiction, when reading an historical memoir, the reader does not have an easy option to dismiss, minimize, or sanitize the events. The shroud of fiction affords latitude; the grounding of reality creates a deeper impression. So when Lewis vividly describes the excessive and amoral nature of naked, unfettered capitalism (as he calls it), the image carries greater weight. When he chronicles the persona "of the slick profiteering Wall Street trader"[83] it impresses because he experienced the depravity first-hand, had a moment of conversion, and now repents of his past sins. However, Lewis did not simply inventory the palpable greed, the boorish behavior, nor did he confine his analysis to the gluttony, envy, lechery, and cruelty of the jungle. To this litany of abuse, he added another damning ingredient. Ignorance.

This ignorance was not primarily the domain of the traders (although one sees many examples of ignorance here as well), but rather in the entire financial sector, including the commercial bankers (especially those running thrifts), bond salesmen (Lewis himself included), regulators, rating agencies, analysts, and really the entire edifice supporting the financial system of complicated securities, bonds, derivatives, and mortgages. The stereotype of the narrow-minded but competent, boring, conservative merchant thus gave way to the huckster, the charlatan, the imbecile, the ridiculous, the dangerous, and the ignoramus. In this reading, most members of the finance industry were not only immoral but stupid as well.[84] Page after page mentions the rampant stupidity of the clients, traders, managers, salespeople, and the firm itself. Lewis repeatedly uses the words "fools," "dummies," "dupes," "stupidity," "blessed ignorance" and a host of other unfavorable terms. To be fair, Lewis couches his critique and reminds the reader that not all employees at Salomon Brothers fit that mold—some decent people existed—but they receive almost no attention. Moreover, bond traders represent a small slice of the complicated financial industry, but, by extrapolation, the entire network becomes toxic. Lewis directs attention to his own fallow, inexperienced beginnings:

> I was niggled during those first few months by the feeling of being a charlatan. I kept blowing people up. I didn't know anything. I had never managed money. I had never made any real money. I didn't even know anyone who had made real money, only a few heirs. Yet I was holding myself out as a great expert on matters of finance. . . . The only thing that saved me in meeting after meeting in the early days at Salomon was that the people I dealt with knew even less.[85]

The earliest depictions of the merchant and entrepreneurial class found in the medieval and Renaissance periods tended to highlight the obsessive amount of time and effort required for success in the world of business—a commitment so intense that it left little time for other pursuits such as family, friends, and faith. The more recent depictions, colored with the veneer of learning and intelligence, invoke the ghost of Machiavelli and a conspicuous lack of intelligence and prudence to create the prevailing stereotype.

The film industry has also focused its cameras on the business and merchant class. The rapid transformation of the stereotype on film took only a generation. In 1946, Frank Capra released "*It's a Wonderful Life,*" one of the most successful and endearing movies in history. The film, starring Jimmy Stewart as George Bailey, the lovable, modest president of the family-owned Building and Loan. George Bailey displays remarkable virtue—he is fair, kind, compassionate, sacrificial, and oriented toward the community and not only profit. These character traits make him admirable, of course, but no match for the greedy banker Henry F. Potter, the richest man in the town of Bedford Falls. Potter, the clear antagonist, has other values and mocks George in his time of crisis (famously telling him that he is "more dead than alive"), setting off a crisis and leaving George with thoughts of suicide. The plot, ultimately, gets resolved and George reflects on his own wonderful life and the myriad blessings he has received—not to mention the opportunities he provided for others in the community. In this case, honesty, integrity, and ethics triumph over avarice, gluttony, and pride, making the movie a favorite of the Christmas season.

But the movie, for all its undeniable charm and pathos, seems quaint, even saccharine, when compared to presentations of business professionals on film today. One does not need to be an expert in movie history to see this conspicuous departure. Oliver Stone's *Wall Street* (1987), starring Michael Douglas and a young Charlie Sheen, was not the first movie to depict such corporate excess, but with a single line, the film captures the anti-capital sentiment which dominates the film: "Greed is Good." When Gordon Gecko addresses the shareholders at the annual meeting, he rails against incompetent corporate governance and launches into his homily on greed. According to this gospel, the primal sin of corporate America is incompetence and too many bureaucrats and vice presidents creating a tangled web of rules, procedures, and policies. This new theology advocates the conspicuous implementation of greed—both corporate and personal varieties, as greed is not only a good, but a saving grace. Gekko, a self-proclaimed "liberator of companies," waxes philosophical when he states that "greed is right, it works. Greed clarifies, cuts, and captures the essence of the evolutionary spirit."[86] In his view, only the strong survive in the Darwinian battle for corporate America and only those companies and individuals fed on the diet of greed can withstand the ordeal. His impassioned and choreographed speech receives thunderous applause and a knowing wink. Machiavelli would be proud.

For its time, *Wall Street* was shocking enough, and Oliver Stone clearly tried to equate the cancer in the film with the Reagan administration and those who favored a free market and free trade among nations. And as a form of propaganda, it clearly worked. Scores of dutiful scribes from the mainstream media took the bait and began making trendy and pseudo-sophisticated comparisons. For sheer lurid excess, however, *The Wolf of Wall Street* far surpasses *Wall Street* for its use scenes of excessive corruption, drugs, and sex. The movie holds the dubious "record" for the most uses of the F-bomb in cinematic history for a feature film.[87] From what I've been told, the movie, loosely based upon a true story, shows nothing redeeming about the activities of Wall Street and the traders act without any moral compunction, any sense of fiduciary responsibility, any vestige of conscience or a smattering of genuine human decency. The movie—an ostensible condemnation of such excesses, makes another point indirectly. The conspicuous stereotyping and bias against the world of commerce and industry continues to this day. Heated rhetoric railing against "millionaires and billionaires" saturates political indoctrination. Surveys suggest that employee engagement is at an all-time low, and the pandemic exacerbated an already fraught situation. Younger people especially feel alienated, and many young men simply have stopped looking for meaningful work, opting instead to work the gig economy, and thus making it harder and harder for them to achieve financial self-sufficiency. Perhaps we do indeed need to revisit the life of St. Omobono and try to recapture, once again, a sense of the theology of work. Work does enable and work also ennobles. A canonization in 1199 provided a model for those ideals.

Chapter 5 Endnotes

1. https://w2.vatican.va/content/john-paul-ii/en/speeches/1997/june/documents/hf_jp-ii_spe_19970624_nicolini.html.
2. Thomas Kuhn, *The Structure of Scientific Revolutions* (Chicago: University of Chicago Press, 1962) introduced the term "paradigm shifts" to explain advances in scientific knowledge. Although imprecise when applied to technology, many scholars use the word to describe sudden and abrupt changes, as when one worldview replaces another or one way of providing goods and services replaces a previous method. In this sense, it seems synonymous with "disruptive innovation."
3. For a fascinating account of the history of Netflix, see March Randolph, *That Will Never Work: The Birth of Netflix and the Amazing Life of an Idea* (New York: Little, Brown, 2019). See also, Peter H. Diamandis and Steven Kotler, *Bold* (New York: Simon and Schuster, 2105) who explore in a compelling fashion the optimistic side of disruption and innovation. The book largely ignores the negative impact of disruption, the losers, including the thousands of jobs lost as a result of new advances in technology. The book provides a death spiral of the Six D's of Exponential Technology: Digitalization, Deception, Disruption, Demonetization, Dematerialization, and Democratization.
4. According to Mary Harvey Doyno, *Lilies Among the Thorns: Lay Saints and Their Cults in Northern and Central Italian Cities, 1150–1350*, Unpublished Dissertation (New York: Columbia University, 2010), "as the first non-royal layman to be canonized by Rome, Omobono has received a fair amount of scholarly attention."
5. In support of her assertion, Doyno cites a few books containing chapters or parts of chapters, including the important work by Vauchez and Piazzi. Neither work has been translated into English. Diana Webb, in *Saints and Cities*, and Don Prudlo have written about Omobono in English. In spite of this impressive research, the life of St. Omobono remains largely unknown to the English-speaking world.
6. Augustine Thompson, O.P., *Cities of God: The Religion of the Italian Communes, 1125–1325* (University Park: Penn State University Press, 2005), 7 and 191. Fr. Thompson calls lay saints "exceptions," as they appear very rarely in this period. He also includes two other lay saints, Facio of Cremona and Pietro Pettinaio of Siena.
7. Christopher Hibbert, *Rome: The Biography of a City* (New York: Penguin, 1985), 90. The Cult of St. Omobono was active in Rome centuries

later, when a fourteenth-century church located near the foot of the Capitoline hill in rione Ripa was given to the Guild of Merchants. The guild dedicated the church to St. Omobono in 1575. Although the church still exists, it is currently closed, awaiting repairs.

8   Alban Butler, *The Lives of the Saints: Complete Revised Edition*, ed. Herbert J. Thurston and Donald Attwater (Naples: Ave Maria Press, 2008).

9   Doyno, 43.

10 Both character and characterization are complex terms and they carry many levels of meanings, including "flat" and "round" characters, static and dynamic, one-dimensional and two-dimensional. For a useful overview of the term, see A Handbook to Literature, ed. William Harmon, 12th edition (Pearson Education 2010), xx.

11 Vincent F. Hopper, *Chaucer's Canterbury Tales: An Interlinear Translation* (New York: Barrons, 1970), ix.

12 Chaucer obviously did not invent the "collection of stories" format, as there are famous earlier examples, including the *Arabian Knights* and Boccaccio's *Decameron*.

13 This passage comes from a delightful "retelling" in Peter Ackroyd, *The Canterbury Tales* (New York: Viking, 2009). For a comprehensive academic edition, see *The Riverside Chaucer*, ed. Larry D. Benson, 3rd ed. (Boston: Houghton Mifflin, 1987). Here is the passage in the original:

> A MARCHANT was ther with a forked berd
> In mottelee, and hye on horse he sat;
> His bootes clasped faire and fetisly,
> His resons he spak ful solempnely,
> Sownynge alwey th'encrees of his wynnyng.
> He wolde the see were kept for any thing
> Bitwixe Middelburgh and Orewelle.
> Wel koude he in eschaunge sheeldes selle.
> This worthy man ful wel his wit bisette:
> Ther wiste no wight that he was in dette,
> So estatly was he of his governaunce
> With his bargaynes and with his chevyssaunce.
> For soothe he was a worthy man with alle,
> But, sooth to seyn, I not how men hym calle. (270–84)

14 The Oxford English Dictionary lists a number of definitions for winning, including the now obsolete sense of "getting of money or wealth; gain, profit; money making" (2.b).

15 John 17: 14–19.
16 In the numerous depictions of Omobono in art—the various frescos and icons still prominent in Cremona—the saint is indeed depicted in rich clothing, bright colors, and lush fabrics.
17 Hopper, 238.
18 *English Mystery Plays*, ed. Peter Happe (New York: Penguin, 1975). See pages 9 and 11.
19 Glynne Wickham, *Early English Stages 1300–1660*, Vol 3 (New York: Columbia UP, 1981): 35. See also, Alfred W. Pollard, *English Miracle Plays, Moralities, and Interludes* (Oxford: Clarendon Press, 1927); Murray Roston, *Biblical Drama in England from the Middle Ages to the Present Day* (London: Faber and Faber, 1968); John D. Cox, *The Devil and the Sacred in English Drama, 1350–1642* (Cambridge: Cambridge UP, 2000).
20 Barara Traister, *Heavenly Necromancers: The Magician in English Renaissance Drama* (Columbia: University of Missouri Press, 1984).
21 Jose M. Ruano de la Haza. "Unparalleled Lives: Hagiographical Drama in Seventeenth-Century England and Spain." *Parallel Lives: Spanish and English National Drama, 1580–1680*. Ed Louise and Peter Fothergill-Payne (Lewisburg: Bucknell UP, 1991), 252–66. According to de la Haza, *The Virgin Martyr*, by Decker and Massinger, is the only exception.
22 A wealth of recent scholarship, much of it revisionist in nature, explores this topic. Among the many, see, for example, the influential work of Eamon Duffy, *Stripping of the Altars: Traditional Religion in England, 1400–150* (New Haven, Yale UP, 1992); John W. O'Malley, *Trent and All That: Renaming Catholicism in Early Modern England* (Cambridge: Harvard UP, 2000); Lucy E. C. Wooding, *Rethinking Catholicism in Reformation England* (Oxford: Clarendon, 2000). See also the collections of essays and lectures assembled in Eamon Duffy, *Saints, Sacrilege, and Sedition: Religious Conflict in the Tudor Reformations* (New York: Bloomsbury, 2012).
23 Robert E. Scully, S.J., "The Unmaking of a Saint," *Catholic Historical Review* 86.4 (Nov 2000): 579–602.
24 See the compelling analysis in Patrick Collinson, *From Iconoclasm to Iconophobia: The Cultural Impact of the Second English Reformation* (Reading: University of Reading, 1986).
25 Louis B. Wright, *Middle-Class Culture in Elizabethan England* (Chapel Hill: U of North Carolina P, 1935), 1–18.
26 I use the plural "reformations" following the recent magisterial work of Carlos Eire, *Reformations: The Early Modern World 1450–1650* (New Haven Yale, 2016). Eire provides a comprehensive bibliography, unrivaled in scope or scale as well as a compelling argument.

27 A vast amount of research examines this important period from a Protestant perspective, and it falls outside the scope of this analysis to review it here. Among the many important works, see Sir G. R. Elton, *Reformation Europe 1517–1559*, 2nd ed. (Oxford: Blackwell, 1985); A. G. Dickens, *The English Reformation* (University Park: Pennsylvania State UP, 1964); Patrick Collinson, *The Religion of the Protestants* (Oxford: Oxford UP, 1982); Peter Lake, *Moderate Puritans and the Elizabethan Church* (Cambridge: Cambridge UP, 1982); Kevin Sharpe, *Remapping Early Modern England* (New Haven: Yale, 2000).

28 Richard Lederer, *The Miracle of Language*. (New York: Pocket Books, 1991): 93.

29 Scores of recent books and articles examine this topic from a wide variety of perspectives, including Shakespeare's intriguing biography and the obvious links to Catholicism and the residual Catholicism found in his plays. See, for example, *Beatrice Groves, Texts and Traditions in Shakespeare, 1592–1604* (Oxford: Clarendon, 2007); Alison Shell, *Shakespeare and Religion* (London: Methuen, 2010). For an impressive overview of the vibrant Catholic literary culture that survived during the English Reformation, see Alison Shell, *Catholicism, Controversy, and the English Literary Imagination, 1558–1660* (Cambridge: Cambridge UP, 1999); see also, Paul J. Voss, "The Catholic Presence in English Renaissance Literature," *Ben Jonson Journal* 7 (2000): 1–26. For a superb collection of Catholic writing from the period, see Robert S. Miola, ed., *Early Modern Catholicism: An Anthology of Primary Sources* (Oxford: Oxford UP, 2007).

30 All references to the plays are from *The Riverside Shakespeare*, edited by G. Blakemore Evans (Boston: Houghton Mifflin) 1997.

31 For a compelling, but in the final analysis, unconvincing discussion of this scene, see Stephen Greenblatt, *Hamlet in Purgatory* (Princeton: Princeton UP, 2001).

32 W. W. Greg, *A Bibliography of the English Printed Drama to the Restoration*, 4 vols. (London: Bibliographical Society), 1939–59.

33 *An Index of Characters in Early Modern English Drama*, ed. Berger, Bradford, and Sondergard (Cambridge: Cambridge UP, 1998).

34 After this explanation, his other companion suggests that love is the root cause of Antonio's melancholy. Antonio rejects this explanation as well. For a useful collection of essays on the play, see *The Merchant of Venice: New Critical Essays*, edited by John W. Mahon and Ellen Macleod Mahon (New York: Routledge, 2002).

35 Peter Ackroyd, *Venice: Pure City* (New York: Doubleday, 2009), 110–11. According to Ackroyd, over forty different trading guilds operated near the Rialto.

36 William N. Goetzmann, *Money Changes Everything: How Finance Made Civilization Possible* (Princeton: Princeton, UP, 2016).
37 Ibid., 227.
38 For an illuminating discussion of the blocking character in comedy, see Northrop Frye, *A Natural Perspective* (New York: Columbia UP, 1995).
39 Tim Parks, *Medici Money: Banking, Metaphysics and Art in Fifteenth-Century Florence* (London: Profile Books, 2006). Parks examines the way Catholics developed a banking system, complete with offering loans at interest, in light of tradition and scriptural injunctions.
40 All references to the play are from Christopher Marlowe, *The Jew of Malta*, in *Drama of the English Renaissance*, ed. Fraser and Rabkin (New York: Macmillan, 1976).
41 Pope Paul IV promulgated the *Index Librorum Prohibitorum* in 1559. The original list contained over 550 titles. Many Catholics considered the list too encompassing and it was replaced by the *Tridentine Index* in 1564. *The Prince* was included on both lists.
42 See John Roe, *Shakespeare and Machiavelli* (Cambridge: DS Brewer, 2002).
43 Citations from the text come from Niccolo Machiavelli, *The Prince*, trans. Robert Adams, 2nd edition (New York: Norton, 1992) 3. Isaiah Berlin, "The Question of Machiavelli," New York Review of Books (4 November 1971).
44 Leo Strauss, *Thoughts on Machiavelli* (Chicago: University of Chicago Press, 1958) 3.
45 Alistair McAlpine, *The New Machiavelli: The Art of Politics in Business* (New York: Wiley and Sons, 1998), 98.
46 Ibid., 98.
47 Michael A. Ledeen, *Machiavelli on Modern Leadership: Why Machiavelli's Iron Rules are as Timely and Important Today as Five Centuries Ago* (New York: Truman Talley, 1999).
48 Ibid., xix.
49 Charlotte Coker Worley, "The Character of the Merchant in English Drama from 1590–1612," unpublished dissertation, University of Mississippi, 1985.
50 Ibid., 60.
51 For an analysis of the complexities of the character, see Audrey Jaffe, "Spectacular Sympathy: Visuality and Ideology in Dickens's *A Christmas Carol*," *PMLA* 109.2 (Mar 1994): 254–65. For an expressly religious reading of the novella, see Cheryl Anne Kincaid, *Hearing the Gospel through Charles Dickens's A Christmas Carol* (New Castle: Cambridge Scholars, 2011).
52 See Robert T. Tally, Jr., "Reading the Original: Alienation, Writing,

and Labor in 'Bartelby, the Scrivener,'" in *Bloom's Literary Themes: Alienation* (New York: Infobase, 2009): 1–10. Naomi C. Reed, "The Specter of Wall Street: 'Bartelby the Scrivener' and the Language of Commodities," *American Literature* 76.2 (2004): 247–73 explores the Marxist implications of the tale.

53 Horatio Alger, *Ragged Dick* and *Struggling Upward*, ed. Carl Bode (New York: Penguin, 1985), x.
54 See, for example, the collection of essays in *Major Literary Characters: Willy Loman*, ed. Harold Bloom (New York: Chelsea House, 1991).
55 Colby H. Kullman. "*Death of a Salesman* at Fifty: An Interview with Arthur Miller" in *Bloom's Modern Critical Interpretations: Arthur Miller's Death of a Salesman*, Harold Bloom, ed. (New York: Chelsea House, 2007), 67–76.
56 All references to the play are taken from Arthur Miller, *Death of a Salesman* (New York: Penguin, 1999). Here, p. 3.
57 Linda Uranga, "Willy Loman and the Legacy of Capitalism." *Arthur Miller's Death of a Salesman*, ed. Eric J. Sterling (New York: Rodopi, 2008): 81–93.
58 Miller, 10.
59 Ibid., 22.
60 Ibid., 60.
61 Ibid., 61
62 Thomas E. Porter, "Aces and Diamonds: *Death of a Salesman*" in *Critical Essays on Arthur Miller*, James E. Martine, ed. (Boston: G. K. Hall, 1979), 24–43.
63 Miller, 65. Juan Ignacio Guijarro-Gonzalez and Ramon Espejo, "Capitalist America in Arthur Miller's *Death of a Salesman*" in *Arthur Miller's Death of a Salesman*, ed. Eric Sterling (New York: Rodopi, 2008), 61–80.
64 Tom Wolfe: *The Bonfire of the Vanities* (New York: Bantam, 1987). All citations from the novel will refer to this edition. Wolfe's first novel, a robust 690 pages, was a critical and popular success. Reviews were largely positive, with a few exceptions. See, *The Critical Response to Tom Wolfe*, ed. Doug Shomette (Westport CT: Greenwood Press, 1992), 181–206.
65 See, for example, Donald Weinstein, *Savonarola: The Rise and Fall of a Renaissance Prophet* (New Haven: Yale UP, 2011); Lauro Martines, *Fire in the City: Savonarola and the Struggle for the Soul of Renaissance Florence* (Oxford: Oxford UP, 2007); Christopher Hibbert, *The House of Medici: Its Rise and Fall* (New York: Harper Collins, 1974); Miles J. Unger, *Magnifico: The Brilliant Life and Violent Times of Lorenzo de' Medici* (New York: Simon and Schuster, 2008).

66 The title also includes a clear reference to the beginning of *Ecclesiastes* 1:2: "Vanity of Vanities! All is Vanity."
67 *Conversations with Tom Wolfe*, ed. Dorothy M. Scura (Jackson: University of Mississippi, 1990), 275. The conversation with Bill Moyers took place 27 October 1988.
68 "Protagonist" might not be the correct word here. McCoy emerges as the central figure around which the plot revolves, but William McKeen, *Tom Wolfe* (New York: Twayne, 1995), calls it "a novel without a hero" (117). Kevin T. McEneaney, *Tom Wolfe's America* (Westport CT: Prager, 2009), states that McCoy "is certainly an anti-hero" (see p. 109).
69 Wolfe, 12.
70 Ibid., 13.
71 Ibid., 61.
72 Ibid., 55.
73 Friedrich Nietzsche, *Thus Spake Zarathustra*, trans. Graham Parkes (Oxford: Oxford UP, 2005); Laurence Lampert, *An Interpretation of "Thus Spake Zarathustra"* (New Have: Yale UP, 1989).
74 Wolfe, 62.
75 Ibid. One could easily add to the list of characters who celebrate individualism and advocate for a free economy, especially in the works of Ayn Rand, including Howard Roark in *The Fountainhead* (Indianapolis: Bobbs-Merrill, 1943) and Dagny Taggart, Vice President of Taggart Intercontinental Railroad in *Atlas Shrugged* (New York: Random House, 1957).
76 Clayton Christensen, *How Will You Measure Your Life?* (New York: Harper Collins, 2012) observes that many graduates of the Harvard Business School, among the most prestigious programs in the world, end up in failed marriages, estranged from family, or even in jail. His book tries to explain that troubling observation. As we shall see in the next chapter, this lack of a current, compelling, and sophisticated vocabulary of business contributes to this behavior.
77 Nate Silver, *The Signal and the Noise: Why Most Predictions Fail—but Some Don't* (New York: Penguin, 2012).
78 Michael Lewis, *Liar's Poker: Rising Through the Wreckage on Wall Street* (New York: Norton, 1989).
79 Ibid., 77.
80 Ibid., 85.
81 Ibid. 86.
82 Ibid., 86–87.
83 Ibid., 141.

84 The same sense of ignorance and arrogance infused the culture of Enron, leading to one of the most extensive bankruptcies in history. See, for example, Bethany McLean, *Smartest Guys in the Room* (New York: Penguin, 2003).
85 Lewis, 214. Lewis continues to examine this notion of abject, reckless, and even illegal ignorance in *The Big Short* (New York: Norton, 2011).
86 For another perspective of greed, see Paul J. Voss, "Occupy Wall Street is Greed vs. Envy," *Atlanta Business Chronicle* (11 October 2011).
87 According to Wikipedia, and those who collect this type of data, *Swearnet: The Movie* holds the *Guiness World Record* with 935 instances. *The Wolf of Wall Street* ranks third (after a documentary), with only 569.

Chapter 6
THE PURPOSE OF BUSINESS AND THE MEANING OF WORK: AN ECONOMIST SPEAKS

On 13 September 1970, the famous economist Milton Friedman (1912–2006) published a short essay in the *New York Times Magazine*.[1] This lucid and provocative declaration, "The Social Responsibility of Business is to Increase Profits," set off a passionate debate about the proper nature of business—a debate that reverberates to this day. Friedman, a staunch libertarian, enjoyed a prestigious and distinguished career at the University of Chicago, authored scores of books and articles, advised presidents and prime ministers, became a television personality, wrote a regular column for *Newsweek*, and won the Nobel Prize for economics in 1976. He published on a remarkable variety of topics, including public policy, consumption theory, the free market, exchange rates, military conscription, income tax, and school choice, to name only a few. Friedman rejected Keynesian economics, state intervention, and the use of political (rather than market) mechanisms for the allocation of scarce resources. He remains one of the most influential economists from the second half of the twentieth century.

The modest essay employs the characteristic Friedman style stripped free of sentiment while possessing a certain charm that belies the rhetorical force of the argument. Friedman defines business as an endeavor designed to make a profit, and he rightly notes that any business not focused on profitability will almost surely fail.[2] In fact, he offers a robust defense of profit earned properly—within the rule of law and without deception or fraud.[3] Thus, profit stands as a *signal* that a business both uses resources efficiently and produces goods wanted by society.[4] The primary target of the essay is the so-called "social conscience" of business, at that time only in an embryonic stage of development and now evolved into a fully-grown discipline.[5] Friedman does not believe a "social conscience of business" makes logical sense (for only people can have consciences) and argues that the "catchwords of the contemporary crop of reformers" is nothing other than "preaching pure and unadulterated socialism." Although largely left unstated, Friedman directs his remarks at professors, economists, and corporate executives who parrot that language and use money earned by the corporation for social causes outside the proper scope of business. According to Friedman, only when acting as an individual (principal) and not as an agent can one rightly contribute resources to a social cause or toward a public function. Thus, a CEO undermines the foundations of a free society when acting in a unilateral fashion to allocate resources toward social concerns and away from business concerns. In this understanding, members of that corporation have no choice in these decisions, but rather are compelled to support the favored social priorities of the executive or the whims of a board of directors. When acting as individuals, people have free scope to support any types of social activity they desire—and he encourages people to invest, *as individuals*, in schools, churches, civic clubs, hospitals, and other acts of philanthropy. But when a corporation acts, it must always act in a fiduciary fashion for the shareholders and not give away money that could be spent to improve financial results. Thus, we have the basis for a limited "shareholder theory" of business (exclusively focused on the investors) in contrast with the more expansive "stakeholder theory" (which considers the people, planet, profits, and the community at large).[6]

Friedman sees this growing trend toward "social" responsibility as a proxy for increased government regulation, redistribution of corporate wealth, and a conspicuous threat to the free economy and private enterprise. Following this argument, the political principle that underlies the market mechanism is unanimity:

> In an ideal free market resting on private property, no individual can coerce any other, all cooperation is voluntary, all parties to such cooperation benefit or they need not participate. There are no values, no "social" responsibilities in any sense other than the shared values and responsibilities of individuals.

According to Friedman, a drastic change (i.e., the emphasis upon *coerced* social responsibility) has started to undermine the free economy, and this misguided behavior grants too much ground to anti-business critics by tacitly admitting that the profits must be dispersed throughout the community in a more explicit fashion. If, for example, one grants the social responsibility argument, it gives succor to the belief that the pursuit of profit is inherently tainted, even wicked and evil and in need of some redress. Once this position gains currency, the external force used to curb such excess will not be social conscience, but rather "the iron fist of Government bureaucrats." As such, it is a "fundamentally subversive" doctrine.

Friedman ends the short opinion piece by noting the corrosive effects of "social responsibility" ("it does not differ in philosophy from the most explicitly collectivist doctrine") and offers a concise defense of the proper function of business: "There is one and only one social responsibility of business—to use its resources and engage in activities designed to increase its profits so long as it stays within the rules of the game, which is to say, engages in open and free competition without deception or fraud." Friedman's essay produced a torrent of critical commentary, with many people condemning him for his heartless, soulless approach to business. But without hyperbole, it remains a seminal article for any discussion on the topic. In fact, according to John Hood, "it is no exaggeration to say that, with very few exceptions, every major article on or analysis of corporate social responsibility since publication of Friedman's article has cited, mentioned, or challenged it."[7] To this day, it remains the foundational text for "shareholder theory" (some even call it the "Friedman Doctrine"), the advocacy of maximum profits and a return of a portion of those profits to the shareholders of any enterprise. Not surprisingly, Professor Friedman does not cite St. Omobono, the patron of business executives and entrepreneurs, in any of his published works. But he continues the discussion started in 1199 about the nature of work and the role of profit.

A Poet Speaks

In 1994, English poet David Whyte published *The Heart Aroused: Poetry and the Preservation of the Soul in Corporate America*. The tenor and tone of Whyte's book differs in nearly every conceivable way from Friedman; Whyte does not discuss profit in any direct or indirect fashion. It sold a respectable 15,000 copies and became a surprise best-selling business book. Although a "business book," it did not deal with economic matters or theories of corporate governance, but rather focused on the individual worker within a corporation. The title might mislead, however, for when Whyte uses the term *soul*, he does not employ it in a religious sense (meaning the immortal essence of the human being), but in a generic psychological sense of "well being." It's primarily a book about psychology and not philosophy or theology. Whyte wrote the book "for those who have chosen to live out their lives as managers and employees of postmodern Corporate America, and who struggle to keep their humanity in the process."[8] Whyte sought to find a symbiosis between the poetic imagination (defined as creativity, freedom, experimentation, and play) and the realities of the corporate world (and its emphasis upon data, metrics, profits, order, and rationality). He notes that both camps viewed each other with suspicion. As we witnessed in the previous chapter, many writers and filmmakers often assume that all business endeavors have the single aim to maximize profits and thus destroy individual creativity and imagination; business leaders often view poetry (if considered at all) as vain, idle, and frivolous. In fact, before he could begin, Whyte admits that he needed to address his own bias against the universe of business, "a world I was taught to view with suspicion," a world in which "I expected to be at least a little corrupted by my immersion."[9] Old stereotypes die hard, even among the enlightened.

Yet, as Whyte freely admits, the experience of working in corporate America changed his perspective dramatically, and he discovered much about his own "arrogance" after working for "seven humbling years in which I have been forced to drop, one by one, many of the prejudices against the corporate world my personal history had generously provided me. I found my image of contemporary business as outdated and clichéd as the business world's image of my own world of poetry and poets."[10] Whyte did not expect to work among so many intelligent people striving to maintain a proper work-life balance, let alone the cultivation of an inner life; he did not expect to see such a hunger for and openness to the poetic imagination and the desire to integrate beauty and work. Everywhere he looked, businessmen and businesswomen longed for a deeper meaning and connection between the personal and the professional. These observations mirrored my own. Over the years as a consultant, the vast majority of my clients have displayed intelligence, passion, curiosity, and a hunger for learning. Far from mindless drones, cultural philistines, or corporate conformists only concerned with money (the common stereotypes), the executives and managers I work with seek tools to help them be better connected with families, co-workers, and clients. Whyte clearly identified a genuine human need.

The interest became so palpable that Whyte began a successful consultancy aimed at facilitating conversations geared toward the human person fully involved in the world of business. Although popular for a brief time and instrumental in creating awareness among executives and managers, *The Heart Aroused* did not fully succeed in its aim. His "soulful approach" to work includes insightful discussions of passion, meaning, creativity, desire, drive, and purpose, but provides little philosophy and almost no practical measures for implementation. It's a poet's book, written by a poet for would-be business poets eager to abolish routine and repetition from the daily grind of work. Make no mistake: It's an admirable goal. Yet business leaders need books that go beyond sparkling gems and brilliant insights. In the final analysis, a collection of poems and stories, without transformational application, becomes a cliché. A random passage illustrates this difficulty:

> In my experience, the more true we are to our own creative gifts the less there is any outer reassurance or help at the beginning. The more we are on the path, the deeper the silence in the first stages of the process. Following our path is in effect a kind of going *off* the path, through open country. There is a certain early stage when we are left to camp out in the wilderness, alone, with few supporting voices. Out there in the silence we must build a hearth, gather the twigs, and strike the flint for the fire ourselves.[11]

While the prose may be beautiful and full of rich allusions and metaphors, it's hardly the concrete raw material around which a robust personal and corporate culture can be formed. Whyte deserves, however, ample credit for trying to find a synthesis between these two disparate, and often isolated, worlds.[12]

A PHILOSOPHER SPEAKS

In 1996, theologian Michal Novak published a modest book titled *Business as a Calling: Work and the Examined Life*.[13] At just over 200 pages, *Business as a Calling* stands among the first serious *philosophical* attempts to form an intellectual argument for the value and dignity of work.[14] As a result, the book provides a *humane* basis (not primarily an economic basis) for business, free enterprise, and capitalism. The title of the book merits some reflection. Novak used the word "calling" in both a professional and religious sense. One often uses a "calling" or a "vocation" (from the Latin *vocare*—"to call") in an expressly religious manner. Members of the clergy, for example, frequently discuss their "calling" to the priesthood. People who feel compelled or driven to a certain task, function, or job also use the term in the sense of a "higher calling." A calling, in this fashion, often suggests nobility, altruism, sacrifice, and service; teachers, nurses, social workers, and artists often employ this vocabulary to define their careers. However, using this term to define the essential nature of business radically departs from the traditional view of business (discussed above) as detached, mindless, and even corrupt. By using the term, Novak directly challenges that stereotypical bigotry often directed against the world of work and private enterprise.

Some businesspeople, of course, are indeed driven primarily by materialism. Some businesspeople engage in morally suspect or criminal activity. But this type of behavior is not exclusive to the world of commerce (as the news makes abundantly clear each day), and only a small minority of successful business owners engage in illegal conduct—especially given the importance of market reputation and "brand equity." The market tends to punish such suspect behavior, especially given the ubiquity of social media platforms and the large number of customer reviews widely available.[15] Moreover, every profession can cite examples of corruption (as can be seen in all levels of government from town, city, county, parish, district, state, and federal) and avarice. Business does not have a monopoly on bad behavior, abuses of power, exploitation, or myopic thinking. News stories appear each day with tales about unethical or morally dubious behaviors in primary schools, universities, law enforcement, hospitals, governments, courts, and every other type of voluntary association. However, just as vice can attach itself to any human endeavor, so can virtue—as St. Omobono so clearly demonstrated and stressed by Butler: "All lawful secular professions have furnished heaven with saints, that the slothful in all states may be without excuse." The tenor and tone of Novak's book suggests a deep and abiding respect for business as a "morally serious" enterprise and for business leaders who display conspicuous virtue and manifest charity in their stewardship.

Novak consciously attempts to create a new language for business by incorporating a vocabulary from philosophy. This point bears some emphasis. As we witnessed in the preceding chapter, the traditional language of business did not employ philosophical terms such as meaning, virtue, ethics, morals, and prudence. The language of business was almost exclusively professional and technical. Novak attempts to synthesize these two vocabularies, in effect baptizing the realm of work in a manner like the earlier way in which Christianity baptized Greek and Roman philosophy, Hebrew law, and even the contemplative life (once the sole purview of the scholar and now also the realm of the religious). This rhetorical move—the attempt to animate the language of business with meaning accessible to business professionals and to provide a deeper level of understanding—will have a profound impact in the subsequent understanding of the proper role of business. In fact, Novak uses a vocabulary not dissimilar from the documents of St. Omobono's life, and in a very real sense, recaptures that language in order to reclaim the nobility of business.

In this sense, Novak addresses a philosophical shortcoming recognized in 1981 by Alasdair MacIntyre in his influential book *After Virtue*.[16] MacIntyre convincingly argued that we no longer possess a nuanced vocabulary to appreciate, yet alone transmit, genuine human virtue. We may have the appearance of morality, but not the actual substance. According to MacIntyre, the language of morality remains present, but in a state of "grave disorder," while the "integral substance of morality has to a large degree been fragmented and then in part destroyed."[17] One sees a conspicuous fragmentation in both language and substance when exploring ideas of the free market and the life of business professionals. The business profession includes so many varied and distinct camps, factions, philosophies, tribes, vocabularies, practices, approaches, schools, and personalities that finding a common language eludes the best of efforts—even among like-minded individuals. Novak seeks to build a compelling and efficacious vocabulary in order to have a meaningful conversation; our own project seeks to contribute to that effort by providing the first Church documents and historical context for understanding the morally serious business life.

Novak does not demonize or condemn business, a striking departure, for many in the academic community demonstrate a palpable distrust of business. In fact, when properly considered, business profits enrich the lives of millions of people each day. For example, critics often overlook the millions and millions of dollars that businesses give away each year to various charitable causes. Most civic organizations—including the high-profile organizations such as symphonies, zoos, museums, theaters, and schools—receive grants and gifts from businesses. Smaller civic organizations, such as Boys and Girls Clubs, little league teams, Rotary, Lions, Optimists, the Salvation Army, and hundreds of others also benefit from the largesse of private enterprise. Even the so-called "robber barons" of the late nineteenth century, including Frick, Rockefeller, Morgan, Vanderbilt, Mellon, and many others, gave away millions and millions of dollars. Andrew Carnegie famously pledged to give away his vast resources before he died. He was so wealthy that despite his best efforts (and the power of compound interest) he still had money left over, but by the time of his death, he had funded and built 1,946 libraries in small communities across America (and 865 in other countries). Novak cites Carnegie's other charitable activities (he paid for 7,689 pipe organs around the world) and examines Carnegie's philosophy of philanthropy in some detail.[18] In spite of the prevailing stereotypes found in literature and film depicting all business leaders as narrow-mined, selfish, or even rapacious, ample evidence suggests a compelling counterargument. A slight digression on this topic proves illustrative.

Instances of the generosity of business leaders abound in our world today. In June 2010, Warren Buffet and Bill Gates formally announced the Giving Pledge campaign, an attempt to recruit billionaires from all over the world (and specifically from the USA, China, and India) to agree to give a majority of their accumulated wealth away before they die. This effort has voluntarily turned the "giving pledge" into a massive transfer of wealth, above and beyond the not incidental commands of governments and tax authorities. According to the official website, 236 billionaires have agreed to give away a reported $600,000,000,000. That's a staggering, impressive number by any calculation. Critics who merely state "so what, they still have millions left over," obviously fail to understand the nature of gifting. In short, as Novak emphasizes, businesses remain a robust and important supporter of our civic world and the common good. It's worth pointing out that none of this transfer would be possible without the wealth creation of the free economy. Moreover, this wealth helps fund programs often not provided by the government and develop social bonds among people. Without private wealth funding hundreds of programs, the programs simply would not exist.

The Catholic community also teems with charitable giving from successful business leaders and executives. Catholic Charities always ranks as one of the most efficient philanthropic groups. Hundreds of St. Vincent de Paul chapters provide food for the needy in local communities. Tom Monaghan built one of the most widely recognized restaurant chains in North America; after building the company for 38 years, he sold Domino's Pizza in 1998 for a reported $1 billion dollars. He pledged to give away his entire fortune to found Ave Maria University, Ave Maria Law School, and Legatus, an organization of Catholic business leaders dedicated "to study, live, and spread the Catholic faith in business, professional, and personal lives." He even sold most of his private possessions—including the Detroit Tigers, expensive art and fancy cars—to support those efforts.[19] Tim Busch recently donated $12 million to the business school at Catholic University for research and support for Catholic business ethics. Roberto Guizetta, Donald Keough, Karl Karcher, Barron Hilton, and many others have given away millions of dollars to charitable causes.[20]

Kenneth Langone, co-founder of Home Depot, recently made headlines when he challenged Pope Francis and his views (discussed below) on income inequality. Estimates place Langone's personal wealth at about $2.1 billion, and his impressive history of philanthropy gives him immediate credibility. He made an enormous amount of money, to be sure, but he also voluntarily gave away—feely and of his own volition—enormous amounts of money. As a Roman Catholic, Langone clearly provides both corporal and spiritual works of mercy and uses his network to encourage others to give generously as well. So it obviously came as a shock to Langone when Pope Francis made a number of sharp, pointed attacks against the greed of business leaders and the corruption of the market. Langone bristled at the pope's blatant generalization that wealth made people "incapable of feeling compassion for the poor." Langone, a primary fund-raiser for the renovations of St. Patrick's Cathedral, directed his concerns to Archbishop Timothy Dolan of New York and said some wealthy donors were reluctant to give money as a result of the pope's erstwhile attack on free enterprise. As Novak makes clear, many, many business leaders invest themselves heavily in charitable and philanthropic endeavors; it's equally clear that millions and millions of dollars generated by businesses end up serving the needs of the larger community and the disadvantaged.[21] Novak does an excellent job demonstrating the positive social impact created by this voluntary transfer of wealth.

The subtitle of the book, where Novak conspicuously links "work and the examined life," might be even more audacious. As this book demonstrates, critics of the business world have often railed against the mechanical, practical, efficient, and routine aspects of business, claiming that total immersion in business and the quest for profit absolutely precludes any role for thought, reflection, philosophy, or the life of the mind. This tension exists conspicuously in the liberal arts, the very academic area dedicated to questions about the human condition. Many college campuses literally separate the humanities and the college of business, driving a figurative wedge between the two communities. Novak, himself an academic, notes that "many persons educated in the humanities (with their aristocratic traditions) are uncritically anticapitalistic. They think of business as vulgar, philistine, and morally suspect."[22] As we have seen, even a brief survey of the movies and literature from the period demonstrate this bias. Yet Novak, the winner of the 1994 Templeton Prize and author of over 25 books, makes a rather different claim: "A career in business is not only a morally serious vocation, but a morally noble one. Those who are called to it have reason to take pride in it and rejoice in it."[23] This sympathetic stance marks a major shift in serious philosophy in trying to understand the complex nature of business and the many talented people engaged in the world of commerce.

Novak does not argue that business necessarily creates philosophers, but that business does indeed require philosophic virtues, especially the cardinal (or hinge) virtues discussed by Aristotle in *Nicomachean Ethics*.[24] The four virtues—prudence, justice, temperance, and fortitude—form the basis for ethical life in any area of life, including family, community, and church. Clearly, these virtues form the basis of many business decisions and strategic plans. Ample experience defends this assertion, for few, if any, business succeed by accident. Likewise, few, if any, businesses succeed from sheer luck or good fortune. The world of commerce is simply too competitive, too full of smart and hard-working people, for the lazy, undisciplined, profligate, or uniformed to flourish. Novak also argues for the creation of three uninformed *business* virtues necessary for any successful enterprise. When Novak rightly calls these activities *virtues*, it casts them in a decidedly different light and, indirectly, turns business leaders into philosophers.

Novak begins with the "virtue of creativity." Aristotle famously argued that virtue requires specific habits and habituation; Novak believes the virtue of creativity requires the habit of enterprise, defined as "the first moment, the inclination to notice, the habit of discerning, the tendency to discover what other people don't yet see. It is also the capacity to act on insight, so as to bring into reality things not before seen."[25] This talent, of course, requires hard work, thought, and imagination. It is the virtue of the entrepreneur and resembles, in many respects, the creative power of artists and writers to bring forth something unique into the world. In his beautiful apostolic "Letter to Artists," St. Pope John Paul II praised artists for their creativity in "creating something new, *ex nihilo sui et subjecti*, and bringing forth beauty into the world for others to use and enjoy."[26] It's this intellectual habit, the creation of the good and the useful, which also helps define the entrepreneur. Novak rightly identifies this as a virtue and a nearly essential characteristic of successful business leaders.[27] Moreover, he provides a compelling vocabulary to describe the process—a vocabulary that economists often lack.[28]

This insight has enormous implications for our understanding of work and economic history. Marx famously (and erroneously) argued for a labor theory of value—a system where labor of the worker created surplus value exploited by capital and the ruling class. With modern technology, physical labor no longer plays a central role in manufacturing. Machines literally do most of the heavy lifting and thinking now. Success now requires more than brawn; intelligence, grit, and enterprise stand as essential attributes in the modern economy. Businesses now find themselves in an "Ivy-League street fight" with their competitors, where education, intelligence, ideas, execution, and enterprise have replaced knives and guns. In this economy, intellect and agility become essential skills. In fact, John Paul II recognized this fact in *Centesimus Annus*: "In our time, in particular, there exists another form of ownership which is becoming no less important than land: the possession of the know-how, technology, and skill. The wealth of the industrialized nations is based much more on this kind of ownership than on natural resources."[29] Economic historians have called this new phase the *experience economy*, as distinct from an agricultural, manufacturing, or service economy. The experience economy, as the name implies, places a premium on addressing human needs and creating something more than a mere service, for most services can be provided easily and by a wide variety of firms. Businesses must focus on *how* they operate even more attentively than on *what* they produce.[30] More than ever, business will need to pay attention to the human dimension of that experience.

Novak defines the second virtue as "the virtue of building community." Business gurus make millions of dollars writing books and conducting seminars of "corporate culture." In this sense, business is seen as much more than a sterile profit-seeking endeavor. In fact, it's becoming widely accepted that culture (defined as *how* one conducts business) plays a crucial role in viability and sustainability. Consultants such as Clayton Christensen, Dov Seidman, Marshall Goldsmith, Patrick Lencioni, Dan Pink, Tom Rath, and many others explore the nature and function of business culture. Some companies are far more successful than others and corporations spend enormous money trying to find the secret sauce of healthy, productive cultures. As Novak observes, when assessing a healthy business organization (or culture), "profitability is not the only indicator of its condition."[31] Other factors include employee engagement, employee safety, ethical history, brand equity, and even social media footprint.

For Novak, "the third cardinal virtue of business is related to the classical cardinal virtue of practical wisdom."[32] Aristotle called this virtue prudence, and St. Thomas Aquinas considered prudence the queen of all virtues, for through its exercise we acquire the moral knowledge necessary to form all other actions into virtues. One develops practical wisdom through experience and this "business sense" obviously plays a central role in creating a successful company. Business is geared toward action and prudence requires that one place the needs of the firm over the needs of the self. Jim Collins, in his international best-selling book *Good to Great*, describes his "Level 5 Leader" as one who "builds enduring greatness through a paradoxical blend of personal humility and professional will."[33] These successful executives all displayed large amounts of practical wisdom born from experience. Hubris, pride (the deadliest of the seven deadly sins) stands opposite of humility and a strong will overcomes inertia and sloth. Business leaders also must deal with concrete realities, the practical nature of day-to-day operations, and the cultivation of this virtue remains essential for success.

In retrospect, *Business as a Calling* stands as a foundational point of departure for a serious and sustained Catholic investigation into the role of business and the inner life of business professionals. For the first time, a serious lay thinker made a successful attempt to find a synthesis between the *negotium* and *otium* of life using a full assortment of philosophical and theological arguments. The book deftly repositioned the conversation from one utterly dominated by efficiency, costs, metrics, production, and other important business considerations into a larger, more robust discussion about the meaning of work, the inherent value in work, and the proper understanding of the "philosophy of work." The reverberations of 1197 and the death of a successful merchant in Cremona were starting to be felt.

Novak's book appeared in print one year before the publication of *If Aristotle Ran General Motors: The New Soul of Business*, written by University of Notre Dame philosophy professor Tom Morris.[34] The book was so well reviewed that Morris resigned his academic position (after 15 years) and started a successful (and lucrative) business consultancy. The title of the book at once marks its unique territory by invoking Aristotle, perhaps the most famous and least read philosopher in history. Linking Aristotle with leadership of one of the world's largest and best-known companies creates an intriguing intellectual hook, and the subtitle invoking the soul adds the dimension of deeper meaning than abstract philosophy. Morris grounds his argument on the bedrock of philosophy and the collective wisdom of great thinkers:

> The philosophers of the centuries, from Plato to Aristotle to the present day, have left us the equivalent of a huge bank account of wisdom that we can draw on for a wealth of insight applicable to both business and the rest of life. We can invest this intellectual capital in our own careers and experiences and reap tremendous returns of new wisdom as a result.[35]

Morris then begins to describe what he calls the "inner foundations for excellence," the core ideas or principles upon which a successful professional life can be built. For without this inner foundation of intellectual work, without an animating principle, any endeavor will likely fail.

Morris displays remarkable clarity in his version of "applied philosophy," beginning with a clear definition of terms and then provides concrete examples. For example, he cites the "four dimensions of human experiences" common to all people and all cultures across the globe. He defines them as:

> The Intellectual Dimension, which aims at Truth
> The Aesthetic Dimension, which aims at Beauty
> The Moral Dimension, which aims at Goodness
> The Spiritual Dimension, which aims at Unity. . . .

Anyone who has studied even remedial philosophy will at once recognize the categories and see the value if applied to the inner life of the mind. These terms, also known as the four transcendentals, exemplify timeless values. Morris, however, takes the terms and applies them to the active world of business. Once again, we have *otium* brought into conversation with *negotium*.

The Intellectual Dimension at work aims at Truth. The world of business appreciates the mandate of truth, even if this mandate at times gets ignored. The business world is full of rules, laws, procedures, and policies directed toward open, honest, and transparent transactions. Employees who lie on their professional résumés will lose their jobs; the SEC punishes companies who knowingly provide false information. Volkswagen will pay out over $15 billion dollars in penalties for using software to cheat on emission tests. Wells Fargo faces many, many millions in fines and lost brand equity for illegal banking activities. In a world of sophisticated technology, it becomes more and more difficult to hide transgressions and the cost associated with such dishonesty provides a decent (if imperfect) deterrent against most overt dishonesty. In this sense, the Intellectual Dimension ought to serve as a self-correcting measure, guiding individuals and companies toward the good and profitable and sustainable.

But Morris does not primarily focus on this important but obvious notion of the truth—that of honesty and truth telling. He relates the Intellectual Dimension with Truth as a question for excellence and human flourishing. Morris makes quick work of a basic misconception regarding pleasure and happiness (spoiler alert—they are not the same and the former does not cause the latter). Here Morris discusses the value of "competitive thought" and the notion that steel sharpens steel. It's become commonplace to say, "if you are the smartest person in the room, it's time to find a new room." Competitive thought combats solipsism and the drift toward self-absorption. In this sense, one ought to differentiate between "selfish" and "self-interest." Selfishness requires a zero-sum mentality, attempting to secure a larger and larger share of resources. Enlightened self-interest, properly understood, stands as an engine of growth and can foster better relationships among people and the common good. Aristotle wrote movingly on the value of friendship, calling it a supreme virtue. Genuine friendship, a second self, allows for constructive criticism and prevents vanity. Wise and respected counsel facilitates the discernment process and helps avoid myopia and tunnel vision. In this sense, friendship serves as a steward to truth.

At first glance, one may not see the importance of beauty in the world of work. Humans love and cherish beauty, to be sure. Millions and millions of people each year seek the beauty of nature at parks; we decorate our homes and strive to make them appealing to the eye. Museum collections proudly display the products of the human imagination from every conceivable time period and culture. We treasure, value, and crave beauty in our lives, but few people require or acknowledge the need for beauty at work. In fact, beauty, genuine beauty, can distract and the minimization of distractions at work makes sense. Aesthetically pleasing rooms and offices increase productivity and emotional wellbeing. So how ought we bring a sense of the Aesthetic Dimension into work? Morris suggests reflecting on a career as the "art of work"[36] and crafting career deep with meaning and even beauty in its service and the quest for excellence in all things.

The Purpose of Business and the Meaning of Work

Most men and women who find success in the world of business (or athletics or entertainment or academics) tend to take seriously their work and they rightly take a sense of pride from their career. But careers, even the most robustly successful, generally do not follow a straight path from unmitigated success to another unmitigated success.[37] The complete definition of the word *career* captures the sense of progress, of success and failure, over a long course of struggle and sacrifice. According to the *Oxford English Dictionary*, the words possessed a number of different meanings over the centuries:

ca·reer \kə-'rir\ *n* [fr. ML *carraria* road for vehicles]
1 a: speed in a course <ran at full ~ >
b: COURSE, PASSAGE
2: ENCOUNTER, CHARGE
3: a field for or pursuit of consecutive progressive achievement
4: a profession for which one trains and which is undertaken as a permanent calling
<a ~ in medicine> <a ~ diplomat>

As the above definitions suggest, a career meant a course or passage—something that could both provide a gateway or a blockade. The passage might at times be free and clear while at other moments be fraught with danger or uncertainty. Today, perhaps more than ever, this fluid nature of career manifests itself. According to a report in the *Wall Street Journal* from September 2010, a recent college graduate can expect to have seven distinct careers in his or her lifetime. Today college graduates expect to switch job numerous times with various companies—a professional form of serial monogamy.

When people first meet one another, the first question is often "what do you do?" It's a common question and it betrays the obvious importance we attach to our jobs. In some cases, it's a polite form of asking "how much money do you make?", for wealth remains a conspicuous measure of success. But the question betrays a misconception, for it no longer actually matters *what* you do. The "what" actually provides us with very little important information. In other words, many people can do *what* you do, as the world is full of talented people. We are all replaceable. But if we focus on "how" you do something—how you conduct your affairs as an employee, an owner, a husband, wife, brother, sister, son, or daughter—the question takes on a new dimension. In this sense, we can talk about the art of work. Scores of books, many using the premise of positive psychology, examine the value and dignity of work. People who can do both what they love and what they excel at tend to be far more engaged and productive while working.[38]

Morris calls this fusion between leisure and work "the art of living well" and he directs his attention to business endeavors: "Like a family, a neighborhood, and even a city, a business should be thought of as a partnership for living well. . . . A business is not primarily a building, or a collection of buildings . . . it is a partnership of people creating in many ways a better life for others as well as themselves."[39] Morris clearly has moved away from the parochial definition of business provided by Friedman that begins this chapter. This subtle and refined definition of business communities stands in stark juxtaposition to the dreary perspective found in the novels of Dickens or the plays of Arthur Miller. The ideal philosophical definition, as distinct from the reductive and stereotypical depiction in literature, suggests the inner life and complexity of work. As Abraham Maslow's "hierarchy of needs" (1943) reminds us, we all have needs—some are bodily and physical while others require love, acceptance, understanding, and meaning. When properly considered, business can help supply the materials for all of these needs: "The beauty of business is that within its structures, these human needs can be addressed with great power and results—if we keep them in focus."[40] In other words, work both enables, and it ennobles. Work *enables* us to earn a living and provide for ourselves and others; work *ennobles* by providing an outlet for creativity, meaning, and accomplishment.[41]

The Moral Dimension of Work does not merely concern itself with business ethics. Scores and scores of books examine the role of business ethics and the return on investment that derives from an ethical business culture. Some of these books focus on rules, policies, procedures, and proper guidelines. These books tend to be the least efficacious or interesting. Others make the human case for ethics in business, including the work of Stephen Young and the Caux Roundtable, dedicated to "Moral Capitalism at Work."[42] Elaine Sternberg, another philosopher deeply steeped in Aristotle, argues in *Just Business: Business Ethics in Action*, for an applied ethics grounded in philosophy.[43] Sternberg believes that a trained philosopher ought to replace the myriad lawyers, compliance officers, auditors, and risk managers. Unlike Morris, she spends considerable time with actual business cases and specific issues, such as hiring and termination, discrimination, finance, junk bonds, insider trading, corporate governance, accounting systems, executive compensation, and a host of other pressing concerns. Her (admittedly) narrow definition of business, "maximizing owner value over the long term by selling goods or services," largely ignores much of the language employed by Whyte, Novak, Morris, and others, and yet she arrives at similar conclusions.[44] Moreover, Sternberg asserts "business does not exist to foster employees' physical or psychological wellbeing; still less is its goal their ultimate fulfillment. . . . Such positive benefits routinely result from business, but they do not constitute its defining aim."[45]

Morris has a different perspective, of course, when it comes to the Moral Dimension and the resulting "goodness" of business. Ethics, Morris writes, suffers from a prevailing misconception: many view ethics simply as a collection of "thou shall nots" and a litany of prohibitions. Yet, ethics seeks the avoidance of evil and the enhancement of goods and services for the betterment of life. Resource allocation then becomes a major ethical issue. Morris argues for a dynamic symbiosis between "inner substance and outer greatness."[46] In fact, the two must have a complementary relationship for any healthy, flourishing enterprise. Ethics in this sense concerns our public behavior and the decisions made in a corporate setting. These decisions have a major impact on external actions, reputation, and success.

Finally, Morris arrives at the Spiritual Dimension at Work. It is here, most profoundly, that business moves into a realm not generally considered proper to its function. We tend to refrain from discussing religion or politics at the office. In fact, it's often discouraged for the sake of harmony and office civility. These topics tend to bring passion and conviction, and they can often result in friction and even hostility. The safest way to avoid a "crucial conversation," is often simply not to have one.[47] Both Novak and Morris seek to baptize the realm of business and place it under the rubric of philosophy—striving to find a synthesis between the world and personal growth, happiness, and meaning. Their efforts provide a context and vocabulary for investigating the complex and profound nature of work and human life. In this way, they build upon the forgotten tradition of St. Omobono of Cremona.[48]

Morris does not write from a specifically Catholic perspective (in the book, he identifies as a Southern Baptist who admires the beauty of the Catholic Faith), and he does not attempt to place his argument within a Catholic context—historical or religious. Thomas Woods, however, forcefully brings the concepts of the free economy (including private enterprise and private property) in direct conversation with the history and expressed teachings of the Catholic Church. The result, *The Church and the Market: A Catholic Defense of the Free Economy*, is a concise, compelling, and lucid argument that combines an impressive knowledge of Church teachings and a stunning command of economic theory.[49] Woods' analysis marks a watershed in the synthesis between Church teaching and economic theory—a serious and unstinting examination of the often confused and vexing topics of religion and economics. A trained historian (Woods attended Harvard as an undergraduate and earned his Ph.D. in history from Columbia University), he also has affiliations with the Austrian School of Economics (Woods serves as a Senior Fellow at the Ludwig von

Mises Institute), and perhaps no single writer brings such impressive credentials to the topic.

Woods begins his project with an admission: Although a faithful and practicing Catholic, he finds many of the Church's teachings regarding economics based more on *sentiment* than on expertise or logic. He does not focus on errors in expression (about which reasonable people might differ), but errors in fact and in consequence. He does not concede, for example, the ubiquitous *a priori* suspicion of the market that colors many perspectives within the Church. He notes that his "argument may well be unique in Catholic literature in that it makes no such concession, offering instead a principled and unapologetic defense of the free market."[50] Moreover, he asserts that the complexity of economic thinking as expressed in many documents, especially papal encyclicals, "is very far from the Church's competence," as it falls "several levels removed from the areas of faith and morals."[51] Thus, an analysis of the economic *consequences* of these various documents is not merely licit, but a moral imperative. As such, Woods presents his case for the "lawful diversity of opinions," since no Papal pronouncement passes definitive judgments, "for this does not fall *per se* within the Magisterium's specific domain."[52] In order to achieve clarity, expert economic analysis, and not mere sentiment or impassioned rhetoric, must be deployed.

It would be outside the scope of this analysis to provide a careful review of each argument put forth by Woods and others; in fact, Catholics interested in the topic ought to read the book entirely. Some of the topics covered by Woods, including foreign aid, the welfare state, and reserve banking, involve complex federal and state legislation and demand careful consideration. Other topics, however, pertain largely to the individual, the corporation, and the common good—the very issues suggested by the canonization of 1199. As such, we can see a thread of continuity weaving together the centuries into a larger tapestry. This analysis rather seeks to examine the rhetoric used (by the Church) regarding the free economy and capitalism. The rhetoric does indeed seem grounded in sentiment and feeling, rather than in consistent and informed economic analysis and this, at times, confuses rather than clarifies.

Woods begins with a "defense of economics," where he introduces and defines some key terms (including opportunity cost, marginal utility, praxeology, and the demand curve, among others) while demonstrating the value of economics as a social science different from hard sciences such as physics and chemistry, for "the very existence of human choice and free will preclude basing social analysis on such a model, since human beings are fundamentally unlike inanimate objects."[53] Economics is thus comparative rather than absolute and subject to significant variation from precise and predictable models. Central to his analysis is a free economy, rule of law, the right to private property, and sound currency. But economics concerns human action as well, and as such requires actors in the drama. In contrast to "central planners" of Marxism and socialism (where economic decision are made by state-ordered fiat and not by rational calculation of self-interest), dynamic economies need dynamic individuals, agents capable of making creative decisions about the highest and best use of capital allocation. Morris quotes Murray Rothbard regarding the essential nature of the rational entrepreneur in any healthy economy:

> It is precisely this central and vital role of the appraising entrepreneur, driven by the quest for profits and the avoidance of losses, that cannot be fulfilled by the socialist planning board, for lack of a market in the means of production. Without such a market, there are no genuine money prices and therefore no means for the entrepreneur to calculate and appraise in cardinal monetary terms.[54]

Once again, we return to the role of the agent—the rational, acting individual serving as a model of virtue—who employs wit, invention, discovery, and enterprise to satisfy a need in society. As we have seen, successful business leaders need intelligence, skill, talent, vision, and grit in order to succeed.[55] If they strive to find sustaining success and fulfillment, they also need virtue.

But economic theory must likewise be grounded in rationality and analysis—not merely sentiment, emotion, or feelings. If governed largely by sentiment, the law of unintended consequences will certainly intrude. In official Church documents, according to Woods, sentiment often plays a role. According to Catholic social teaching, Christians must recognize the plague of poverty, and they must work to alleviate the suffering caused by it. Nearly everyone *feels* badly for the poor and we as a nation *feel* that something ought to be done regarding poverty. Since 1965, the USA has spent over $5.4 trillion dollars on various federal, state, and local welfare programs—despite mounting evidence that they do not work and have not really ended poverty in any concrete fashion. Yet, for many people, the problem of poverty would vanish could we simply muster the moral or political will to solve the problem. Often, critics of business assert that if people just cared more, if they just gave more, these intractable social problems would, somehow, magically disappear. Such charges demonstrate a palpable ignorance regarding the complexity of these vexing economic issues.

Without the virtuous entrepreneur, the state often lacks a sufficient vocabulary for virtue. Federal and State regulations strive to efface any language that suggests virtue as an animating principle. Laws tend to focus exclusively on compliance with the legal mandate—offering no compelling justification for the mandate. Consequently, business leaders must find a vocabulary for virtue (and not simply compliance) elsewhere. They must look to other sources for guidelines in creating a moral framework and vision for business. The Church has reluctantly entered this discussion and with mixed results—especially since very few Church leaders have any genuine training or expertise in complex economic matters. Woods examines these conflicting signals through an economic lens and finds many of the adjurations lacking in sophistication or efficacy. Once again, asserting that solutions to these problems are self-evident hinders real conversation and attributing bad motives to others obviously hampers the coherence of any argument.

The case for the economic blessings of capitalism has been made many times by scores of thinkers. This is not the place to cover that extraordinary amount of material. In short, no economic system in history has produced more wealth, health, prosperity, and peace than market-based capitalism. I will, however, end this section with an optimistic passage from *Abundance: The Future is Brighter than You Think*, by Peter H. Diamandis.[56] In the book Diamandis makes a compelling argument in favor of innovation resulting from freedom of information, ideas, and capital. He provides persuasive data to show how by almost every conceivable measure, the world population, taken as a whole, is better off today than one hundred years ago. Most homes have electricity, plumbing, heating, refrigeration, phone, television, internet connections, and other modern devices. The cost of goods and services continues to plunge for basic necessities and utilities.

> Today light will cost less than a half of second of your working time if you are an average worker: Half a second of work for an hour of light! Had you been using a kerosene lamp in the 1880s, you would have had to work for 15 minutes to get the same amount of light. A tallow candle in the 1700s: over six hours of work. And to get that much light from a sesame-oil lamp in Babylon in 1750 BC would have cost you more than 50 hours of work.[57]

But light only represents one area of abundance. Diamandis looks at water treatment and desalinization efforts, health care, hydroponics and agriculture, computing, and every other area of human endeavor. In fact,

> The vast majority of people are much better fed, much better sheltered, much better entertained, much better protected against disease and much more likely to live

to old age than their ancestors have been. . . . Even allowing for the hundreds of millions who still live in abject poverty, disease, and want, this generation of human beings has access to more calories, watts, lumen-hours, square-feet, gigabytes, megahertz, light-years, bushels per acre, miles per gallon, food miles, air miles, and, of course, dollars, than any that went before.[58]

Most of these innovations result from the ideas and enterprise of individuals working within a free economy. One does not find this innovation in command economies directed by central planners. One does not see this creative disruption coming from the governments of the world. One finds this abundance of creation in places like Austin, Ann Arbor, Boston, San Francisco, and other cities where the marketplace of ideas allows for competition and reward. It bears repeating that young people must be free to move to these robust markets, and such freedom of movement (for both people and goods) is a crucial part of the capitalist order. In this case, people literally "vote with their feet" and relocate to areas that afford better opportunities. No legal or political coercion is needed. This is the beauty and promise of the market economy in action. It works. The evidence is overwhelming. But in order to fulfill the promise for all, in order for the blessings and abundance to spread continually, individuals must act with a spirit of generosity, a notion of virtuous action, and a clear understanding of the common good. This is the domain of the Church—dynamic intersection where Omobono the successful entrepreneur and merchant meets Omobono the man of virtue, intelligence, compassion, stewardship, enterprise, and agency.[59]

Entering into the Discussion: The Church Speaks

On 15 May 1891, Pope Leo XIII issued his encyclical *Rerum Novarum* (On Capital and Labor).[60] This seminal document remains a foundational text for modern Catholic social teaching and today continues to generate much discussion and commentary. Pope Leo, born Vincenzo Luigi Pecci in 1810, reigned from February 1878 until his death in 1903, making his tenure the third longest in Church history. Historians refer to him as the "Rosary Pope," for he issued eleven encyclicals on the rosary. *Rerum Novarum*, however, sought to identify and ameliorate the harsh conditions placed "upon the teeming masses of the laboring poor a yoke little better than that of slavery itself."[61] Pope Leo notes the difficult nature of his task ("the discussion is not easy, not is it void of danger") and he tacitly admits that economics, generally, falls outside of the realm of faith and morals. In fact, the document does not interrogate current economic theory or even cite major economic thinkers. The encyclical thus offers very few specific monetary or fiscal proposals, opting rather for guidelines and core beliefs. This does not prevent the pope from making strong assertions, but it also helps create a complex, even economically incoherent document. In short, Pope Leo presents rhetorically mixed signals and thus does not offer a unified, theoretically sophisticated argument.[62]

Significantly, Pope Leo does not address the encyclical to the workers of the world, to the managers of those workers, or to the owners who employ the workers. Rather, he addresses the encyclical to "Our Venerable Brethren the Patriarchs, Primates, Archbishops, Bishops, and other ordinaries of places having Peace and Communion with the Apostolic See." As such, it's a high-level, executive document intended to circulate among senior church leaders in order to help them as they minster to the faithful in their local dioceses. The text provides scant references to any important works of economic theory and clearly does not seek to partake in the examination of economics *qua* economics. The audience matters here, for he was not entering into conversation with policy experts, academics, or professional economists. This was a document for the faithful, and Pope Leo makes abundantly clear two primary points that inform the basis of this analysis: the utter rejection of socialism and the inherent, natural right to private property.

In other encyclicals, Pope Leo condemned socialism in the strongest possible language. In *Quod Apostolici Muneris* (1878),

Diuturnum (1881), and *Graves de Communi Re* (1901), the pope denounced socialism as incompatible with Christian life. In *Rerum Novarum*, Leo reasserts his objections. Socialism is a false teaching that attempts to destroy, thwart, and undermine natural rights and values. To remedy economic inequalities,

> The socialists, working on the poor man's envy of the rich, are striving to do away with private property, and contend that individual possessions should become the common property of all . . . but their contentions are so clearly powerless to end the controversy that were they carried into effect the working man himself would be among the first to suffer.[63]

According to Pope Leo, socialists are "emphatically unjust, for they would rob the lawful possessor" while undermining and distorting the functions of the state while creating confusion in the community. Moreover, the well-connected and influential rarely suffer from the abrogation of private property; it's generally the lowest rung of society that suffers most from socialism. Thomas Woods calls Leo's strong denunciation an "especially courageous move, flying as it did in the face of intellectual fashion."[64] The pope specifically mentions envy as a primary animating principle within socialism.

The pope's use of the word envy merits special attention. According to Helmut Schoeck, envy exists in all societies, cultures, historical epochs and languages.[65] At a robust 427 pages, this book stands as one of the most comprehensive treatments of envy ever written. Schoeck believes that envy can spur competition and even help societies maintain social control, but at the same time it can also overshoot its mark and turn man to destruction, especially when used to direct social, economic, and fiscal policy. His book has two primary aims:

> First, envy is much more universal than has so far been admitted or even realized, indeed that envy alone

makes any kind of social co-existence possible; secondly, however, I believe envy as the implicit or explicit fulcrum of social policy to be much more destructive than those who have fabricated their social and economic philosophy out of envy would care to admit.[66]

It does not take much imagination to see the manifestations of envy in social policy arguing in favor of redistribution of wealth, the handwringing over economic inequality, and the impulse behind the short-lived Occupy Wall Street movement.[67] Demanding something (under the guise of "fairness" or "equality") from others largely because they have surplus and you have a deficit betrays the insidious effects of envy. Ethics and religion possess clear vocabularies to help combat the excessive nature of envy. The Decalogue, for example, expressly prohibits "coveting" in two separate commandments. Christopher Marlowe, in his famous play *Doctor Faustus*, personifies envy in his acute bitterness toward others. The pageant of the seven deadly sins reveals the nature of envy: "I cannot read, and therefore wish all books burned. I am lean with seeing others eat."[68] Envy is unique among these deadly sins, as it is the only sin that does not provide even a measure of pleasure. But even as the Marxists can identify expressions of envy, Schoeck argues, "it is hard to see how the totally secularized and ultimately egalitarian society promised us by socialism can ever solve the problem of residual envy latent in society."[69] In fact, without private property and material reward for labor, resentment grows, and any society that forbids this natural desire "would become extremely distasteful to the individual."[70] Envy produces bitterness and division, hardly the basis of sound economic or social policy.

Novak also examines the pernicious effects of envy, calling it "the most destructive passion in any free society . . . anything that incites envy—or seems to support the arguments of those moved by envy—is a danger to the free society."[71] But Novak takes the argument a bit further and offers an antidote to envy in the form of freedom of opportunity afforded by the market. Novak asserts that if business seeks indeed to be a "morally serious calling," it must define and exhibit moral responsibilities. To that end, he lists seven "corporate responsibilities" required of all legitimate business enterprises. The fifth responsibility concerns envy and the most efficacious way to eliminate envy: "To defeat envy through generating upward mobility, and putting empirical ground under the conviction that hard work and talent are fairly rewarded."[72] In other words, the free market, if truly free, should give everyone the opportunity to succeed through talent and enterprise. When people succeed thusly, through "earned merit," envy diminishes and increased emotional well-being results. Envy fixates on the unattainable and on ways to dislodge others from possession of the desired object; entrepreneurs, rather, focus on what could be and what is possible as they seek to add and create value (rather than confiscate from others).

Modern social science seems to support this contention. In a widely cited paper, psychologists Daniel Kahneman (primary founder of the emergent "positive psychology") and Angus Deaton examined how rises in income might impact both "evaluation of life" (i.e., how an individual thinks about the current overall quality of life) and "emotional well-being" (the frequency and intensity of experiences of joy, stress, sadness, anger, and affection).[73] In this study, the authors show that high income improves the "evaluation of life" and thus money can initially "buy" a portion of happiness. While emotional well-being rises with income, there is very little progress beyond an annual income of $75,000. In other words, increased money cannot buy increased happiness, as the law of diminished returns takes effects: The person with ten cars is not 10x happier than the person with one car. An enhanced valuation of life diminishes envy—for when one is content and at peace with one's own life, there is little reason to feel envy of another. Crucially, the most efficacious way to raise income and increase both evaluation of life and emotional well-being is the free economy itself. It is not the command economy, punitively progressive tax codes, or vast redistributions of wealth. The proposals for a "universal income" will likely fail to create a more "equitable" society (however one defines that complex term). The most obvious and humane method remains to provide ample opportunities for meaningful work and job creation. And the best vehicle for such economic richness is through the free market and private enterprise.[74]

Pope Leo also offers an impassioned defense of private property as a right natural and sacred to the individual, the family, and, by extension, to the benefit of society. Without a right to private property, humans would not only lack motivation to work hard and save, but they would also lose a sense of place, home, dignity, security, community, and motivation:

> It is surely undeniable that, when a man engages in remunerative labor, the impelling reason and motive of his work is to obtain property, and thereafter to hold it as his very own. If one man hires out to another his strength or skill, he does so for the purpose of receiving in return what is necessary for the satisfaction of his needs; he therefore expressly intends to acquire a right full and real, not only to the remuneration, but also to the disposal of such remuneration, just as he pleases. Thus, if he lives sparingly, saves money, and, for greater security, invests his savings in land, the land, in such case, is only his wages under another form; and so, consequently, a working man's little estate thus purchased should be as completely at his full disposal as are those wages he receives for his labor. Socialists, therefore, by endeavoring to transfer the possessions of individuals to the community at large, strike at the interest of every wage earner, since they would deprive him of the liberty of disposing of his wages, and thereby of all the hope and possibility of increasing his resources and of bettering his condition in life.[75]

In this long quote, Leo incorporates the "self-interest" discussed by Adam Smith under a Catholic banner. Such a robust defense of private property and the rule of law required to protect private property suggests a similar defense for the economic system best suited for the accumulation of capital necessary to secure private property. No other economic system can approach the power of a free economy in providing real opportunity to create jobs through innovation, enterprise, and creativity. Yet the encyclical does not endorse a *laissez faire* economic system. It does not condemn a market-based system, but it does support regulations, limits, and other restraints—even if left unstated with precision.[76]

During the last days of the Cold War, 1 May 1991, then Pope John Paul II published his ninth encyclical, *Centesimus Annus* on the 100th anniversary of *Rerum Novarum*—in part to honor that ground-breaking document, as well as to refine, update, and enlarge the social teaching of the Church.[77] The document was both an example of continuity and disruption, part of a continual tradition (offering "an invitation to look back") while recognizing that the unique historical moment required new understandings and formulations ("a look to the future"). John Paul echoed Pius X in praising Leo and his "immortal document,"[78] and he clearly understood the profound historical moment required asking new questions about the very nature and function of society and the world of business. As Russell Hittinger explains, *Centesimus Annus*

> was the first major encyclical that treats the modern state for what it is, at least as recent history has disclosed it: namely, a potentially dangerous concentration of coercive power that requires the most exacting juridical and structural limitations lest it engulf the economic sphere on the one hand, or the cultural-religious sphere on the other. The political state depicted in *Centesimus Annus* is no longer the classical or medieval *civitas*.[79]

In the encyclical, John Paul takes seriously his role as a pastor and the text stands clearly within the tradition of "teaching" documents. He asserts with modesty that he has no precise principles to offer and no concrete economic theories to eliminate or even reduce the scale and scope of human suffering: "The Church has no models to present," but rather "an indispensable and ideal orientation."[80] Indeed, for the pope, "the can be no genuine solution to the 'social question' apart from the Gospel."[81] The pope then spends considerable time reviewing and reflecting upon *Rerum Novarum* and retrofitting the encyclical into the modern world. *Centesimus Annus* again defends the natural right to private property, rejects socialism and statist economies, argues in favor of trade unions, and teaches about the universal destination of material goods. He reviews the traditional tension between capital and labor, and he discusses the two traditional forms of ownership found in history—work and land. The growing chasm between work (labor) and land ownership (capital) created a rift with significant social consequences discussed in many previous social encyclicals. But then John Paul notices something fundamentally unique about the current time.

A third agent has been added to the dynamic between capital and labor, a third "form of ownership" that will disrupt the binary and create new opportunities for wealth, productivity, freedom, advancement, and autonomy: The knowledge and skills of the *individual*. According to the pope, "in our time, in particular, there exists another form of ownership which is becoming no less important than land: *the possession of know-how, technology, and skill*. The wealth of the industrialized nations is based much more on this kind of ownership than on natural resources."[82] He continues to praise those who have the "ability to foresee both the needs of others" and the technology skill to satisfy those needs. He then offers a concise account of the working of the free economy and the power of collaboration: "Organizing such productive effort, planning its duration in time, making sure that it corresponds in a positive way to the demands which it must satisfy, and taking the necessary risks—all this too is a source of wealth in today's society."[83] It's a crucial insight and one that anticipates prophetically the power of innovation and disruption found in the world today—an economic force unleashed with power previously unseen in human history. It sets the foundation for a profound "theology of work."[84] The free economy requires and allows for freedom of occupational mobility. Excessive government regulations often hamper this mobility and yet this freedom offers employees an additional layer of protection: If they suffer abuse at the hand of an employer, they have the freedom to change jobs. If they do not find certain policies agreeable (e.g., for maternity leave, sick days, vacations, wages, etc.), freedom to move and find a new employer benefits the worker, thus using the power of the market to secure more favorable treatment.

The pope then precisely frames this type of virtuous activity: "In this way, the *role* of disciplined and creative *human work* and, as an essential part of that work, *initiative and entrepreneurial ability* becomes increasingly evident and decisive."[85] It's a stunning observation and one that sits at the very heart of a free economy. No longer will people be bound to the land, as serfs or slaves. In fact, fewer than 2% of the population in the industrialized world works in farming. Today, the Internet and other forms of technology allow millions and millions of people across the globe to participate in the production and distribution of goods and services—people who would have been excluded only a generation ago. The emergent virtues of initiative, fortitude, grit, resiliency, imagination, and creativity will allow millions and millions of people to share the promise of a better life.[86] The workings of a free economy and the entrepreneurial mindset allow virtually anyone with a computer and Internet connection to participate. Such technology, once the domain of the rich and privileged, is now available to a larger and larger percentage of the world's population. In fact, around the globe, more people have direct access to a cell phone than a toilet.[87] This provides a powerful computer in their hands and creates the possibility for endless forms of disruption and economic development, from medicine, sales, communication, travel, finance (especially microlending and crowd-funded projects), and nearly every other human endeavor.

Thus, in a remarkable way, the new economic realities, far

from alienating and excluding, can refocus attention on humanity itself. While many remain marginalized and alienated, the free economy coupled with technology will continue to erase barriers and constraints on the individual. According to John Paul, beside the planet, our greatest resource is *man himself*, for our "intelligence enables [us] to discover the earth's productive potential and the many different ways in which human needs can be satisfied."[88] It's a point worth considering. This rupture—or paradigm shift, to use a word coined for the hard sciences—provides a remarkable opportunity for individuals working alone and together to find new methods of creation and distribution. No longer will large monopolies protect and exclude the majority of people; the barriers to entry in almost any field are rapidly crumbling and new entrepreneurial immigrants arrive daily—without ever leaving their homes. Innovative technology, both incremental and disruptive, holds great promise for humanity, from both the production and consumer aspects. In fact, the "modern *business economy* has positive aspects. Its basis is human freedom exercised in the economic field."[89] Of course, many millions still suffer and remain excluded, but the free economy, coupled with technology and human initiative, offers a promising avenue for the remediation of such suffering and blight.

Did the pope foresee and even predict this new economy? Does this new economy offer solutions to the ravishing poverty in the world? According to the encyclical, "the answer is obviously complex,"[90] but the animating principles behind the "free economy," "business economy," or "market economy" (the pope uses all three terms) offer the most promise and measured results for humanity. Others echoed his remarks, even if guardedly. Irving Kristol applied his phrase "two cheers for capitalism" after reading the encyclical.[91] Kristol praises capitalism for two primary reasons: 1) as an economic system, it works very well in the material world, and 2) the system supports a large expression of individual liberty. Thus, it deserves two cheers, but not, perhaps, three. For at the same time, the free economy can produce a "psychic burden" of responsibility upon the individual to work, earn, budget, and largely control the teleology of an individual life. Clearly the market cannot be society's *sole* animating or organizing principle, for they are not perfectly self-correcting, self-regulating economic systems, and thus we must rely on prudence and the collective judgments of experience and tradition. But the free economy can indeed work to reduce poverty and increase wages, standards of living, and overall health.

An initiative by the Acton Institute recognizes the possibilities. The Institute, led by Fr. Robert Sirico, strives to integrate Judeo-Christian Truths with Free Market Principles. It stands as one of the most important, effective, and intelligent organizations dedicated to liberty, responsibility, and the human person within a free economy. Its most recent program, The Poverty Cure, explores the fascinating way in which free economy principles can help eliminate poverty via the use of micro-credit and finance.[92]

Others advocate a similar salutary role for the free economy and market forces as efficacious means of solving social problems. Muhammad Yunus, winner of the 2006 Nobel Peace Prize, is a social entrepreneur, banker, and economist. He specializes in the creation of microcredit and micro-financing in poverty-stricken areas in his home of Bangladesh and around the world. In his best-selling book *Building Social Businesses*, Yunus advocates using market principles in the creation of "social businesses"—a new kind of business that expressly seeks to solve social problems by using business methods.[93] The subtitle of the book, *The New Kind of Capitalism that Serves Humanity's Most Pressing Needs*, also merits some attention. The economic system employed—the system deemed the most promising in alleviating poverty in the poorest areas—was not Marxism, socialism, neo-statism, of the new welfare state. The principles of the market, including finance, enterprise, innovation, creativity, and autonomy, hold the most promise for raising people out of poverty. Yunus articulates seven animating characteristics for social businesses, including the solving of a problem, financial stability, full repayment of seed capital, all future profits return to the business, environmental consciousness, market wages or better for employees, and joyful work.

Each of these characteristics finds expression, either directly or indirectly, in John Paul's encyclical. Moreover, the entire system is a concrete and efficacious example of subsidiarity in action.

St. John Paul II proved to be exceptionally astute in his observations about the changing nature of work and the world economy—the newly emergent reality often called the "sharing economy" or the "experience economy." He recognized, before many professional economists and philosophers, the true renaissance of humanity and the need for creativity, intelligence, initiative, and resilience. He also urges the active cultivation of prudence, justice, temperance, and fortitude—those classical virtues required for human flourishing and enriched by the Christian virtues of faith, hope, and charity. But St. John Paul II also vividly recognized the power of tradition and the models of heroic virtue expressed in the communion of saints, specifically in his recognition of St. Omobono in 1997.[94]

The *Catechism of the Catholic Church* (second edition, 1994) likewise sends some rhetorically mixed signals in matters economic.[95] This impressive publication, the summary of Church doctrine, has remarkably little to say about specific matters of business and industry, including economic systems, taxes, profits, regulation, or the free market. The *Catechism* clearly echoes Leo's condemnation of socialism, but it also introduces some uncertainty regarding capitalism. The following paragraph is the most detailed:

> The Church has rejected the totalitarianism and atheistic ideologies associated in modern times with "communism" or "socialism." She has likewise refused to accept, in the practice of "capitalism," individualism and absolute primacy of the law of the marketplace over human labor. Regulating the economy solely by centralized planning perverts the basis of social bonds; regulating it solely by the law of the marketplace fails social justice, for "there are many human needs which cannot be satisfied by the market" (*CA*, 34). Reasonable regulation of the marketplace and economic initiatives,

in keeping with a just hierarchy of values and a view to the common good, is to be commended.

While rejecting communism and socialism as incompatible with human dignity and the autonomy of each person, this paragraph also suggests "reasonable regulation" of the marketplace. This vague phrase, of course, contains all sorts of mischief, as both "reasonable" and "regulation" covers a wide spectrum of possible behaviors.[96]

The passage repeats a primary critique of centralized planning (perverting the basis for social bonds) while rejecting the atheism associated with communism and socialism. The caution directed toward capitalism is muted, in comparison, especially with certain qualifications. Moreover, the passage might contain a straw man, for few economists subscribe to a totally unfettered capitalism—an economic system free from any restraint or regulation. Fewer argue for the "absolute primacy" of the market over human labor. Slavery, an example of market considerations taking primacy over the dignity of human beings, was abolished in the United States in 1865. Child labor, another example of a perverted relationship between market and human labor, was largely abolished in 1938 with the passage of the Fair Labor Standards Act. The passage creates enough ambiguity, however, to create confusion and misunderstanding among the faithful, even as it urges a measure of prudence in all undertakings.

THE MOVE TOWARD A NEW UNDERSTANDING OF FAITH AND BUSINESS

In 2012, the Pontifical Council for Justice and Peace published a 30-page pamphlet called "Vocation of the Business Leader: A Reflection." The document, complete with a Foreword written by Cardinal Peter K. A. Turkson, president of the Council, marks a conspicuous shift in sympathy within some quarters of the Church when addressing the world in business. Although Michael Novak used the term "vocation" in his book *Business as a Calling* (as discussed above), this document used the word expressly to describe the role of the businessperson as an opportunity for personal sanctification and holiness—connecting it back to the canonization in 1199. The document examines with seriousness and intelligence the nature of business and strives to understand the dynamic synthesis that can exist between the world of business and the life of authentic faith. The authors, an impressive collection of academics and religious, challenge the commonly held view that the realms of morality and business must remain separate, and they attempt to replace the "divided life" with an integrated one—business practices informed by and animated by a moral foundation and Catholic teaching. Consequently, the document started a discussion and filled a conspicuous void for Catholic men and women who desire some guiding principles and concrete application to settle these nettlesome and vexing questions.

A most striking aspect of the *Reflection* is the tone of respect and even admiration for the world of business and the business leader—when properly ordered. The Introduction makes several claims explicitly: "Businesspeople have been given great resources . . . This is your vocation. In this young century alone many businesses have already brought forth marvelous innovations which have cured disease, brought people closer together through technology, and created prosperity in countless ways."[97] The text continues to state that when managed well, business can actively help in the "development of virtues" just as families ("the first school of societies") do.[98] Perhaps even more directly, the document asserts what many in business have long understood and accepted as obvious, namely that "the vocation of the businessperson is a genuine human and Christian calling. Its importance in the life of the Church and in the world economy can hardly be overstated."[99] The language used here is extraordinary. Never before had Church leaders referred to the unique and essential role business plays in the life of the Church. The sentiments here obviously go well beyond the financial role and the collection plate and suggest a more integral and foundational function. The canonization of 1199 focused on a single individual; this document addresses the entire profession.

The serious *Reflection* recognizes the myriad challenges facing the business leader attempting to synthesize the *negotium* and *otium* as it identifies a primary challenge for many: Chief among these obstacles at a personal level is a "divided life" or what Vatican II described as the "split between the faith which many profess and their daily lives."[100] Indeed, this challenge, the work-life balance or the compartmentalized reality of life, can create a real barrier between the activities of life. At its heart, the *Reflection* desires to move from theory to practice, to propose concrete solutions to vexing questions. Recognizing the difficulties is more than an effective rhetorical posture and stands as the first step toward examination and remedy. It is here where stands an example of heroic virtue—the type of integrated life achieved by St. Omobono, for the saint faced similar challenges and obstacles, including strife within his own family, as he attempted to find harmony between and among the various mandates.

The document also addresses one of the most contentious topics in the world of business: profit. As we have seen, the common caricature of business includes a narrow-minded focus solely on the bottom line and a fixation with profits, profits, profits. The caricature, so ingrained in the anti-capitalist mythology, fails to recognize a fundamental truth about business and profit: Making a profit is not unlawful or sinful. The point seems so obvious to business leaders that it seems superfluous to mention, but a strong undercurrent undermines and even distrusts the profit motive. Church documents have largely ignored the topic. The pamphlet, however, presents a genuine appraisal of profit as an indication of business acumen and health:

> Entrepreneurs exercise their creativity to organize their talents and energies of labor and to assemble capital and other resources from the earth's abundance to produce goods and services. When this is done effectively, well-paying jobs are created, profit is realized, the resulting wealth is shared with investors, and everyone involved excels. The Church acknowledges the legitimate role of

profit as an indicator that a business is functioning well.[101]

Profit qua profit is neither moral nor immoral—but how one secures that profit and what one does with that profit both contain a clear moral dimension. The guiding principle for both making profit and distributing the profit must be, first and foremost, human dignity.

The *Reflection* praises the freedom of the market and the freedom of the business leaders but recognizes that with freedom also comes responsibility. Here we see the stark contrast between the "Friedman Doctrine" and Catholic Social teaching as expressed in the Reflection. Instead of profit being the primary (and only) measure of social responsibility, Catholic business leaders are reminded that every action (job, wages, products, services) must conform to the general principal of human dignity. "Businesses are therefore essential to the common good of every society and to the whole global order. They contribute best when their activities are allowed to be oriented toward, and be fully respectful of, the dignity of people as ends in themselves who are intelligent, free and social."[102] This important work continues, and various resources are now readily available for Catholic business leaders. In 2014, Andrew Abela and Joseph Capizzi edited *A Catechism for Business: Tough Ethical Questions & Insights from Catholic Teaching*. This edition provides an excellent guide for navigating the difficult practical questions that arise while running a business.

The document also sounds note of optimism concerning the opportunities for individuals to pursue the integrated life more fully: "Fortunately, new movements and programs have been developed in an effort to take more seriously the moral and spiritual life in relation to business," including "faith and work groups, spirituality of work programs, business ethics training, and social responsibility projects."[103] The laity continues to lead the way in this renaissance, in the quest for rediscovering the harmony between work and the spirit. For example, Legatus, a network of Catholic CEOs and senior executives founded in 1987 by Thomas Monaghan, continues to expand. In fact, 2022 saw the addition of new chapters across the United States. Legatus now has over 80 chapters around the world and sees its mission at the nexus of faith and business. Its mission statement, "To study, live, and spread the Catholic faith in our business, professional, and personal lives" emphasizes the conspicuous attention paid to the world of business. The monthly *Legatus* magazine has regular features on business ethics, case studies, and Church documents. The organization hosts an annual gala conference (attended by luminaries of the Catholic world) as well as seminars, retreats, and pilgrimages throughout the year.

Over 1800 Catholic colleges and universities exist world-wide and approximately 800 have business programs. In this way, the "Church has invested herself in the formation of future business leaders," presenting a rich opportunity to continue to find harmonies and synergy with young professionals seeking a deeper connection between work and the world at large. Catholic Business Conferences, almost unheard of a generation ago, continue to proliferate around the country, with thousands of people attending each year to hear Mass, network, and learn from distinguished speakers. Catholic social service organizations offer job training programs, career counseling and mentoring, as well as abundant opportunities to find work in the non-profit sector. Indeed, there is much room for optimism. The Reflection concludes with an uplifting, positive adjuration: "Entrepreneurs, managers, and all who work in business, should be encouraged to recognize their work as a true vocation and respond to God's call in the spirit of true disciples."[104] This Reflection, finally, offers a "Discernment Checklist" for business leaders to conduct an examination of current business practices and ways to improve and suggestions for further discovery. Taken together, the modest publication provides an enormous opportunity for a renewed consideration of the inherent possibilities for virtue and the life of business.

This recognition of the virtuous nature of the well-ordered business and the exciting opportunities for a deeper understanding and collaboration between business and religion received a sudden jolt with the election of Pope Francis. The Jesuit from

Argentina wasted little time in making powerful pronouncements on a wide range of topics. Since his election on 13 March 2013, in his published encyclicals, in his apostolic exhortations, in his homilies, and in the numerous unscripted, off-the-cuff press conferences (many of which occur on airplanes), he has generated enormous attention from Catholics and non-Catholics across the globe. He offers opinions and thoughts on a wide range of topics, including those not normally associated with the competency of the Church over the realm of faith and morals. Many of these remarks, often wrenched from context or presented for maximum controversy, engender debates and polemics, especially in the areas of economics and the environment. The strong rhetoric against capitalism and the market has created confusion and misunderstanding both within and without the Catholic community.

Pope Francis directly addressed the question of the free market in his encyclical *Lumen Fidei* (*The Light of Faith*) issued on 29 June 2013. The encyclical, lengthy and largely conversational, moves between and among various topics of importance. The pope decries the disposable culture—a culture where goods and humans are used and the discarded when no longer possessing a full and vibrant utility. According to the pope, the disposable culture creates vexing social problems.

> In this context [the disposable culture], some people continue to defend trickle-down theories which assume that economic growth, encouraged by a free market, will inevitably succeed in bringing about greater justice and inclusiveness in the world. This opinion, which has never been confirmed by the facts, expresses a crude and naïve trust in the goodness of those wielding economic power and in the sacralized workings of the prevailing economic system. Meanwhile, the excluded are still waiting.[105]

Economic growth is indeed seen by many as a tide that can lift all boats; business leaders see economic growth as a sign of a healthy company or economy. But very few, if any, see economic growth as bringing about greater justice (a legal claim) and inclusiveness (a social question) in the world. One activity does not necessarily lead to another. Some economists believe that growth will lead to more jobs and higher wages for workers: "Economic power continues to justify the current global system in favor of markets . . . as a result, whatever is fragile, like the environment, is defenseless before the interests of the deified market, which becomes the only rule."[106]

The pope also neglects to consider a primary component of the free economy. Economic historians call it "creative destruction," and the term is often associated with Joseph Schumpter, who described the process by which a "gale of innovation" can render entire products, skills, traditions, methods, and industries obsolete in a short period of time. In a dynamic, growing economy, an economy marked by vitality and innovation, such disruption (and built-in obsolescence) occurs. In such cases, the result is always winners and losers. Innovation tends to offer benefits for many—as the printing press, the steam engine, the mechanical loom, and digital photography suggest. Millions and millions have benefitted from these innovations. Yes, some people have lost as well. The most astute thinker on innovation, Clayton Christensen, understands this fact and points out a common mistake made by companies (or individuals) who strive to innovate. In his influential book *The Innovator's Dilemma* (1997), Christensen makes the basic distinction between "sustaining technologies" and "disruptive technologies." Sustaining technology (or incrementalism) seeks to improve on already-existing products, making them better, cheaper, faster, and less expensive. The free economy rewards individuals who can "make a better mousetrap" and add improved products and services in the marketplace. Sustaining technology, according to Christensen, accounts for the majority of all innovation and continues to generate new ideas and create jobs and wealth in the process.

Disruptive technologies, as the name implies, arise when products or applications displace an entire established method of conducting business or completing a particular job. History is replete with examples of new disruptive technology replacing, with surprising speed and precision, entire industries. When Johann Gutenberg invented movable type in the 1440s—and with it the technology called the printing press—he ushered in a new era, an era scholars call "print culture" which lasted nearly 500 years as the dominant method for producing and disseminating information. Print culture had a profound impact on learning and literacy rates; it also had an equally profound, and deadly, impact on Manuscript Culture. Quite suddenly, the market began to shrink for parchment, for quills, for ink, and other implements of a manuscript culture. The role of the scribe, while not totally eliminated, was eventually replaced by the printing press, then the typewriter, today by the word processor, and tomorrow solely by voice activation. As a result of this disruptive technology, small armies of talented scribes (who had spent many years struggling to perfect their craft) were soon displaced and out of work. Those who made a living making and selling ink and the quills used as writing implements also lost market share and jobs. Collateral damage took place in all businesses that supported the scribe and his profession. Ultimately, the printing press produced far more winners than losers and society reaps the benefits conferred by literacy and the widespread dissemination of knowledge. The printing press, it bears repeating, also created a category of the displaced.

This phenomenon of "creative destruction" also occurred with the transcontinental railroad (the Pony Express disappeared), the telephone (the telegraph was soon obsolete), the internal combustion engine (no more horses and buggies), hydraulic engineering (eliminating limited cables), digital photography (film is becoming an historical artifact), and e-mail (snail mail becomes almost antiquated). Our new "digital culture" is rapidly putting an end to the stunning 500-year reign of print culture (thanks for the memories, Gutenberg) as the primary medium for exchanging ideas and information. Consider, for example, the Library of Congress, the world's largest library, holding 155.3 million printed items on 838 miles of shelves. Each day, the Library adds another 11,000 new printed items. However, as tablets and E-Books will continue to capture a larger and larger percentage of the market from printed newspapers and printed books, that impressive number will stagnate and fall. The ubiquitous smart phone has already displaced, and will continue to displace, scores of suddenly redundant technologies as the IT revolution continues unabated.

Revolution is indeed the proper word—for it's a total reconfiguring of our daily lives and the way we relate with other human beings. One can hardly over-estimate this point. The speed with which the IT revolution took place (and it's nearly reached in culmination) caught many by surprise. It's been estimated that the agricultural revolution took about 3000 years to reach fruition and allow the world to produce sufficient food for the expanding population; the industrial revolution in the West took about 300 years in order to remake and remold our everyday lives. The IT revolution, by contrast, will need only about 30 years (1995–2025) to irrevocably change the entire landscape of human activity. The promises of AI will add further speed and capacity to this shifting landscape. Think about it: In less than three short decades, the entire way we create, process, and disseminate information, not to mention the basic and fundamental way we communicate with each other, has changed. Forever. It's stunning in many, many ways. New technology is now so common, that legendary Cisco CEO John Chambers (and as CEO, he has seen revenues increase from $1.2 billion in 1995 to $48.6 billion in 2013) can state with certainty that "our industry [IT] is going to be one in *constant disruption*, which you are now starting to see across all industries, it doesn't matter which one." And from all available evidence, Chambers is almost certainly correct about this new state of affairs. Chat GPT and Generative AI will only increase this phenomenon.

When Christensen examines disruptive technology, he attempts to understand why so many leading firms stumble, and stumble badly, when confronting the disruptions in their industry. It's not that the leadership of these grand companies suddenly got stupid or lazy, but rather the new technology or product did not make sense in their current reality. The disruptions often produced (at least initially) an inferior product, with lowers margins, that current customers did not even want. Just consider digital photography. Ironically an invention from Kodak's own laboratories, digital photography literally displaced film in a matter of years. Digital photography initially resulted in worse product performance (compared to high quality film), with far lower margins, no defined market, and it was something Kodak's current customers did not want. It's little wonder why they ignored the product. Such displacement can happen with surprising speed.

Peter Diamandis charts the process used by "exponential entrepreneurs" (contrasted with "linear-thinking executives") as they change the world by leveraging technology and innovation. In his book *Bold* (2015), Diamandis and co-author Steven Kotler provide numerous thought-provoking examples of the process used to render a product or service obsolete: digitization, deception, disruption, demonetization, dematerialization, and democratization. To understand more clearly this process, consider the case of Kodak—one of the most iconic and respected companies in the pantheon of American history. As *Wall Street Journal* writer Philip Delves Broughton summarizes:

> First came the technology that allowed photographs to be taken and stored digitally rather than on film—digitization. But it seemed too trivial for a giant like Kodak to worry about—an act of self-deception. Then came disruption, when digital photography grew from a tiny niche into a big business and then surpassed print photography. People no longer needed to pay to store or share their photographs because free digital services had sprung up. Kodak found itself demonetized. Then photography was dematerialized, as cameras were built into phones and the physical materials of the darkroom were replaced by digital tools. Finally, the entire process was democratized, since anyone with a phone can (at no additional cost) take pictures, edit them and share them.

History is replete with examples of this process and the way that "sustaining technology" helps refine and improve products until, at some future point, the disruption changes the environment completely.

This is not the time nor place for an extensive review of Christensen's influential research (Eric Reis's *The Lean Startup* [2011] provides such an analysis), but it is worth noting again that sustaining technology accounts for the majority of all innovation. In other words, companies and individuals seeking innovation will, most likely, engage in incremental changes that make existing products faster, cheaper, safer, and stronger. Most of the world's improvements will be to existing products, goods, and services. Sustaining innovation, as a result, must be part of the job description for all employees, since all employees can be and should be expected to look for more efficient, safe, and inexpensive ways to perform their assigned tasks. If that's what we mean by innovation, then innovation is a job shared by all. This emphasis will help mitigate against a culture of complacency (and the most tired refrain that "this is the way we've always done things around here"). Emphasizing sustaining innovation will also help fight the battle of inertia. But, make no mistake, some people will be displaced and left behind as new technology disrupts and destroys traditional business and industries. In this case, workers need to pivot and adapt; business looking for talent will need to retrain and provide opportunities.

The pope's broadside against the free market failed to consider this phenomenon. The emphasis ought to be on retraining and enterprise, along with the ability to pivot and adapt with grit and resiliency. His words thus created such confusion, and even outright disagreement, that Cardinal Timothy Dolan, Archbishop of New York, took the rather extraordinary step of writing an op-ed in the *Wall Street Journal* in order to "clarify" the pope's remarks. On 22 May 2014, the archbishop restated the Catholic teaching (as presented in the Catechism) in clear and concise terms. The archbishop asserted that although the free market is not perfect, business can be a "noble vocation" when in conformity with human dignity and genuine virtue.

> Yet the answer to problems with the free market is not to reject economic liberty in favor of government control. The Church has consistently rejected coercive systems of socialism and collectivism, because they violate inherent human rights to economic freedom and private property. When properly regulated, a free market can certainly foster greater productivity and prosperity. But, as the pope continually emphasizes, the essential element is genuine human virtue.
>
> The Church has long taught that the value of any economic system rests on the personal virtue of the individuals who take part in it, and on the morality of their day-to-day decisions. Business can be a noble vocation, so long as those engaged in it also serve the common good, acting with a sense of generosity in addition to self-interest.[107]

Genuine human virtue. It's precisely what St. Omobono demonstrated during his lifetime and the Church officially recognized in 1199. Genuine human virtue requires freedom in order to operate willfully and with full volition. Thus, any economic system that limits freedom of trade, of movement, of ideas, of innovation, or of creativity does not conform to the dignity of the human person. The free economy is not perfect (even its most ardent supporters admit this), but it is the economic system most in conformity with the constitution of the human person and the inherent dignity of all people.

Pope Francis released his most anticipated and controversial encyclical *Laudato Si* (Praise be to You) on 18 June 2015—only one year after Cardinal Dolan's essay in the *WSJ*.[108] The primary aim of the encyclical was to address the issue of global warming and humanity's stewardship of the planet. The encyclical generated enormous attention but produced, perhaps, more heat than light. In a truly catholic gesture, he addresses the encyclical to "every person living on the planet."[109] and indeed the document is epic in scope. In a very lengthy fashion (this encyclical runs a rather robust 183 pages), the pope considers an array of topics, including environmental, economic, and moral concerns. The pope modestly notes that the "Church has no reason to offer a definitive opinion."[110] on any specific issue, and that a wide diversity of perspectives exists on almost every issue he addresses. Moreover, he encourages, on many occasions, "honest debate."[111] and he "welcomes dialogue with anyone."[112] The media reviewed the encyclical with fervor (it stands as the most reviewed encyclical in history) and immediately began exploiting divisions among predictable fault lines.

The Wall Street Journal, for example, reviewed the encyclical with a banner headline: "Pope Blames Market for Environmental Ills."[113] The piece, written by veteran journalist Francis X. Rocca, notes the pope's "passionate language" as he "offered a broad and uncompromising indictment of the global market economy." Rocca's white-hot rhetoric perhaps does a disservice to the encyclical. The pope's language is indeed passionate, and he clearly distrusts the free market and those who hold to the Friedman Doctrine of profit. He expressly directs his remarks to "some circles," a code for proponents of the free economy: "Some circles maintain that current economics and technology will solve all environmental problems, and argue, in popular and non-technical terms, that the problems of global hunger and poverty will be resolved simply by market growth."[114] I am not aware of any serious economist, or philosopher, or business leader who maintains this position. Many advocate for a crucial role played by a free economy in alleviating poverty but, quite obviously, simple market growth is not the only method. The red herring distracts from the real issue. But he continues to criticize the unnamed villains: "Their behavior shows that for them maximizing profits is enough. Yet the market cannot guarantee integral human development and social inclusion."[115] The pope again laments the disposable culture and the excessive consumerism that creates, in his opinion, a vicious cycle of consumption and waste.

But Pope Francis also offers a few positive remarks about work as well. Work "should be the setting for rich personal growth,"[116] and we are "created with a vocation to work."[117] Moreover, he repeats previous claims that work must recognize the dignity of each individual. But he quickly returns to a criticism of the role of profit by making wide, sweeping generalizations without nuance or qualification. For example, when he rails against "maximization of profit," he claims that "as long as production is increased, little concern is given to whether it is at a cost of future resources or the health of the environment; as long as the clearing of the forests increases production, no one calculates the losses entailed in the desertification of the land, the harm done to biodiversity or the increased pollution. In a word, businesses profit by calculating and paying only a fraction of the costs involved."[118] If true, that would indeed be a strong indictment. The pope then quotes himself (cited above) in condemning the "deified market" and the way "economic powers continue to justify the current global system where priority tends to be given to speculation and the pursuit of financial gain," causing further damage to the world.[119] Ultimately, the encyclical falls victim to sentiment and the naïve belief that if we only care a little more, these problems would go away.

The pope does not confine his remarks about business and the market to official Church documents. He is famous for speaking "off the cuff" and without reflection, for he admits to speaking whatever comes into his heart. These candid remarks often inflame the media and create sensational headlines, followed by the invariable "clarification" from the Vatican. On 9 July 2015, the pope delivered an address critical of capitalism. The headlines screamed "Pope calls Capitalism 'the dung of the devil.'" Once again, if true, the strong remark seems careless and overtly divisive. The reality was less shocking. While some defenders claim that the true meaning of his words were "lost in translation," they appear in every way consistent with previous comments about the free economy and the insidious nature of the market—a market that can only exploit, destroy, pillage, pollute, overwhelm, and rape. In many ways, it's a shockingly misinformed document.

The tone of the encyclical departs in significant ways from previous encyclicals and the modern conventions found in such documents. Papal encyclicals tend to be pastoral documents, primarily attempts to teach, govern, and sanctify—the three primary tasks of the Episcopal office. As such, popes generally use a kind, compassionate, and loving tone, full of encouragement, understanding, and compassion. The tone of this document, however, departs from that tradition, and often harsh, judgmental, and condemning. As R. R Reno notes in "The Weakness of *Laudato Si*," this encyclical comes from the homiletic tradition with very little teaching, substituting "exhortation and denunciation" for sustained rational argument.[120] Now, as Reno admits, we all need exhortation from time to time, and we could all improve our individual acts of charity, stewardship, empathy, and works of mercy, but a hectoring document becomes a screed when it sounds only a single note.

CHAPTER 6 ENDNOTES

1 http://www.colorado.edu/studentgroups/libertarians/issues/friedman-soc-resp-business.html.
2 Friedman acknowledges that a group of persons might establish a corporation for an eleemosynary purpose and thus not have profit but rather a service as an objective.
3 For a different defense of profits, see Paul J. Voss, "The Ethics of Profit and the Profit of Ethics," *Atlanta Business Chronicle* (25 May 2009).
4 Nate Silver, *The Signal and the Noise: Why So Many Predictions Fail—But Some Don't* (New York: Penguin, 2012) makes the useful distinction between "noise" (all data broadly defined) and signal (important data that holds genuine promise for making predictions). Many forecasts fail, according to Silver, from the inability to differentiate between the data pools. For Friedman, profit provides a compelling (but not the only) signal in forecasting future business success.
5 The Corporate Social Responsibility (CSR) movement has indeed

expanded since 1970, and it constitutes its own academic discipline, complete with a glossy publication (*CR: Corporate Responsibility Magazine*), scores of academic journals, and hundreds of academic conferences around the globe.

6   Friedman's view of profit-maximization might be too narrow even by strict libertarian standards. Shareholders, for example, might want the corporation to engage in profit-making while emphasizing various social considerations. If shareholders do not like these values, they have the freedom to leave. Focusing solely on profits actually limits the freedom of others to buy and sell as they deem proper.

7   John Hood, "Do Corporations Have Social Responsibilities?" *The Freeman* (48 November 1998): 680–84. 682. The immense secondary literature on the topic is outside the scope of this chapter. For a very useful summary and critique, see Richard W. Wilcke, "An Appropriate Ethical Model for Business and a Critique of Milton Friedman's Thesis," *The Independent Review* IX (Fall 2004); 187–209.

8   David Whyte, *The Heart Aroused: Poetry and the Preservation of the Soul in Corporate America* (New York: Doubleday, 1994): 4.

9   Ibid., 8.

10 Ibid., 9

11 Ibid., 87.

12 I applaud this work of "applied humanities" and advocate such an approach in my own professional life. See, for example, Paul J. Voss, "How Successful Companies Do Something is far More Important than What they Do," *Atlanta Business Chronicle* (21 July 2015). Other academics make similar claims. See, for example, John McCumber, "How the Humanities Can Help Fix the World," *Chronicle of Higher Education* (2 October 2016): http://www.chronicle.com/article/How-Humanities-Can-Help-Fix/237955.

13 Michael Novak, *Business as a Calling: Work and the Examined Life* (New York: The Free Press, 1976).

14 This work builds upon Novak's earlier book, *The Spirit of Democratic Capitalism* (New York: Simon and Shuster, 1982). Novak explores with intelligence the theological assumptions and values of democratic capitalism and addresses an audience of fellow academics. *Business as a Calling* speaks directly to business leaders and has a conspicuously practical application.

15 See, for example, Gary Vaynerchuk, *The Thank You Economy* (New York: HarperCollins, 2011).

16 Alasdair MacIntyre, *After Virtue* (Notre Dame: University of Notre Dame Press, 1981).

17 Ibid., 5.
18 See especially pages 191–99.
19 See James Leonard, *Living the Faith: A Life of Tom Monaghan* (Ann Arbor: University of Michigan Press, 2012); Peggy Stinnet, *A Call to Deliver* (Franklin, TN: Clovercraft, 2015).
20 For a Catholic perspective on philanthropy, see Frank J. Hanna, *What Your Money Means* (New York: Crossroads, 2008).
21 Americans have displayed this civic-mindedness from the earliest days of the republic. Alexis de Tocqueville, *Democracy in America*, ed. Eduardo Nolla, 2 vols. (Indianapolis, Liberty Fund, 2012), famously observed this unique trait of the Americans to serve the common good: "Americans of all ages, of all conditions, of all minds, constantly unite. Not only do they have commercial and industrial associations in which they all take part, but they also have a thousand other kinds: religious, moral [intellectual], serious ones, useless ones, very general and very particulars ones, immense and very small ones; Americans associate to celebrate holidays, establish seminaries, build inns, erect churches, distribute books, send missionaries to the Antipodes; in this way they create hospitals, prisons, schools" (896).
22 Novak, *Business as a Calling*, 7.
23 Ibid., 13.
24 Aristotle, *Nicomachean Ethics*, trans. Martin Oswald (Upper Saddle River: NJ: Prentice Hall, 1999).
25 Novak, 120.
26 Letter to Artists," 4 April 1999 accessed at: vatican.va/content/john-paul-ii/en/letters/1999/documents/hf_jp-ii_let_23041999_artists.html.
27 Cf. Ibid.
28 The rise of the "celebrity entrepreneur" often undermines serious attempts to define and explore this crucial function in the free economy, often reducing the role of the entrepreneur, and the essential characteristics of the entrepreneurial activity, to energy and personality. For a learned account of the character necessary for entrepreneurship, see Israel Kirzner, *Competition and Entrepreneurship* (Chicago: University of Chicago Press, 1978). See also Clayton Christensen, *The Innovator's Dilemma* (New York: Harper, 1997); Eric Ries, *The Lean Startup* (New York: Crown, 2011); Neal Thornberry, *Innovation Judo* (New York: Evolve, 2016).
29 John Paul II, *CA*, N. 47.
30 See, for example, Dov Seidman, *How: Why How We Do Anything Means Everything* (New Jersey: Wiley, 2007). See also, B. Joseph Pine and James H. Gilmore, *The Experience Economy* (Boston: HBR Press, 2011).
31 Novak, 126.

32 Ibid., 128
33 Jim Collins, *Good to Great: Why Some Companies Make the Leap . . . And Others Don't* (New York: Harper Collins, 2001).
34 Tom Morris, *If Aristotle Ran General Motors: The New Soul of Business* (New York: Henry Holt, 1997).
35 Ibid., ix.
36 Ibid., 80.
37 Many books explore the unpredictable nature of the modern career. See, for example, Spencer Johnson, *Who Moved My Cheese?* (New York: Putnam, 1998).
38 See, for example, Tom Rath, *Strength Finders 2* (New York: Gallup Press, 2007); Dave and Wendy Ulrich, *The Why of Work* (New York: McGraw Hill, 2010); Marshall Goldsmith, *Mojo*.
39 Morris, 103.
40 Morris, 110. See also, Abraham Maslow, "A Theory of Human Motivation," in *Psychological Review* 50: 370–396.
41 For a provocative account of the world of work and the *vita activa* (the active life), see Hannah Arendt, *The Human Condition* (Chicago: University of Chicago Press, 1958). In this award-wining book, Arendt re-examines the active life and explores the fundamental modes of being-in-the-world: Labor, Work, and Action. According to Arendt, one must cultivate each mode in order to live a truly fulfilled human life.
42 Stephen Young, *Moral Capitalism: Reconciling Private Interest with the Public Good* (Oakland: Berrett-Koehler, 2003).
43 Elaine Sternberg, *Just Business: Business Ethics in Action* (Oxford: Oxford University Press, 2000).
44 Sternberg rejects including social aims or personal fulfillment in her consideration: "A definition that incorporates all social goals into the purpose of business, risks making business meaningless" (33).
45 Ibid., 36.
46 Morris, 119.
47 See Kerry Patterson, et al., *Crucial Conversations: Tools for Talking When the Stakes are High* (New York: McGraw Hill, 2002).
48 One ought to distinguish the work of Novak and Morris from other approaches to this question. Scores of books deal with topics of motivation, happiness, work-life balance, and other attributes of positive psychology. See, for example, Shawn Achor, *Before Happiness: The 5 Hidden Keys to Achieving Success, Spreading happiness, and Sustaining Positive Change* (New York: Crown, 2013). I do not mean to dismiss these types of books, full of lists, slogans, and promises, but rather to discriminate between psychology and philosophy.

Recently, the Kingdom of Bhutan developed a "Gross National Happiness" metric. According to this measurement, The Kingdom of Bhutan rates number one in the world for Happiness and this impacts the world of business and productivity. Many view these efforts with skepticism because of the inherent subjectivity in calculating present-day happiness.

49   Thomas Woods, *The Church and the Market: A Catholic Defense of the Free Economy* (Maryland: Lexington Books, 2005).
50   Ibid., 2.
51   Ibid., 3–4.
52   Ibid., 4.
53   Ibid., 15.
54   Ibid., 22.
55   The "psychology of success" seeks to understand the necessary characteristics used by high achievers. A fascinating body of research explores a wide variety of success in many endeavors. See Angela Duckworth, *Grit: The Power of Passion and Perseverance* (New York: Scribner, 2016).
56   Peter H. Diamandis and Steven Kotler, *Abundance: The Future is Brighter Than You Think* (New York: Free Press, 2012).
57   Ibid., 41.
58   Ibid., 42.
59   In many ways by a variety of measures, the world is getting healthier, safer, and sustainable. See, for example, Has Rosling, *Factfulness: Ten Reasons We're Wrong About the World, and Why Things are Getting Better* (Flat Iron, 2018).
60   Pope Leo XIII, *Rerum Novarum: On Capital and Labor* (Lexington: St. Athanasius Press, 2016).
61   Ibid., nn. 6–7.
62   The profound text, replete with the weight of Christian tradition, also creates ambiguity. For example, who, precisely, bears responsibility for the plight of the worker? There is a call for a living wage, but it's not clear if this falls to various governments to legislate into existence, or if business owners have a moral responsibility to make it a reality. This ambiguity may be a virtue, for it places emphasis upon subsidiarity—which itself implies that it is not appropriate for the pope to place blame—or solutions—for economic problems on the shoulders of any particular group.
63   *RN*, n. 4.
64   Woods, 51.
65   Helmut Schoeck, *Envy: A Theory of Social Behavior* (Indianapolis: Liberty Fund, 1987).

66 Schoeck, 4.
67 See, for example, Paul J. Voss, "The Ethics of Profit and the Profit of Ethics *Atlanta Business Chronicle*, 21 May 2009.
68 Christopher Marlowe, *Dr. Faustus*, in *Drama of the English Renaissance*, ed. Fraser and Rabkin (New York: Macmillan, 1976), 2.2.140–41.
69 Schoeck, 5.
70 Ibid., 373.
71 Novak, 11.
72 Ibid., 143.
73 Daniel Kahneman and Angus Deaton, "Emotional Well Being Increases with Salary up to $75,000 and then Plateaus," *PNAS* 107 (September 2010): 489–93.
74 For a popular account of motivation and the differences between extrinsic and intrinsic motivation, see Dan Pink, *Drive: The Surprising Truth About What Motivates Us* (New York: Riverhead Books, 2009). Pink argues that relying solely on extrinsic motivation (such as money) sharply diminishes job performance and employee engagement.
75 *RN*, n. 5.
76 This imprecision might very well be intentional—the principle of subsidiarity at work. The encyclical contains very few, if any, actual policy prescriptions.
77 Pope John Paul II, *On the Hundredth Anniversary of Rerum Novarum* (Boston: Pauline Books, 1991).
78 Ibid., 1.
79 Russell Hittinger, "The Problem of the State in *Centesimus Annus*," *Fordham International Law Journal* 15 (1991–92): 956.
80 John Paul II, 43.
81 Ibid., 5.
82 Ibid., 32. Emphasis in the original.
83 Ibid., 48.
84 See also, Clayton Christensen, *How Will You Measure Your Life?* (New York: Harper Business, 2012). Christensen, a professor at the Harvard Business School, also strives to find meaning in work—a higher vision—and uses some of the same vocabulary.
85 John Paul II, 32.
86 Not all scholars view the future with optimism. See, for example, Tyler Cowen, *Average Is Over: Powering America Beyond the Age of the Great Stagnation* (New York: Dutton, 2013). Cowen argues that for the upper 15% of Americans, the future is indeed bright and quality of life will remain high. The other 85% will stagnate and fall behind.

87 *Abundance*, 283. Over 6.5 billion cell phones are active in the world today—nearing an 80% penetration rate.
88 John Paul II, 32.
89 Ibid.
90 Ibid., 42.
91 Irving Kristol, *Two Cheers for Capitalism* (New York: Basic Books, 1978).
92 http://www.povertycure.org/.
93 Muhammad Yunus, *Building Social Businesses* (New York: Public Affairs, 2010). For a comprehensive account of the history of finance and the seminal role finance (and credit) played in the development of civilization, see William N. Goetzmann, *Money Changes Everything: How Finance Made Civilization Possible* (Princeton: Princeton UP, 2016).
94 https://w2.vatican.va/content/john-paul-ii/en/speeches/1997/june/documents/hf_jp-ii_spe_19970624_nicolini.html.
95 *Catechism of the Catholic Church*, Second Edition, Revised in Accordance with the Official Latin Text promulgated by Pope John Paull II (Vatican City: Liberia Editice Vaticana, 1994).
96 While the *Catechism* is rather scant in commentary on the free economy, in 2004 the Pontifical Council of Justice and Peace released an extensive *Compendium of Social Doctrine*.
97 "Vocation of the Business Leader: A Reflection," Pontifical Council for Justice and Peace, 2012.
98 Ibid., 3.
99 Ibid., 5.
100 Ibid., 10.
101 Ibid., 51.
102 Ibid., 35.
103 Ibid., 25.
104 Ibid., 87.
105 *Lumen Fidei*, n. 54.
106 Ibid., n. 56.
107 http://www.wsj.com/articles/SB10001424052702304198504579572571508689630.
108 *Laudato Si* (Brooklyn: Melville House, 2015). The official publication is listed as 24 May 2015, but the actual release occurred on 18 June 2015.
109 *LS*, n. 3.
110 Ibid., n. 61.
111 Ibid.

112 Ibid., n. 64.
113 Francis X. Rocca, "Pope Blames Market for Environmental Ills," *WSJ*, 18 June 2015.
114 *LS*, n. 109.
115 Ibid.
116 Ibid., n. 127.
117 Ibid., n. 128.
118 Ibid., n. 195.
119 Ibid., n. 56.
120 https://www.firstthings.com/web-exclusives/2015/07/the-weakness-of-laudato-si.

Conclusion

Late in 1197, in a small parish church in Cremona, a devout merchant — a person admired for his honesty, generosity, fidelity, and compassion — died peacefully during Mass. This layman, Omobono Tucenghi, was both a successful merchant and a devout Catholic. He worked diligently, offering his products of high quality at a fair price; his labors allowed him to maintain a home and provide for his family. He experienced change and disruption—economic, political, social, religious, and familial—and rightly earned his reputation for holiness. His daily life, in many ways, was typical and not too dissimilar from the lives of many today. Shortly after his death, he became Saint Omobono—patron of businesspeople and entrepreneurs. After 800 years, his story remains largely unknown to the English-speaking world. This project hopes to rectify that shortcoming by making a modest contribution to the treasury of the world's knowledge.

The story of Omobono, however, is more than the story of a medieval saint—even a unique saint, taken from the world of the market and the hectic life of business. The story resonates today with an unexpected poignancy for the contribution it makes to the pressing issues of economic justice, free markets, work-life balance, the "theology of work," and Catholic history. These issues will continue to engender considerable discussion and heated debate in the coming years as economic concerns become more and more conspicuous. The Church enters these discussions carefully and with knowledge of its own limitations in proposing concrete solutions to these vexing problems. But if the Church is to be truly catholic and universal, it cannot remain ignorant of its own rich history. This book attempts to recapture this lost history, and we believe that the discussion turns upon the critical year 1199, when the universal Church recognized one man for his heroic virtue, at a time when the Church was refining the theology of sainthood and settled on a merchant from Cremona to serve as the model of heroic virtue for succeeding generations.

The canonization, of course, raised many questions about the proper role and aims of the commercial life, including the nature of work, the realization of profit, the lending of money, the virtues needed for moral capitalism, and the tension between *otium* and *negotium*. It's a serious intellectual and philosophical undertaking, to be sure, but it cannot occur without a comprehensive understanding of the teachings and traditions developed over the previous 3000 years. The death of a modest, saintly, compassionate, charitable, and successful merchant seems like an exceptional place to start.

Index of Names and Terms

Abela, Andrew 282
Abraham 4, 9, 30–31, 213
Acton Institute 277
Adhegrin, monk 47
Alain, of Lille 61–62
Albert the Great, saint 161–162
Albigensian Crusade 96
Alexander III 92
Alexander, of Hales 161, 167
Alexis, saint 71–72
Alfred the Great, king 53
Al-Ghazali 37
Alighieri, Dante 79
Alger, Horatio 218–219
Ambrose, bishop, saint 26
   De Officiis 60
Amos viii, 3, 9, 14
Arians
   Opus Imperfectum in Matthaeum 149
Arnold, of Brescia 69–70
Anthony, of Egypt, saint 24, 28, 46
Aquinas, Thomas, saint 87, 127, 164–167, 171–174, 255
   Summa Theologiae 172
Asaph 3
Augustine, of Hippo, saint 31–35, 39, 70
   Confessions 35

Basil, of Caesarea, saint 24, 26, 46
Battle of Legnano 80
Beaumont, Francis 217
Becket, Thomas, saint 93, 195, 200

Beowulf 38
Benedict, of Nursia, saint 24, 46, 68
   Rule 68, 195
Benedict XII, pope 178
Broughton, Philip Delves 288
Brown, Peter 31, 34, 38, 91
Bruno, saint 64–65
Buffett, Warren 250
Burghers 55, 159
Busch, Tim 251
Butler, Alban 190–191, 248

Camaldolese 64
Canonization, process of 15, 92–95
Capet, Hugh 48
Capitalism viii, 6, 51, 53, 220, 222, 229–230, 247, 261, 263, 266, 276, 278–279, 284, 292, 302
   Latin America vii
   proto-capitalism 39, 78, 148, 165
Capizzi, Joseph 282
Capra, Frank 231
Carmina Burana 61
Carthusians 64
Casole, Rainerio de, bishop 177
Catechism of the Catholic Church 278, 279
Catherine, of Siena, saint 50
Cathars 70, 73, 95–97, 151, 153, 173, 177
Caux Roundtable 261

Cavalcanti, Aldobrandino 159
Caxton, William 194
Chambers, John 287
Charlemagne, emperor 45, 48
Chaucer, Geoffrey 194–197, 200
Chrysostom, John, saint 27, 30, 60, 149, 175
Christensen, Clayton 255, 285, 287, 289
Clement, pope, saint 16–17, 60, 150
Clement, of Alexandria, saint 19–21, 23
  Quis Dives Salvetur? 19
Clare, of Assisi, saint 87
Cluny 47, 58
Codevilla, Angelo M. 214
Collins, Jim 255
  Good to Great 255
Comune 79, 88, 102, 147
Conversi 71, 84–85, 157
Consortium of Saint Omobono (*Consorzio*) 178
Constantine, emperor 22–24, 69
Cromwell, Oliver 214
Contemptus mundi 25, 164
Cum orbita solis [COS] 82–83, 86, 92, 94, 124–125, 131, 142–143, 146–147, 197, 206
Cyprian, of Carthage, saint 21–22, 28
  De Lapsis 22
Cynics 8

Damien, Peter, saint 58
David, king 2, 4
Deaton, Angus 271
Deloney, Thomas 217
Diamandis, Peter H. 266, 288
Dickens, Charles viii, 217, 260
Didache 17
Diogenes the Cynic 7

Dives and Lazarus 9, 31
Docetism ix
Dolan, Timothy, cardinal archbishop 252, 289–290
Doyno, Mary Harvey 191
Durand, of Huesca 151
Duns Scotus 173, 175

Edict of Milan 22
Egidio, of Cremona 83, 136
church of 91, 98, 107, 142, 147, 178
Eustathius, of Sebaste 28–29

Fair Labor Standards Act 279
Felix, of Nola, saint 31
Francis, pope vii, viii, 251–252, 283–284, 290, 292
  Laudato Si 290, 293
  Lumen Fidei 284
Francis, of Assisi, saint 73, 151–153, 157, 159, 170, 172
Francis, of Sales, saint 145
Frederick I, emperor 80
Frederick II, emperor 148, 214
Friedman, Milton 214–215, 242–245, 260
Friedman Doctrine 245, 282, 291

Gangra, Council of 29
Gates, Bill 250
Ghibellines 80, 148
Gilbert, of Tournai 159
Giles, of Lessines 167
Gnosticism ix, x
Goldsmith, Marshall 255
Gratian 59–61, 149–150, 164
Greg, W.W. 204
Gregory, of Nyssa, saint 26–27
Gregory, of Tours 38
Gregorian Reform 58–59, 62–63, 67, 70, 80, 84
Greene, Robert 217

Grosseteste, Robert 161
Guelfs 80
Guizetta, Robert 251

Happe, Peter 199
Harmony of Discordant Canons, The 59
Haza, Jose M. Ruano de la 199
Henry, of Ghent 174
Henry IV, king 214
Henry VIII, king 199–200
Hilton, Barron 251
Hitler, Adolph 214
Hittinger, Russell 273
Hood, John 244
Honorius, of Autun 146
Hugh, of St. Cher 159–161
Huguccio 164–165
Humbert, of Romans 159
Humiliati 71, 151
Humility 16, 89, 138, 152–153, 156, 161, 170, 172, 255
Hussein, Saddam 214

Innocent III, pope 73, 81–82, 84, 91–93, 102, 109, 149–150, 187–188
    Mitrale 81
Insurance 52–53, 169, 208, 222

Jacob 4, 31
James, apostle, saint 14
Jerome, saint 27, 30–31, 62
John, apostle, saint 11, 13, 198
John XXII, pope 171
John, of Paris 172–173
John, the Baptist, saint 113–114
John Paul II, pope, saint 185–187, 254, 273–274, 276, 278
Joint-stock Company (*commenda*) 53
Jonson, Ben 217

Joseph, saint 8
Joseph II, emperor 179
Joseph, of Arimathea, saint 12, 114

Kahneman, Daniel 271
Karcher, Karl 251
Khadijah 36
Keough, Donald 251
Kristol, Irving 276

Labentius annis [*LA*] 82, 193
Langone, Kenneth 251–252
Lateran Basilica 23, 108
Lateran Council 158
Lateran Council III 72–73
Lateran Council IV 47, 144
Lawrence, martyr, saint 23
Lederer, Richard 201
Lencioni, Patrick 255
Leo I, pope, saint 60
Leo IX, pope 59
Leo XIII, pope 267–269, 272–273, 278
    Diuturnum 269
    Graves de Communi Re 269
    Quod Apostolici Muneris 268
    Rerum Novarum 267, 269
Legatus 251, 282–283
Lewis, Michael 227–231
Licinius, emperor 22
Lombard, Peter 60, 149–150
Louis the Pious 45
Lazarus, of Bethany 9–10, 12, 32

Machiavelli 212–216, 231, 233
MacIntyre, Alasdair 249
    After Virtue 249
Magnanimity 34, 38, 162, 209
Map, Walter 72
Marlowe, Christopher 211, 270
Martha, of Bethany, saint 111

Mary, of Bethany, saint 12, 111
Mary, Mother of God, saint ix, 8
Maslow, Abraham 260
Matilda, of Tuscany 79
Medieval Warm Period 48, 50
Mendicants 155, 161, 170, 172, 177
Meun, Jean de 156
Middleton, Thomas 217
Miller, Arthur 219–220, 260
   Death of a Salesman 215
Minoritas 152, 170, 172
Monaghan, Tom 251, 282
Morris, Tom 256–258, 260–262, 264
   If Aristotle Ran General Motors: The New Soul of Business 256
Monte di Pietá 170
Montes Pietatis 170
Muhammad 36–37
Mussolini, Benito 214

Napoleon 214
Negotium 191, 196, 226, 256–257, 281, 302
Nicholas I 45
Nicolini, Giulio, bishop 185
Nietzsche, Friedrich 226
Novak, Michael 247–249, 256, 261–262, 270–271, 279
   Business as a Calling 247

Olivi, Peter John 175, 202
Opus Dei 145
Origen 19
Osberto, of Cremona 89–91, 102, 107, 132, 139
Otium 19, 196, 220, 226, 256–257, 281, 302
Otto I, emperor 48

Pallavicini, Umberto 148
Paul, saint 14, 17, 23, 25, 67–68

Paulinus, of Nola 31, 39
Pelagians 31
Penitenti 84
Peripatetics 8
Peter, apostle, saint 13, 16, 23
Peter, of Chobham 158
Peter, the Chanter 158
Pink, Dan 255
Pius X, pope, saint 273
Plato ix, 7, 20, 161, 256
   Republic 7
Pontifical Council for Justice and Peace 279
   Vocation of the Business Leader: A Reflection 279
Popolo (middle class) 136
Poverty 8, 11, 24–25, 28, 30 *passim*
Puritanism ix

Quia Pietas [*QP*] 94, 97, 144, 187–188, 193, 211
Quem Quaeritis 200
Quoniam Historiae [*QH*] 82–83, 87–89

Rath, Tom 255
Reconquista 60
Reis, Eric 289
Reno, R. R. 293
Robert, of Arbissel 66–68
Robert, of Courçon 149, 158
Rocca, Francis X. 291
Romuald, saint 64–65
Rothbard, Murray 264

Savonarola, Girolamo 224
Scarlet Whore of Babylon 15
Schoeck, Helmut 269–270
Scully, Robert 200
Second Agricultural Revolution 39, 49
Seidman, Dov 255

Index of Names and Terms

Septuagint, Greek 4, 32
Shakespeare, William 10, 78–79, 199, 201–208, 210–211, 214
Shepherd of Hermas 17, 21, 28
Sicard, of Cremona 81–82, 89, 91–94, 98, 102, 104, 109, 144, 146–148
Simon the Magician 13, 58
Simony 13, 17, 57–59, 70
Sirico, Robert 277
Sixtus II, pope 22
Smith, Adam 53, 272
   Wealth of Nations 53
Solomon, king 2–4
Stalin, Joseph 214
Stoics 8
Stone, Oliver 232–233
Sternberg, Elaine 261
Strauss, Leo 215
   Thoughts on Machiavelli 215

Tertullian 21–23, 28, 70
Thompson, Augustine 188
Thomas, of Chobham 158
Traister, Barbara 199
Treaty of Verdun 45
Trento, Bartolomeo da 148
Turkson, Peter K.A. 279

Ugolino, bishop 178
Usury 4–5, 7, 55–56, 166, 168–170, 213

Vauchez, Andre 148, 179
Vetus Itala 4, 32
Vikings 45, 48

Weber, Max 219
Waldo, Peter, saint 71–73, 85, 95–96, 152–153, 174
Waldensians 73, 80, 95–96, 151
Whyte, David 245–247, 261
   The Heart Aroused: Poetry and the Preservation of the Soul in Corporate America 245
Wickham, Glynne 199
Wilken, Robert 16
Wolfe, Tom 224–225, 227, 229–230
   Bonfire of the Vanities 224, 229
Woods, Thomas 262–265, 269
   The Church and the Market: A Catholic Defense of the Free Economy 262
Worley, Charlotte Coker 217
Wright, Louis B. 200

Young, Stephen 261
Yunus, Muhammad 277
   Building Social Businesses 277

Zaccheus 11, 33, 114
Zecharia 121

Index of Scripture

Genesis 3:17–19; 4:17; 6:13; 11; 12:3; 19.

Exodus 7:11–22; 7:14–26; 8:1–11; 32: 15–34.

Levitcus 25:36–37.

Deuteronomy 8:12–13; 19:14; 23:19–20; 26:10–13; 27:17.

1 Kings 11:4.

Job 24:2; 29:16.

Psalms 1:2; 1:3; 2:11; 117:22; 37; 48[49]:14; 67:36; 70[71]: 15–16; 112; 112:3–5; 118:62; 118:67; 123: 7; 145:8.

Proverbs 22:2; 22:28; 23:10.

Song of Solomon 1:3.

Wisdom 3:6.

Sirach 26:29; 36:6.

Isaiah 22:22; 49:1.

Amos 6:4–5.

Zephaniah 3:20.

Matthew 4:8; 5:48; 6:8; 6:20; 6:24; 7:12; 7:15–20; 7:22–23; 8:20; 9:9; 9:18–26; 9:40; 10:1; 10:9; 10:22; 10:24–27; 10:29; 11:11; 11:12; 13:8; 13:43; 17:19; 19:21; 19:22; 19:23–24; 19:26; 19:27–30; 21:21; 22:1–4; 23:5; 24:24; 24:41; 25:14–30; 26:11; 27:57–61.

Mark 12:41; 12:42; 16:20.

Luke 1:20; 1:53; 2:24; 3:16; 6:24; 7:36–50; 8; 9:3; 9:58; 10:7; 10:42; 12:33–34; 12:38–42; 14:21–23; 14:26; 15:4–7; 16:9; 16:19–26; 18:22; 18:24–27; 19:1–9; 19:1–10; 19:11–27; 21:1.

John 2:9, 3; 8:44; 9:1–35; 15:5; 15:13–14.

Acts of the Apostles 4:32–35; 5; 8:20; 16:16–24; 19: 11–16.

Romans 5:20; 11:32.

1 Corinthians 7:9

2 Corinthians 11:4.

Galatians 1:15; 3:22.

Ephesians 4:22–24.

Philippians 2:15; 2:21; 3:13; 3:14.

1 *Timothy* 6:10; 6:17.

2 *Timothy* 2:5; 3:1–8.

Titus 2:12.

Hebrews 11: 1.

James 1:9–11; 2:5–6.

1 *Peter* 2:25.

Revelation 3:17; 3:7; 13:11–18; 14:13; 18:3; 18:15–19.